How to Share an Egg

How to Share an Egg

A TRUE STORY OF HUNGER,
LOVE, AND PLENTY

Bonny Reichert

BALLANTINE BOOKS
New York

Published in the United States by Ballantine Books, an imprint of Random House, a division of Penguin Random House LLC, New York.

BALLANTINE BOOKS & colophon are registered trademarks of Penguin Random House LLC.

Published simultaneously in Canada by Appetite by Random House, a division of Penguin Random House Canada Limited.

Grateful acknowledgment is made to Alfred A. Knopf, an imprint of the Knopf Doubleday Publishing Group, a division of Penguin Random House LLC, for permission to reprint an excerpt from "The Cinnamon Peeler" from *The Cinnamon Peeler* by Michael Ondaatje, copyright © 1989, 1991 by Michael Ondaatje. Used by permission of Alfred A. Knopf, an imprint of the Knopf Doubleday Publishing Group, a division of Penguin Random House LLC.

Hardback ISBN 978-0-593-59916-7
Ebook ISBN 978-0-593-59917-4

Printed in the United States of America on acid-free paper

randomhousebooks.com

1st Printing

FIRST US EDITION

Book design by Mary A. Wirth

For Dad, finally

"It's dark because you are trying too hard. Lightly child, lightly. Learn to do everything lightly. Yes, feel lightly even though you're feeling deeply."

—ALDOUS HUXLEY

Imagine two boys—a couple of skeletons, really—roaming the German countryside. One is fourteen, the other, a little older. It's the spring of 1945, and they haven't eaten much besides potato peels and coffee grounds for three years. They knock on door after door until they find a farmer who goes into his kitchen and brings something back: a single brown egg. One egg for two starving boys.

The day before begging for the egg, my dad and his cousin Abe were hiding in a hayloft. The date was May 7. The boys could hear planes through the barn's patchy roof; they didn't know it, but the gates of concentration camps throughout Europe had already been pried open. The soldiers in charge of guarding my dad's dwindling cohort were running—running from the Russians and running from the Americans, running from their own certain capture or death—and they were taking their prisoners with them. The SS didn't want Jews talking about all that had happened to them, and the German war machine counted on their slave labor to the bitter end. Dad's march had begun at Gleiwitz, an Auschwitz subcamp, where he had been forced to carry steel railway ties with his emaciated shoulders and bare hands.

Each evening, the soldiers found a farmer to house them for a few hours before hurrying off in the morning, dragging along any prisoners who'd survived the night. The prisoners often slept in open fields, but on this particular night, my dad and his cousin slipped into a barn. They climbed to the hayloft and brought up the ladder behind them.

"*Raus, raus,*" the soldiers called in the morning, the standard come-out-before-I-shoot-you greeting. Dad and Abe didn't move. The soldiers must have counted their prisoners. They must have known two were missing. They came into the barn with pitchforks, piercing and tearing at the ground below the hayloft. The boys stayed hidden, and the steel tines found nothing but hay.

Dad thinks it might have been the next morning when voices called to them again. *"Raus!* Come out! We want to help you!" After five and a half years of abuse and terror, the boys were not convinced, and they stayed hidden. Only when the voices switched to English did Dad and Abe tumble down from the hayloft and out the barn door to find a jeep with a white star on it. Standing in the field were not the SS but American soldiers. The Germans had just surrendered, and the Americans were sweeping the countryside, searching for survivors. What does my father remember about this moment of liberation, eighty years ago? What he ate, of course. "I was so hungry, but the only food they had was a big jar of green relish," he says. "I ate and ate until I was sick."

WHEN YOU HAVE A FATHER with stories like these, and you happen to be a writer, you know what you're supposed to do. I was always going to write Dad's book, to tell his incredible story. Capturing the tale of survival for future generations was not only my role, but my duty. My privilege. And yet, there was always a reason to put it off. "When are we going to start the book?" he'd ask.

"Soon, Dad. Soon."

My dad is a charming and persuasive man. He is short and handsome and warm, with a ready smile and big dimples. He is the kind of person everyone remembers after one meeting. "Say hello to your dad from me," my friends are always saying. "Oh, I just love your dad." He's a force, an optimist, a lover of life. He's not someone you want to disappoint.

I had every intention of fulfilling my role, but I couldn't find the right time. First, I was too young. Then I was busy with university. My children came along—one, two, three—taking up my every waking moment. After that, I was overwhelmed at work. The years pressed down on us. Dad was sixty; he was seventy-five.

Whenever someone in the family said, "Aren't you writing the story?" a guilty thrum pulsated through my bloodstream, and I changed the subject.

A few times, Dad and I sat down together. I knew a lot of what had happened to him, but I didn't have all the facts and details I would need for a book. My pen shook in my hand. He would have told me anything, but there were certain words and sentences I couldn't stand to hear him say.

More than too busy, what I had always been was too scared. As soon as I was old enough to understand what the Holocaust was, I was sick at its mere mention. The soldiers and their snarling dogs, the gas chamber belching human smoke. That this thing had existed was frightening enough; that my very own father had been trapped inside such a hell was too much for me to bear.

THE BOY FROM THE HAYLOFT is now ninety-four. I've waited until the last possible moment, but still, the book you're holding is not quite the book I was supposed to write. Instead of a straightforward tale of Holocaust survival, it traces a more subtle struggle. It's not always a life-and-death struggle. It's not necessarily a unique struggle. It's simply the story of a daughter trying to figure out who she is in the shadow of something bigger.

Again and again, I've asked myself: Do the tiny machinations of my own life matter in comparison to everything my father has seen and done? Truthfully, I still don't know. But I've come to realize this is the only story I can tell, and my own the only lens I can see through.

THE BOOK YOU'RE ABOUT TO read is a tale of hunger and sorrow and love. It's a mishmash of what happened to my dad and what's happened to me; a portrait of a parent and a child, a father and a daughter. It's both a small story and an enormous one, a study of contrasts. And because it's my family, it's a story about food—

sumptuous meals and meals of almost nothing at all; food that is simple and complicated, basic and bountiful. Food that is rife with meaning.

How does a daughter reconcile her privilege when her father had nothing? How does she set her table, heavy with plenty, when her ancestors were lucky to share a single egg? As much about survival as sustenance, the story you're about to read is about a family that lost everything and built itself up again, one meal at a time.

PART ONE

Warsaw

2015

1

Borscht

We are starving. It's midafternoon on a rainy Wednesday, and our tour guide's gray Skoda lurches and pauses—go, stop, go—as we crawl away from the cemetery through narrow backstreets. Squished in the back between my sister Julie and my dad, I feel like a little kid—hot, claustrophobic, nauseous.

"If I don't eat something right now, I'm going to faint," Mom says from the front. My sister and I scroll and tap on our phones. It's well past lunchtime, and places have closed for the afternoon. Why didn't Ewa book a reservation? She's our tour guide in Warsaw, after all, and what could be more important than feeding hungry people who are depending on you?

"Okay, here." Ewa jerks the car to the right and drives up on the sidewalk with two wheels. She hits the brakes and yanks up the emergency. The car tilts precariously.

"Where are we?" I ask.

"You'll see."

Julie cracks open her door and steps out to help Mom. I slide out next, relieved to put my feet on the ground. I reach into the car to take Dad's hand, and our palms lock as he works his way onto the sidewalk. The rain has stopped, and his hair glows silver in the flat June light. His belly protrudes a little under his navy blue golf jacket. At eighty-four, he isn't exactly light on his feet, but as we follow Ewa, Julie, and Mom toward a run-down brick building, he seems to almost float.

We walk under an archway and part a pair of dusty black curtains, finding ourselves at the threshold of a dimly lit restaurant. Rectangular tables and beat-up chairs are arranged around the room, every single one empty.

Damn. We are a family that doesn't eat in dead restaurants. After a lifetime in the business, Dad hates them more than anyone. No customers means no money, depressing even if you aren't the one with an empty wallet. But now all I hear is his labored breathing behind me. I turn around to find him staring into space.

"Dad?"

"This is lovely. Let's sit down."

"But look at this place. It's—"

"There." Still tour-guiding, Ewa is pointing toward a scarred wood table and signals to a made-up blonde behind the bar. The woman puts her cigarette in an ashtray and ambles over with menus. The air is blue with smoke. I touch my right temple where a little vein pulsates steadily.

I know the food will be awful, so I don't bother trying to decipher the Polish menu. Across the table, Mom is pale and tiny, wrapped in her shawl from the cemetery. I want to order her a hot coffee, but the waitress spoke only to Ewa, now sitting beside Julie at the other end of the table, and disappeared.

How did I end up here? I planned to live my whole life never setting foot on Polish soil. My father was born here, yes, but to me, Poland has always meant a starving ghetto, a train ride into hell. For my entire forty-six years, Dad all but forbade me from coming, and I was happy to be forbidden. "Let the people who don't know what

happened go," he said when my friends traveled to Europe on Holocaust education trips. "I suffered enough. You don't need to."

A single phone call changed Dad's mind with dizzying speed.
Two weeks ago, a distant relative told Dad a family tomb had been
discovered in Warsaw. "I have to see it," Dad said.

Everything would have been different had that call come before
Mom's memory started to slip. "Poland?" She would've laughed at
the suggestion. Mom likes nice places, comfortable places. They
both do. Misery is not their style. And yet, here we are. The ache in
my head intensifies and I close my eyes.

WE LEFT THE HOTEL FOR the cemetery after breakfast, bundled
against the damp spring air. Buses zoomed up Okopowa Street, and
students from the nearby trade school clogged the sidewalk, but inside the cemetery's iron gates, the headstones were wrapped in
spongy silence.

"We have to find the shomer," Ewa said, her short red hair frizz-
ing up in the dampness. It was strange to hear the Hebrew word on
her lips. "Szpilman. He's the only one who knows which graves are
where."

We came upon him hunched over an ancient computer in a bare
room with a dirt floor. He was younger than I expected, with a kippa
on his head and wire-rimmed glasses. As we crowded into his office,
Ewa lifted her chin and Dad took a roll of zlotys from the pocket of
his pants. Like a maître d' in a Florida restaurant, Szpilman palmed
the money without looking up.

Once, the Jews of Warsaw comprised a third of the city's population, but they were long gone, their houses and entire district razed
to the ground. Ewa wasn't sure how this ancient cemetery survived
and, honestly, I didn't care that much. We were from a little town
near Lodz called Pabianice, not Warsaw. Dad's father had died in
Pabianice before the war, while his mother, sisters, and nearly all his
aunts, uncles, cousins, and extended family had been murdered in

the Pabianice ghetto, the Lodz Ghetto, Auschwitz-Birkenau, or somewhere on the bloody road in between. No vast cemeteries, no special tombs. Just complete and utter erasure. Who could the grave even belong to?

"Spell the name, please," Szpilman said in accented English.

"R-o-t-h-b-l-a-t," Julie said. It was Dad's mother's maiden name.

Szpilman tapped a few keys. "Sector 47, row 7, number 36." He came from behind his rickety desk and strode toward the main aisle of the cemetery as I hurried to keep up. Julie took Mom's arm. Dad walked alone, kicking loose stones out of the way with his white loafers.

When Szpilman left the main path, I followed him into the brush, looking down for tree roots and mud puddles. The others were far behind.

"Okay," he said, stopping abruptly.

The headstones were huge and so tightly arranged, they almost overlapped. Ferns sprung up between a carpet of leaves. For a moment, I thought of my kids at home. This would be a good place to look for frogs.

Szpilman pointed to an ornate stone taller than my shoulders, with pillars on the sides and a curved top. It was gray, with a fine green moss growing near the bottom. I ran my fingers over the engraved Hebrew letters, sounding out the name שלמה ראטבלאט. A crash in my rib cage. "Dad," I yelled. "We found it. It's here!"

My father came up and stood beside me, his face inches from the stone. "Shlomo Rothblat," he said slowly, once, then again. "You see?" he whispered, finally turning to me with tears in his eyes. "It's my name carved into this old piece of stone."

LIKE SO MANY TIMES BEFORE, Dad had been right to believe. His mother was born in Warsaw—a simple fact I'd somehow overlooked amid all the more sinister facts—and this hundred-year-old tomb belonged to her father. Shlomo Rothblat was not some mysterious stranger. He was Dad's grandfather and my own great-grandfather, a pillar of his community and a beloved scholar who died before my father was born. Dad is even named after him: Shlomo translates to Solomon, which Dad shortened, after arriving in Canada, to Saul.

Suddenly, my father became joyful. He raised his arms over his head in triumph and danced around. Mom and Julie walked up and we all joined hands in an impromptu hora, grateful for such an unexpected, beautiful moment.

STILL, ENOUGH IS ENOUGH. I look down the table at Mom, rub my temples, check the time. We did what we came to Warsaw to do, and now it's time to go home. How long do we have to sit in this terrible restaurant?

The waitress arrives, carrying little plates: a pile of pickled cucumbers, carrots, and cauliflower; a saucer of hard salami rounds studded with nuggets of fat. In front of Dad, she places a stack of black bread, thickly cut, with several squares of butter and a little mound of sea salt on the side. Dad picks up a slice and smells it in a gesture I've seen a thousand times.

My shoulders release. Even if the next course is fried horse meat, or a Polish army boot that's been frozen since the war, we will not starve. My mother pulls the pickles closer and pinches a carrot spear between her manicured fingernails. Ewa and Julie nibble at the salami. Dad hands me a slice of bread, lavishly buttered and glittering with salt flakes. He makes another one to pass down to Mom. We wolf everything down in silence.

When our waitress returns, she is carrying a long glass dish with a series of little compartments. One is filled with chopped cucumbers, another with boiled potatoes, a third with purple cubes of beets, a fourth with sour cream, and what's that green at the end—chopped dill?

Hustling a bit now, the waitress comes one more time with five ceramic bowls on an oversized tray, the cook behind her in a jacket that was once white. I hold my breath as he places a bowl in front of me.

"Dziekuje," I say, using one of my two Polish words.

He bows slightly and backs away.

I peer into my bowl, ready for gruel or mush or a greasy hunk of meat. Instead, I discover a broth so clear I can see myself. The dish is cool to the touch, the liquid inside a deep ruby color. I bring my nose down to the rim and breathe in the smell of clean earth. The smell of roots.

A Jew who comes from Poland is Jewish, not Polish, I've always been taught, and yet, I know exactly what to do. I add a few tender pieces of potato, a scoop of cucumber, a little bit of sour cream. I sprinkle dill on top. I look at Dad. His bowl is piled high with garnishes. He motions for the server to come over. "Can we have more sour cream, please?"

I pick up my tarnished little spoon and sink it through the cloud of sour cream, into the burgundy lake of broth below. When I bring the borscht to my mouth, the taste is sweet and sour and honest. The taste is alive.

SOON, I'LL FALL INTO MY husband Michael's arms in the Toronto airport. "I'm never going back to Poland," I'll tell him.

"No, you don't have to," he'll say.

I don't know that this little meal has powers. Not yet. I don't realize this simple bowl of borscht is about to change my everything.

PART TWO

Edmonton, Canada

1970s

2

Roots

I want to go forward, but first I have to go back. Back to a time before the borscht in Warsaw, before the talk of writing the book, even before I found the blue-green numbers inside Dad's arm. What I remember most about that time was my freedom, and how I soaked it up as though I knew I was lucky to have it.

IN THE NEIGHBORHOOD WHERE I grew up, every house had an alley behind it. Once a week, garbage trucks lurched up and down, collecting potato peels and coffee grounds, soup cans, eggshells, all the stuff nobody wanted. The rest of the time, the alleys were empty. My Free Spirit bike was a hand-me-down, with sparkly blue paint and a white padded banana seat. All winter it sat in the garage, but by June, the wheels were in constant motion. We lived far north, and the evenings were like afternoons.

If I had been born in a bigger Jewish center like Toronto or New York or LA, Pittsburgh, Chicago, or Montreal, everything would've been different. Just a dot on the map, our prairie city of Edmonton was a land of big skies and empty spaces, a place with only a handful of Jewish families when my first grandparent, my mother's father, arrived in 1913. He died well before I was born, but his wife was my baba Sarah, who came to escape the pogroms in Ukraine as a motherless teenager, sent for by a male relative.

On the other side, I had no grandparents at all. My father was a seventeen-year-old orphan when he got on a ship bound for Canada at the end of 1947. His war ordeal had taken him from his hometown of Pabianice to the Pabianice ghetto, the Lodz Ghetto, Auschwitz-Birkenau, and a string of slave labor camps. He'd been on a cattle car for ten days with no food or water, and endless marches where to stop moving was to be shot. When he was finally liberated in the German countryside in May, 1945, he had already been without parents for many months.

I had only the vaguest sense of this history as I rode my bike through beams of light and clouds of mosquitos, past peeling fences and bushes heavy with purple lilacs. Lawn mowers droned in the soft twilight as I pedaled home. Dad had a special way of talking about where he'd come from. Let me tell you a story, he would say, and then we'd be off in a mysterious world where the war was the perfect place for him to ply his wit and charm. In these homespun fairy tales, he was strong and daring and clever. Nothing terrible happened and good always triumphed over evil.

But back in 1947, the bare facts were this: Dad's parents were dead. His five sisters were also dead. He had his cousin Abe—they'd kept each other alive through everything—but after two years living together in an abandoned villa in Pegnitz, a town northeast of Nuremberg, they would have to separate. Despite the Canadian government's shameful "none is too many" policy, the Canadian Jewish Congress was compiling a list of 1,123 war orphans who would be sponsored by private Jewish families. Dad was just young enough to apply. Abe, who was older and newly married, was not.

Dad got to the front of the line and the congress representative behind the counter pulled out a map. "There were points, like dots, to show population," Dad says. "Montreal had a lot of points. Winnipeg had a few points. Edmonton had almost no points."

"I'd like to go to Montreal," Dad said.

"No," the clerk behind the counter said. "You've been assigned to Edmonton."

"It's so far away. I hear it's freezing. How about Winnipeg?"

"Maybe," the clerk said, but she was only humoring him. There was a sponsor waiting in Edmonton and Edmonton was where he would go.

DAD SAILED FROM GERMANY TO Halifax in the hold of the SS *Sturgis* on December 29, 1947. People were sick during the fifteen days at sea, but Dad made the most of the ample food and salt air, spending as much time on deck as possible. He'd earned a suitcase full of money smuggling cigarettes from West Berlin into Russian-occupied East Berlin, and he'd spent it on a special outfit for the trip—a white shirt, dotted tie, belted jacket, and pleated trousers. In the photo taken before the journey, he's wearing a fedora perched at a rakish angle over his thin, handsome face. There are two dollars in his pocket.

After he disembarked in Halifax, Dad got on a train heading west, past the beautiful lights of Montreal, past Toronto, all the way to Winnipeg where his sponsor, a dashing businessman named Wolfe Margolus, was waiting to persuade Dad to make the last eight hundred miles of the journey. A respected community leader in Edmonton, Wolfe took an instant liking to my smart, charming father, of course he did. "You're going to love this kid I'm bringing home," he said to his wife, Seda, when he called her from the train station.

IN EDMONTON, DAD MOVED IN with the Margolus family and set his sights on a little grocery store and lunch counter called Teddy's. His education had been sharply truncated, but he knew food. When he wasn't smuggling cigarettes in Germany, he'd worked in the American army's kitchen, peeling potatoes and chopping carrots. "I was their star kitchen boy," Dad says. After the hunger he'd seen and felt, he planned never to be far from food again.

Two years after he arrived in Canada, with help from Wolfe, Dad bought Teddy's. He kept the cook that came with the business and the lunch counter menu—hot turkey sandwiches, chili con carne, milkshakes, and apple pie. He was twenty years old.

THE STORY OF MY PARENTS' life together starts with my grandmother's cooking. Dad and Baba Sarah were two refugees who came from Europe to Edmonton, thirty years apart. Cousin Abe had by then immigrated to New York, but Dad learned that Mickey, another cousin from Poland, had survived and had been living first in a displaced persons camp in Cyprus and then in Israel. Dad had moved out of the Margolus's house and wanted Mickey to join him in Edmonton, but his new apartment was too small. Baba, known around town as Mrs. Taradash, or simply, Mrs. T, was by then a widow as well as a fabled cook and baker who took in boarders to make ends meet. Mickey came to Edmonton and moved into Baba's, where Dad was a frequent guest for meals. "Mrs. T cooked the most delicious Jewish food," Dad still muses, seventy-five years later. "I always left there bursting."

While my mother, Baba's youngest daughter, studied dietetics at the University of Alberta in Edmonton, Baba got to know my dad, a handsome young immigrant who helped his cousin, ran a restaurant, and already had a car. Mom graduated and applied for a dietetic internship at the Jewish General Hospital in Montreal. It was a gutsy move. She knew no one there and had never been on a plane. She hung around at home and waited for word from the hospital. She waited and waited. In the meantime, she liked when my father pulled up in his blue Pontiac to visit his cousin. Soon she asked Dad to teach her to drive. Like some kind of Shakespearean comedy, Mom wanted to marry a Montreal doctor and Dad wanted to marry Mom. When the letter came from the Montreal Jewish General, my parents had started to date, and Baba was overjoyed. She knew what she had to do.

Mom and Dad were happily married when Baba finally told Dad she'd hidden Mom's acceptance letter from the hospital. She was still a little afraid to tell her feisty daughter. By that time, Dad had bought and sold two more restaurants and was planning a fourth, a new take on the delis popular in New York and LA. He recruited Mrs. T, now his mother-in-law, to help him create corned beef and brisket sandwiches, in addition to desserts like lemon meringue pie, flapper pie, and cherry cheesecake.

For several years, Mom continued to wonder why she never heard from the Montreal Jewish General. When at last Baba told Mom what she'd done, it didn't matter because, Dad says, "Mom had a wonderful life."

"Is that what Mom would say?" We're reviewing the story, much later, and I only have access to Dad's version.

"Of course," he says, dimples flashing.

ALL OF THIS WAS ANCIENT history by the time I came along, the youngest of four daughters. My three sisters, Lisa, Suzanne, and Julie, were ten, eight, and six years older than me, and they seemed to do everything together: off they went to school or the ski hill or shopping downtown, while I stayed home with Mom and Dad or, more often, Baba.

Every Friday, she came to stay with us for the weekend and the house brightened. She arrived as though she were fleeing all over again, with parcels and packages and a giant soup pot wrapped in a tea towel, knotted to make a handle. Things were hot or cold or frozen. I didn't know to wonder if she'd stayed up all night rolling and pinching and stuffing for us. Pekeleh, she called her bundles, little packages. Pekeleh also means burdens. Yiddish is like that.

The contents of the packages depended on the season. In winter, she brought rich kishka that snapped and potato knishes that flaked. In warmer weather she made cheese blintzes, fried to a crispy gold and ready to be smothered in syrupy strawberries and sour cream. August was the time for wild blueberry varenikes, pinched closed and boiled like dumplings, ready to squirt their purple juice into your mouth. There was a cherry soup, ice-cold on a hot day. Year round, we ate grieven, crunchy fried chicken skin with crispy onions, as well as beef tongue dipped in sweet-hot mustard. For me, she saved the chicken necks, boiled until the bones were soft and the meat fell off in strips.

It was a lot of food, and I could tell Mom wasn't pleased, but all she would say was "Mama, there's no room in the fridge." Baba didn't answer. She was too busy heaving her enormous pots and containers from shelf to shelf. Mom rolled her eyes at Baba's wide back.

Even when they were side by side, chopping and slicing in our yellow kitchen, it was hard to put Mom and Baba together as mother and daughter. Mom was thin as a stick; hugging Baba was like trying to wrap your arms around the biggest tree in the ravine. Mom wore perfume; Baba smelled like oranges and tea. Mom loved slacks, but Baba wore loose housedresses with a corset underneath to contain her ample parts. Mom's acrylic nails were long and painted whereas Baba's hands were tough and weathered, with strong natural nails. Mom hated her own hair and wore wigs; Baba's dark hair never grayed—she said it was because she washed it with coal when she was a child in Pishchanka. When Baba stayed with us, she slept on a cot in my bedroom, holding my hand until I fell asleep. *"All maf dir,"* she said to me. I didn't need to know what the Yiddish words meant to know she was talking about love.

YOU COULD TELL WHO WAS in charge on any particular night by what was on the table. Friday nights, it was usually a prime rib roast. Mom's. The smell in the afternoon was of roasting garlic and floor polish. But Baba made chicken with a crispy flour and paprika coating everyone liked, and sometimes we ate that instead. Mom drew the line at chicken soup and brisket; dishes she didn't make and didn't want Baba to make, either. They resembled the "poor people food" she'd eaten as a child, and brought back unhappy memories of parents who spoke too little English and had too little money. Rather, she made no-fuss higher-end stuff like steak and salad, lamb chops, maybe a whole salmon on a Friday night.

Mom knew her way around the kitchen but whenever possible, she'd open a box or a can to liberate herself from the stove. She didn't want to slave away, making everything from scratch like her mother had. It was the era of choice and for Mom, freedom wasn't a burned bra but a good can opener. She loved sweet things like glazed baby onions and canned Harvard beets that made a gooey fuchsia stain on my dinnerplate. "Scrumptious," she'd announce, while I fought to choke them down.

Baba was the milder of the two. Nobody hit me, but Mom pinched once in a while, and she yelled. Baba joked about chasing my sisters and me with a wooden spoon, but I didn't even know what "a lickin'" meant. When Mom talked about the mother of her childhood, she drew a picture of an exacting woman who told my mom and her two sisters there was only one way to set a table, wring out a rag, iron a sheet. That this was the same person who rubbed my feet as I fell asleep seemed impossible.

3

The Restaurants

To be the youngest person in such a household was to understand
that food was everything. I knew it was delicious and I knew it
was precious. My father had been forced to scrape and scrounge to
survive and as his daughter, foraging was in my blood. Walking on
the grassy strip beside the road, I wanted to pop every berry, mushroom, and dandelion into my mouth. Kids said you could eat the
white roots of grass, which were mild and earthy. In spring, I squished
the tiny flowers that grew on the neighborhood hedges and licked at
the single drop of syrup.

Mom wasn't the type to fuss with a vegetable garden, but a rhubarb plant sprung up near our back fence every year. Julie showed
me how to brace my feet on either side of the plant, grab a stalk, and
yank upward. *Careful, the leaves are poisonous!* We wet crimson stems
under the kitchen faucet and dragged them through the sugar
drawer, the shock of sweet and sour making my teeth ache. Our
driveway was lined with burgundy trees that produced dark berries,
and their strange juice made my mouth pucker. A few times Baba
got me to collect them so she could make wine in big glass jars.

BABA MUST'VE LOVED TO EAT—SHE was wide enough to hold space for all four grandparents—but mostly I think of her eating melba toast and drinking tea. Dad, on the other hand, ate with obvious relish. He had the girth of a generous appetite: as one of my sisters' boyfriends once said, he wasn't fat, he just had a big stomach. It was a happy kind of hunger, built on gratitude and pleasure and a true appreciation for what was delicious. "What's for lunch?" he said at breakfast or, at lunch, "What's for dinner?"

Was there a dark edge of trauma to Dad's hunger? If I was told I couldn't get up from the table until I finished what was on my plate, it didn't upset me much, except when it was liver. He didn't say the kinds of things he could have: *Don't you know how lucky you are? I would've killed for this food during the war.* But somehow, my sisters and I knew. We just knew. We understood that food was connected to the meaning of life itself; an understanding woven into our very being. "Don't waste that," Dad might have said, pointing a fork at a remaining chicken wing on my plate. Soy sauce and honey made it dark and sticky. He'd pick up the blackened wing and set it aside to be wrapped for lunch the next day. Only rarely did he become the family vacuum cleaner, compulsively eating up the leftovers on everyone's plate. "Saul, stop," Mom said, once in a while. If someone were to dump the remnants of a good steak dinner in the garbage, as I'd heard some families did, he would have become red in the face and loose with the swear words, but it wasn't just him. Food waste was anathema to all of us, an attitude bred right into our bones.

I still don't understand how this dovetailed with my mother's compulsion to be thin. By all logic, it should have been a schizophrenic childhood—one parent preoccupied with food and feeding, the other phobic about being fat. Food should have become fraught, disordered, the last place to look for pleasure. Instead, by some miracle, Mom and Dad balanced each other out. Too little and too much. Stress and stability. Food was the center of our existence, and what I learned from the two of them was that the table was the most important place on earth.

IN ADDITION TO BABA, WE had my mom's two sisters and their husbands and kids, but on Dad's side, there were only those cousins, Abe, who lived in New York, and Mickey, who joined him there before I was born, leaving a gaping hole where the rest of our family should have been. Our restaurants, Teddy's and the Carousel, were almost like two extra family members, each with its own personality, helping to fill the void.

Teddy's was casual and fun and always busy. Suzanne started punching the cash register there on an upturned Coke crate at age five. Years later, I would take her place, thrilled to earn my own pocket money. In those early days, Teddy's was still a luncheonette with a soda fountain and booths against the wall. Every table had a mini jukebox with a knob you could turn to select a song. On the other side of the wall that ran the length of the place was the little grocery with eggs, milk, cigarettes, and chocolate bars. I guess that's why we called it, and every restaurant that came after it, "the store." Outside, there was a huge billboard that said, STOP HERE FOR THE BEST CORNED BEEF ON RYE, and it was. Dad and Baba worked hard to perfect the recipe: what quality of meat, which spices, how long in brine, how slow in the oven.

Sometimes Dad took me to Teddy's and left the motor running. "I'll just be a minute," he said, turning up the heat in the car to keep me warm. I wondered what he'd come back with—a chocolate bar? A bag of corned beef? A foil container of honey-glazed ham? My mouth watered as I thought about the smoky, crispy meat we ate only in the car. We didn't keep kosher, but we didn't go so far as to bring pork in the house.

Most often, he came out carrying paper grocery bags full of bills, crumpled shut at the top. When he closed the door, the smell of grease and cigarettes permeated the car.

At home, we worked together to count the money. I'd seen the green one-dollar bills many times, and the twos, a pretty salmon

color. The fives were blue and the tens purple. The bright red fifties
were rare, popping out at me when Dad dumped the bags. With my
sisters, we were six people working at the low table in the corner of
my parents' bedroom. Dad handed me the ones. "Okay, sweetheart.
Just turn them so all the heads are facing the same direction."

Mom's counting was steady and methodical, but Dad was the superstar. He counted with the bills bent around the fingers of one
hand, thumbing through them so fast, my eyes couldn't keep up.

It seemed like a lot of money, but Dad said it wasn't ours. Mom
wrote the number of ones, twos, fives, tens, and twenties with a
ballpoint pen in a special book. All the money and the book went
into a cloth bag with a heavy metal lock. There was a slot at the
bank, like the one where we returned books at the library, and that's
where Dad dropped the bag.

"Be careful," Mom said, as Dad buttoned his coat and picked up
his keys. Someone could clunk Dad over the head, take the bag, and
that would be it, she said. I wasn't sure what "it" meant, but the hint
of risk felt in keeping with the general air of excitement and mys-
tery Dad carried around with him. Whatever "it" was, I knew Dad
would prevail.

THE CAROUSEL, WHICH OPENED IN 1955 and was by then around
fifteen years old, was a little more serious. I ordered mashed potatoes and covered the mound with more and more butter, peeling the
waxed paper off the little pats. I was waiting for everyone to finish
their French and Western dips, hot sandwiches of corned or roast
beef as big as my head and served with a little bowl of warm dipping
sauce. I preferred the oily, salty things we ate at home, like herring
or anchovies, right out of the jar, or the fatty, crispy skin from Baba's
chicken. I adored the sardines Dad tipped out of a can and drenched
in lemon juice.

The Carousel's booths were orange vinyl, and every table had a
candle that shone in the dim light. In the coming years, it would
become fancier, with thick steaks added to the menu. Mom would
say we should have a salad bar, the newest trend, and swanky cock-

tails like Harvey Wallbangers and Golden Cadillacs. We would even serve lobster tails, brought to the table with melted butter over a little flame.

OUR FAMILY DIDN'T REALLY EAT anywhere else, except the Lingnan. Baba loved Chinese food, so on certain Sunday nights my parents brought her out for dinner with us before she went back to her little apartment with the huge old-fashioned furniture.

We sat at a big round table—my three sisters, my parents, Baba, and me. Something about the hanging lanterns and gold walls made me sleepy, and Baba set up a bed of two chairs for me, and covered me with a coat. Stray words from the grown-up conversation drifted over my head as I looked up at a ceiling of swirling green dragons and imagined myself on a journey far from home. When I heard the clatter of dishes, I sat up. I liked rice and dry garlic ribs, but even better was the way the servers brought the empty plates to the table, warm to the touch. I remember the feeling of laying my cheek on the porcelain's clean white surface.

More often than not, someone—Mom or Lisa, my oldest sister—would say, "Don't lie on your plate. You're going to dirty it." I stared into the plate to look for dirt, but all I could see in its smooth, blank surface was a reflection of myself, shadowy and unformed.

After dinner, the server brought a pot of jasmine tea and a tower of little cups. I hurried to finish the tea and flip my cup face down on its saucer. One, two, three—I turned it the way Baba had taught us. "Pass it to me, Bondles," she said, resplendent in the green shantung dress she'd put on for the occasion. Wise and mystical, Baba read my future in the leaves that clung to the bottom of the cup—how many husbands, how many children, how long my life. I didn't know the first thing about who I was, and it didn't matter. I was the baby— a little separate, a little forgotten—and I trusted Baba to tell me who I was going to become.

4

The Numbers

My memories of childhood are floaty and soft until the summer night I found the numbers inside my father's arm. I was five years old.

We had a built-in barbecue at the side of the house, and Mom had grilled lamb chops for dinner, the fat around the meat smoky and charred. She made a salad of cucumbers, tomatoes, and lots of fresh dill, an herb we called "creepy" for the feathery, persistent way it grew.

"Girls, bring in the plates," Mom said from the kitchen when we'd finished eating. My sisters started to clear but I stayed on Daddy's lap, scooping the oily, vinegary dressing out of the bottom of the salad bowl with a spoon. That was when I noticed something colorful on his skin.

"What's this?" I said, turning his forearm face up. There was a blue-green letter *B*, like my name, and a bunch of numbers. An *O* or a zero. A six.

"Some bad men put that on me."

"Take it off." I started scrubbing him with a napkin.

"It doesn't come off," he said mildly.

I looked into his big open face. "Where are the bad men?"

"Don't worry. They ran away." I had a funny feeling in my stomach, but he shifted me onto his other knee and said, "Let's finish the salad." There were a couple of cucumbers left in the bottom of the bowl, and he spooned them into my mouth.

OUR BRICK HOUSE WAS A block from a river valley that cleaved the city in half. Later that evening, Dad took me to sit on the lone bench facing the ravine. It was dark and we gazed over the treetops at the wet squiggle of river and the glowing buildings on the other side.

"Look at that view," he said. "Isn't it beautiful?"

The buildings sparkled. The river shimmered as it wound its way northeast. Even the air around us felt heavy with possibility.

"I want you to remember this beauty," he said.

I worked on memorizing the skyline.

SOMETHING HAPPENED THAT DAY, SOME kind of transfer, from Dad to me. He shared facts, a few, but more than that, there were feelings; feelings that seemed to move between us like particles in the air. What strikes me most—the thing that tells me, even today, that my father is not quite a regular human, bound by the ordinary limits of heart and mind, is that despite the horrors he'd seen and felt, violence and cruelty and unfathomable suffering, some of those feelings were very beautiful.

I've tried to figure this out my whole life—how the memory of finding those blue-green numbers from Birkenau stirs in me not just fear and grief but also amazement and even a sense of wonder.

"In wonderment, the soul is suddenly taken by surprise, which causes it to consider attentively the objects that it finds rare and extraordinary," wrote René Descartes, the seventeenth-century French philosopher. After surviving what wasn't survivable and finding himself in a brave new life in Canada, my dad's world became, as Descartes wrote, rare and extraordinary.

It seems like we walked to the bench every evening of my childhood. It would be forty years before I'd realize that the sparkly buildings reminded Dad of his first glimpse of Montreal through the train window. The dark past was behind him, the future glowed in the distance. But at five years old, I didn't need an explanation. The river was full of fish. The sky was full of stars. That was enough.

THE NIGHTMARES DIDN'T START UNTIL the fall. Lions chased me down an endless strip of highway; I was running in tall brown grass beside the road. I was tripping. I was falling. I dreamed of towering pines chained together, draped in dark fabric. I started to wake in the night, bewildered and shivering, calling for Mom and Dad. They came to my room and comforted me, but if they recognized that my nightmares were related to my dawning sense of the catastrophe in our background, they didn't say.

WE WENT TO SYNAGOGUE FOR the holidays and Dad gave off a specific, magical energy. His family had been Chasidic in Poland, and although he wasn't so religious anymore, I could feel his joy as he connected to an earlier self, a self with a mother and father and sisters, with safety and security and no inkling of the evil in the world. I leaned on his shoulder and braided the fringes of his tallis, wanting to be inside his cloud of happiness.

Teddy's was close to the synagogue and sometimes Dad got us to services by promising a treat there, after. Perched on a stool in my burgundy corduroy skirt, I watched Tony the cook sizzle clarified butter on the flat top. He pulled four butterhorns out of a plastic bag, split them, and laid them cut-side-down on the puddle of fat. When his sinewy hand slid the green-rimmed dinner plate in front of me, one side of the pastry was deep golden brown and spongy with butter, the other just warmed and sticky with melting white icing.

Synagogue didn't always mean treats. On Yom Kippur, the adults didn't eat, and Dad chanted the prayers with tears in his eyes. I sat on the velvet pew beside him, shivering. I felt God hovering right above us with His big book of life and a rubber stamp. I knew how sorry He felt about what had happened to Dad, and I prayed He'd put us down for another year of life because of it.

5

Stories

"Want to go for a car ride?" It was winter and Dad was holding his huge ring of keys, the belt of his soft camel coat hanging down. I couldn't scamper into my down-filled jacket fast enough and we swung out the door, leaving Mom and my sisters to finish cleaning up from dinner.

Outside, the snow glowed in the moonlight. I climbed into the car and the hard leather seats cracked under me. Dad said he had a story for me.

"Have I told you about Abe and the dog?"

"No," I said, as glimmers of magical energy bounced around the car.

"It was during the war, and we were very hungry, me and Abe. One day we followed a little doggie. We couldn't believe how lucky we were." Dad loved animals, but I knew this story wasn't about playing with the dog. "We thought if maybe we could catch the dog, we could finally eat something."

The streetlights blurred together in a white streak against the dark sky. "You wanted to eat a dog?"

"We were very hungry."

I told Dad I thought eating a furry little dog sounded gross and mean. He glanced in the rearview mirror and smiled. "You're right," he said. He knew I wanted a puppy, but Mom had said no. Within the year, he would drive me out to the country to choose a bunny instead.

It was like that with Dad. You never knew when something wonderful might happen. Once, he took me to his friend's farm, where I milked a cow and fed a horse. I would think I'd dreamed it but there's a photo of me in the short haircut Mom liked, holding a wooden bucket with a horse's nose deep inside. Another time, we went fishing across the river, in Mayfair Park. That Dad didn't know how to fish made no difference at all.

Dad and Abe caught the dog but, in the end, decided to return it to a nearby soldier. "We were lucky," Dad said. "Instead of shooting us, he gave us a few pieces of bread, took the dog, and went on his way."

ANOTHER NIGHT, ANOTHER STORY. DAD spotted a pile of potatoes, just lying there in an open field. *What a wonder!* The guards seemed not to mind when Dad and some other boys rushed over to collect them. There were so many potatoes, Dad stuffed them in his jacket. Suddenly, the soldiers changed their minds and started shooting. "Not shooting to kill," Dad hurried to add. "Just to scare us." He didn't feel anything, nothing at all, but something dripped down his face. A bullet has scraped his forehead.

I stopped breathing, imagining my beautiful father bleeding. "Did it hurt?"

"Not at all! Just a scratch." The tips of my fingers buzzed as I thought of that extra little wrinkle, the scar from that bullet, above Dad's right eye.

I WORKED AT PIECING IT all together—Dad's stories, the numbers and the bad men, the feelings I had inside me. The stories didn't immediately frighten me; not exactly. Or maybe they did, but in the way stories in my big book of fairy tales frightened me. In that safe way little kids almost enjoy.

For his part, Dad wasn't trying to be cryptic but, rather, age appropriate. Even more than that, he got something from these retellings, leaning hard into that sense of wonder, reframing his living nightmares into stories of bravery and triumph. Maybe there was even some healing for him in this recasting, an opportunity to both unburden himself and revise the past in the retelling.

My sisters must've already known a lot more, and Mom knew everything. But the stories in the car were just for me, and I loved that time alone with my father as he painted a picture of who we were.

"DID I TELL YOU ABOUT the pillows full of money?" he said another night. The days were getting longer, and the deep blue sky was streaked with pink.

"What pillows?"

"In the Lodz Ghetto, I had a job, such a good job! The Germans brought in all these pillows and blankets, and my job was to open them. The feathers were everywhere, all in the air. Sometimes there were jewels in the pillows—big diamonds and gold and money, just waiting for me to find them. We did this sorting in a beautiful church." It was strange to think of Dad in a church instead of a synagogue.

"There was a wonderful man named Mr. Sharp in the ghetto," he said that same night, or maybe the next time. "He took a liking to me."

I scanned my mind for *Sharp*, but I couldn't pull up a face.

"Where is Mr. Sharp now?"

"I wish I knew," Dad said. "He helped my whole family. I never found out what happened to him."

I lay down in the car, closed my eyes and let Mr. Sharp slip away.

THERE WERE STORIES FROM BEFORE the war, too. Dad as a little boy in his grandmother's hardware store, falling into a barrel of blue paint. Dad fussed over by his mother and five sisters. And always, stories of food. Dad walking with his mother to the bakery to buy fresh bread. Dad and his father picking berries on a trip to the countryside. Dad eating a magical dish of beans and meat that seemed to make itself on Shabbat. The stories collided and overlapped and knit together to form a secure web in my mind.

6

Bad Dreams

There was a lot of beauty in this childhood, but there was also a sadness inside me that I didn't understand. I was a lucky girl, born in a safe place, with tons of food and loving parents, yet I had stones in my chest, heavy and gray.

Dad worked a lot. He was available when you really needed him, but the little day-to-day stuff was Mom's domain, and my sadness exhausted her. "Don't you get tired of crying?" she said one morning, as I sat on the teal area rug in her dressing room, tears running down my face again. I was still in my nightgown, not yet dressed for afternoon kindergarten. She wore nylons and a sturdy bra, taking her blue Ultrasuede dress out of the closet. "Don't you hate having a runny nose and a sore throat?"

I nodded. Then I shook my head. It was all very confusing because I didn't know where the sadness was coming from. It seemed to be everywhere, just in the air, and I thought everyone could feel it. There were Dad's stories, full of untold sorrow, but I felt something with Mom, too. I could see the unhappiness below her happiness in the tight set of her jaw; I could hear it in the edge in her voice. I was too young to realize she was still wrestling with the pain of her own childhood—a huge immigrant mother who could barely read or write English, a dad who was quick to anger. "I came home from school hurt, so he hit me," she once told me, much later. I was almost an adult by then, but the revelation shocked me, nonetheless. "Can you imagine?" she said with a hard laugh. "I got hurt at school, so he hit me?" I didn't ask her to elaborate and to my guilty relief, she never mentioned it again. I had already been saturated with Dad's story and I didn't have the space to absorb hers.

I was very young when my mind began to play a little trick on me. *Imagine what it would feel like to see someone killed right in front of you*, it told me. *Do it. If you love Dad, it's your job.* Then: *Pretend you're starving. Imagine how it feels to be so hungry, you can't get out of bed, you can't move your body.* At my Auntie Reva's house, I snuck some of her dog's kibble into the bathroom and crunched into it as I stared at myself in the mirror. Then: *What does it feel like to be forced to march barefoot and almost naked in snow?* I opened the back door and tested an icy drift against the sole of my bare foot.

As I moved through the ages Dad was during the war—nine in the first ghetto, eleven in Lodz, thirteen when he last saw his mother and sisters on the platform at Auschwitz—a voice from inside commanded me to try to be him. The more I could put myself in his skin, the more I soaked up his suffering, the less hurt he would be, the voice said.

I grew intimate with hauntings that would be with me forever. The lions had huge manes and sharp teeth. The trees groaned under the weight of heavy chains. I'd think the dreams were gone and then they'd be back, many nights in a row. When I became afraid to go to sleep, Baba taught me to pray for good dreams before bed. Mom applied her own brand of logic as she tucked me in, her hoop earrings glinting in the light from my bedside lamp. "Sleep fast," she said, as the usual tears soaked my pillow. "Fall asleep before the dreams can catch up to you."

BECAUSE OF MY BAD DREAMS and my inexplicable sadness, Mom labeled me "the sensitive one," but she wasn't too interested in breaking my distress into parts and unraveling where it came from. She had three older girls to deal with, plus her own feelings and desires to satisfy. She'd had a meager childhood and what she most wanted was to make up for it. She loved musicals and *Funny Girl* was her favorite movie. Like Barbra Streisand's character, she dreamed of being pampered and spoiled like "Sadie, Sadie, married lady."

It must have been this love of musicals that led Mom to take me to the movie *Jesus Christ Superstar* when it came out in theaters in 1973. The rock opera was a sensation and I had just turned six. Maybe another child would have taken its grown-up themes in stride, or fallen asleep, or just been bored. Maybe if I'd known the Jesus story, the movie would've seemed more like a fable. But I was not those other kids, and I took everything I saw and heard literally. The priests in black robes and pointy black hats sang, "This Jesus must die," and the dissonant guitar chords confirmed it. Those menacing riffs still make the hair on the back of my neck stand up.

About three-quarters of the way through the film, they whipped the golden, beautiful Jesus, tearing up his back and gleefully counting the lashes one by one. I felt vomit at the back of my throat. I didn't know that Daddy had been beaten with a whip, but at the same time, I knew. I felt heavy. I felt hollow. I vibrated with terror.

We stayed to the end, because I remember how my hands ached when they nailed Jesus to the cross, right through his palms. Mom took me to Teddy's for a bite, after. We settled into one of those little booths, but I couldn't eat. "Why are you so sulky?" she asked. I wanted to explain but I couldn't even speak, so sick was I with feeling for Jesus. For Dad.

WHEN MY BAD DREAMS CONTINUED into my early school years, my parents were genuinely puzzled. What could possibly be wrong? We lived in a comfortable, clean house with plenty of food. Mom was organized and clever. Dad was loving, hardworking, upbeat. He didn't rant about the Holocaust or refuse to speak or lock himself in his room. My three sisters were outgoing and bubbly; my sisters seemed fine.

"You're so sensitive," my parents said to me over and over. Soon that became "You're *too* sensitive." In the most literal way, it was true. I sensed many things I didn't even know yet: searing pain and loss, humiliation, isolation, and terror. It all mixed together into a darkness I didn't understand and couldn't describe.

Dad was particularly distressed by my bedtime tears, which he wanted to dry up with love and positive messages. Be happy. That's all you have to do, he told me. I felt a stab of something cold in my chest. To call it guilt would be too simple.

What I knew for sure was that I didn't feel the right way. We were happy and strong. We were normal and well-adjusted. We didn't talk about trauma except to say we didn't have it. "Tramma" was how Dad pronounced it, a bad word he wanted nothing to do with. My parents had a way of modeling pride and hiding shame, of making us strong but keeping us protected, of telling the truth but leaving out the scariest realities. They had never heard of intergenerational trauma, and they had no reason to consider the possibility of information being transmitted, from parent to child, on a cellular level.

7

Molasses

There were a lot of complicated feelings inside my little body. What I needed in order to feel better—maybe what any sensitive child who is overburdened with emotion needs—was a creative outlet. The first one I found was as natural as the air in our house. Cooking was my comfort, my refuge, and my first way to self-soothe.

SATURDAY MORNING, STILL DARK OUTSIDE. The yellow cabinets and white laminate countertops belonged to adults most of the week, but now I had the kitchen to myself. I began with the butter Mom kept on the countertop in a silver dish so it would be soft for Daddy's rye bread. I took a blob with a spoon and slung it into the little blue bowl. I opened the sugar drawer, dug in with the red scoop, and sprinkled sparkly grains over the butter. I mixed until I had a nice paste. The first few times I just ate that, butter and sugar, watching *Scooby-Doo, Where Are You!* on the couch in the family room. A few weeks later, I mixed butter and sugar again. I opened the drawer below the sugar and scooped up some flour. I knew where the cinnamon was—what would that taste like in my dough? The real oven was big and mysterious, but turning the dial on the toaster oven that sat on the counter was easy. You just had to watch out for sizzling sugar. If it touched your finger, it stuck and made a white bubble.

It wasn't long before I found potatoes under the kitchen sink and decided that chips couldn't be too hard to make. I took a frying pan from the lower drawer and stood on a chair to fill it with Mazola oil. I shaved thin slices of potatoes with a peeler and dropped them into the hot oil. Using Baba's slotted spoon, I lifted out my potato strips, blotting them with paper towel as I'd seen Mom do when she fried veal cutlets. The chips curved and curled, with crisp edges and nice soft centers, but they were bland. I made another batch, shaking salt over the potato strips as they bubbled away in the hot oil. I blew on them before placing them on my tongue. Hot. Delicious.

I hurried to clean up before anyone came down, except I didn't know what to do with all the oil I'd used. I couldn't waste it. I found Mom's metal funnel and carefully poured the used oil back into the big Mazola container. It wasn't hot enough to melt through the plastic, but the container seemed to change shape, bulging out a bit where the warm oil mixed with the oil that hadn't been used. Or maybe it always looked like that. I put the plastic jug back in the pantry.

A FEW DAYS LATER, I came home from school to find Mom making the komish broit she and Dad had with coffee every morning. I eyed the yellow Mazola container on the counter anxiously, but all she said was "How was school?"

She soon called me down from my room and my heart leapt. Her twice-baked komish, studded with almonds and chocolate chips, lay in neat rows on baking sheets beside the oven. "Bon Bon, try this," Mom said, handing me a warm komish. "Does it seem salty to you?"

AROUND THIS TIME, MOM AND Dad started to travel. At home, Baba Sarah moved in to take care of us, inhabiting the kitchen so completely, I had to put my Saturday morning experiments on hold. We were good kids, docile and obedient, but watching four of us, rang-ing in age from eight to eighteen, couldn't have been easy. Still, if Baba was stressed, she didn't show it. After fleeing Ukraine as a teenager, she had been left a penniless widow. She had played poker for grocery money, and dipped chocolates to make the rent. Watching four kids was, perhaps, no big deal.

It'd been several months since Mom had asked me to start making my own breakfast. "I'm really quite awful in the mornings," she'd said, to explain why she stayed in bed and arranged for me to go to school in a taxi with a few other kids from the neighborhood. But with Baba babysitting, there was no limit to what I might come down in the morning to find. I'd float into the kitchen in my nightie and swoon from the smell. It might be freshly baked cinnamon rolls with sticky caramel and pecans, or flaky knishes filled with cheese or rice, hot from the oven and covered in cool sour cream. Her hands were constantly in motion, and she seemed to never sleep.

ONE SATURDAY MORNING, I FOUND Baba at work in a housedress and slippers. I climbed up on the counter, careful not to sit in the flour. Into the yellow bowl, Baba poured boiling water over rolled oats. She dropped in a spoonful of butter, a sprinkle of salt, a dark glug of molasses. She mixed and handed me the wooden spoon. It tasted dark and sweet; also a little bitter, a little metallic. I picked up the molasses container and poured more thick black syrup onto the spoon. Baba cracked an egg.

Something was bubbling in the measuring cup and it smelled like feet. Baba stirred it down and added it to the oats, then she started to add flour by the cupful. When she could no longer move the wooden spoon, she turned the whole thing onto the counter. We kneaded by hand until the counter was almost clean, the sticky dough warm under my fingers. She gathered the brown dough into a ball and set it aside under a tea cloth, like a baby under a blanket. In a few hours, she would cut me a thick slice of molasses porridge bread and slather it with butter.

Not every day with Baba was perfect. She was an insomniac and she sometimes boiled organ meats like lung or tongue in the middle of the night, making the kitchen smell like a slaughterhouse in the morning. My sisters gagged and complained, but there was something interesting about that odor. I knew it didn't smell *nice*, yet it was fascinating, the idea that you could eat all those different parts. The one thing I truly hated was liver—Baba cooked a slab of it on brown paper, just for me. She was determined to cure my chronic anemia the only way she knew how. Those days, I missed Mom terribly. I missed her new-country way of doing things and her habit of staying in bed in the mornings, leaving me to find my own way around the kitchen before school.

THE SUMMER I TURNED NINE, Mom organized a birthday party for me in the backyard, and Baba made old-fashioned party sandwiches. She cut the crust off a loaf of bread and sliced it crosswise into long slabs. She gave me the rolling pin to flatten the rectangles before she spread the bread with Cheez Whiz and rolled it around cooked asparagus spears, laid end to end. Cut, cut, cut—Baba moved so fast! How did all the little rolls end up the same size?

The whole class came over, including the new boy. While everyone took turns on our bumpy swing set and teeter-totter, he collected so many caterpillars in a cup. "Look," he said, coming close to me. He had dark hair and huge eyes. The caterpillars were overlapping and inching up the sides of the cup, blue and furry, with a black-and-white pattern on their backs. "Aren't they pretty?" The boy's name was Michael. One day he would be my husband.

8

Lox

My sisters were mostly nice to me, but I knew I wasn't one of them. I was still in the early grades when Lisa and Suzanne were in high school, driving and going out with boys while I had just learned to write in cursive. I didn't quite feel like an outsider in my family, but I often had the sense of being on the periphery. I was little and my role was to fall in line and not take up too much space, sort of like a pet or a mascot. Mom cared for me but didn't want me to be too much trouble. It was Dad who was my constant, keeping me tethered to the group and, especially, to himself.

WINTER IN EDMONTON WAS A Narnia-like deep freeze I still dream about. It began in October, with lacy frost on fallen leaves, and lasted until April, when snowmelt ran through the gutters like rivers on either side of the road. There was nothing sweeter than the smell of wet pavement and hot cedar on those first spring days, but in between, we had to endure profound cold, when the temperature plunged to 40 below for two-week stretches and cars didn't start. Pipes burst in the middle of the night and Dad ran to the restaurants again and again to deal with floods. "Promise me you'll never go into the restaurant business," he said.

WE WEREN'T A SPORTY FAMILY, but with all that snow, skiing was a natural part of life. I lay in bed in the early mornings, listening to my sisters pack for their school trips to Jasper or Banff.

"Who took my ski socks?"

"No, *I'm* wearing those ski pants."

"Don't wear my gray turtleneck. You're going to sweat it up!"

I felt both left out and relieved when Dad loaded their skis and boots and bags into the car and took them to the bus.

The January I was nine, it was my turn. There was a little ski hill maybe an hour's drive from our house and that is where Mom said I would start lessons on Sundays. Being away from home for a whole day seemed a little scary, but Mom said it was time to get started. Maybe she thought skiing was chic and glamorous. Maybe she wanted me out of the house for the day.

Like so many of my memories, there is a food attached to the experience of learning to ski, and that food is lox. Mom and Dad ordered it by the side from British Columbia and it came in a long, flat box. There was a great commotion the day it arrived, as Mom cleared the counter and Dad sharpened the knife. They had their own system for dealing with these boxes that appeared, maybe, a few times a year. Instead of shaving the lox on the angle like you see in certain restaurants or appetizing stores, they cut the huge side of salmon horizontally into a series of portions, five or six inches wide. Mom wrapped up each chunk in plastic and then foil, and put them all in the freezer.

Dad didn't do much of the cooking at home, but on Sunday mornings, he took over the kitchen to make brunch. Into cottage cheese he mixed sour cream, chopped radishes, and cucumber for farmer's salad. He scrambled eggs and, best of all, he sliced that smoky, oily lox and laid it on a plate. It broke my heart to miss brunch and be sent out of the warm, delicious house to learn to ski.

In the frigid dark, I waited for the ski bus with a smattering of kids, stomping my feet and exhaling white puffs of air. The driver took my skis out of my mittened hand, but when it came to climbing the huge steps of the bus in my ski boots, I was on my own. I grabbed the handrail and pulled up my small body and heavy feet.

It was a bad introduction to a sport I would eventually come to love. There was a terrifying rope tow that chewed up your mitts and jerked your whole body when you grabbed it. I was so small, the T-bar hit me in the back instead of under my bum. My toes were numb by lunch, pins and needles as I scrunched and relaxed them the way the man at the ski shop had told me to. The only good part of the day was the hot chocolate machine—its whirr and the fake marshmallow liquid it pumped atop the watery brown cocoa.

Home time couldn't come fast enough. Sometimes I fell asleep on the bus, arriving back in the dark again, waking up to look for our car before we had even stopped moving. One night, a few weeks in, I didn't see it. I got off the bus and the driver handed me my skis. Kids and parents were reuniting, doors slamming, white plumes of exhaust everywhere. When the last set of tires had crunched away, I stood there in the dark, my body growing stiff. I clomped over to a lone phone booth. I had a dime in my pocket, but the telephone receiver was high over my head. I stretched to reach it and let go of the folding door, which snapped shut. I pushed on the door but it didn't open.

I couldn't reach the phone and I couldn't get out. Everyone had gone home. How long was I trapped in that icy box, darkness pressing in from all sides?

When Dad arrived, he found me in the phone booth and drove me home. He brought me straight from the car into the kitchen and sat me on the counter in my ski pants. He took out the orange juice and the farmer's salad, the leftover lox and the carton of eggs. He cut the lox into cubes and put it in a bowl with diced tomato and marinated onions, oil and vinegar and capers. He heated butter in the old frying pan until it gave off that golden smell and scrambled an egg as the snow fell silently all around us.

"Don't cry, sweetheart," he said. "Look, I made your favorite—lox salad." I wiped my tears and ate the tangy dish Dad had invented for me because I didn't like bagels. He made me feel better the best way he knew how, and I had never loved him more. I still don't know if it was him or Mom who forgot to pick me up.

9

Spring Cleaning

I spent so much time alone—reading or playing in the backyard, zigzagging the neighborhood on my bike, or roaming the ravine in a hand-me-down windbreaker. I told myself stories: I was traveling through space and time; I was hosting a cooking show; I was searching for my dad's sisters, my lost aunties. I imagined that finding one would be like looking in the mirror, and I'd bring her home for Dad as a present. He'd cry happy tears! Sometimes the inside of my nostrils froze and my toes grew numb before I remembered to go in.

It's strange that despite my stories and fantasies, I thoroughly believed I was uncreative. The teacher said, "Use your imagination," and I froze, sure I was missing that essential part. Families are systems and within those systems, everyone has a role. The younger you are in the birth order, the more roles have already been taken up by the time you come along. Someone is already the musical one, the artist, the storyteller. You have to settle for what's left, to wiggle into that oddly shaped vacancy that's been left for you. How many of us spend our adult lives trying to sort out who we really are versus the child we were required to be to make the family whole?

As I GREW, I BECAME a voracious reader. More and more, my mind concocted scenarios where I dreamed up alternate realities and found our dead relatives alive and well. But I didn't tell anyone. We already had a storyteller—the best storyteller—and Dad inhabited his role with passion and authority. My little fantasies weren't worth mentioning.

Instead, I wrote them down. I sat at the built-in desk in my bedroom as my pencil roved over notebooks and foolscap. In the nightmare years, the too-sensitive years, I wrote freely. Joyfully, even. Much too quickly, I moved from the unselfconscious realm of childhood to a long adolescence when reading my work over, even to myself, made me cringe. The inner critic had already taken up residence inside me and I found the voice on the page—my own voice—too raw and grating. It was like looking at your face in a magnifying mirror, nostrils and freckles enlarged to scary proportions.

I would discover that writing to please other people was simpler, if you could figure out what they wanted. Soon my school assignments would start to earn good marks and praise. Soon Dad would notice I had a little bit of skill and would wonder how it might be put toward capturing his enormous story for future generations. "For posterity," he would say, and although I didn't know what posterity meant, I was thrilled at the prospect of having a talent that could make him happy. Eagerly, I would give up the role of creator in favor of becoming the scribe.

BUT FOR THE TIME BEING, nobody knew I was writing and nobody cared. I worked at my little desk and chucked my freely scrawled pages into the bottom drawer of my desk.

One early spring, the snow was crusty in the backyard, and we were getting ready for Passover. I wanted to work in the kitchen with Baba—I knew how to peel apples with the little knife and chop walnuts and even separate eggs—but I had to clean my room first. Mom gave me a bag and asked me to throw out my garbage. The smell of roasting Cornish hens wafted up from downstairs. The table was set with gold plates and fancy glasses. I knew I would be asked to chant the four questions in front of my aunts and uncles and cousins, and I was nervous about my voice, which was too thin and too raspy and never quite right. The night before, I'd climbed up to the high cupboard over the fridge to get out the Haggadah and practice.

Mom came in to see how I was doing with my spring cleaning, and I showed off my progress. The top four drawers of my desk were almost empty, and I opened them for her, one after the other. "Very nice, Bon Bon. What about that one?"

I yanked open the bottom drawer, which was deeper, heavier, and still full of loose pages and notebooks. "What's all this stuff?" Mom said. "Do you need it?" When I shook my head, Mom grabbed a pile of my work and put it into the bag. I did the same. My journals, my diaries, those loose pages covered in writing all disappeared into the garbage bag.

A few hours later, I sat beside Dad at the long table and delivered the Ma Nishtana in a quivering voice. We counted out the ten plagues and took turns reading the Passover story from the Haggadah. Dad held up the matzoh and the bitter herbs and the room became silent except for his chanting. He had a beautiful voice.

I didn't feel an immediate sense of grief over my lost work. It has developed over the years, the loss of a freer, earlier self that was captured on the pages we threw in the garbage. I'm not sure what they said, and maybe it doesn't matter. The role of the storyteller would come back to me, in time.

10

Be Happy

As I got older, I developed a clearer understanding of what had happened to Dad; that he'd been rounded up and sent first to a ghetto, then a concentration camp. "But look," he said, dimples flashing, huge hand covering mine. "I'm okay. I'm a living miracle, and you're my miracle child!" I felt special but uneasy. I wasn't sure what a miracle child was supposed to do.

Our household was never steeped in the gray tones of tragedy. In fact, life was painted with almost too much color in an effort to brighten what had come before. My parents liked shiny new cars and modern appliances and "continental" food. Our house wasn't huge or super fancy, but Mom kept it immaculate. She threw everything she had into "gracious living," the name she gave to the idealized way of being she and my dad wanted for all of us. There were plants and paintings and a brilliant cleanliness that, she said, reflected our self-respect. I now see this was part of the striving Mom herself was brought up with. In my mind's eye, her childhood home is dark and threadbare except for Baba Sarah's gleaming teacups in ornate patterns of pink or green or blue, and a floor so well polished it shines in the dim light. Baba has her lady friends over for tea, serving properly brewed Red Rose in those delicate cups. She got up before dawn to bake sour cream coffee cake and Turkish delight strudel and pecan puffs dusted in icing sugar. Leaning heavily on Emily Post, Baba figured out how to behave in her adopted country, how to rise above her lowly economic status and her lack of education with manners and social niceties and flawless domestic skills.

I WAS SURROUNDED BY BUBBLY extroverts and I was expected to be like them: vivacious, outgoing, and happy. And sometimes, I was. Offsetting the small, dark weight I carried in my chest were beams of light, many of them found with my best friend. Her name was Cathy and together we went to a little Jewish school that smelled like glue. In winter, the vents along the walls blew so hot, it took my breath away. Cathy was the smartest kid in the class. If I stuck close to her, maybe I could be the second smartest.

Cathy was Jewish, too, but she had a dad who worked at an office and a mom who was finishing a master's degree. Instead of sisters, she had two older brothers and the talk around the dinner table at her house was quick and clever. Nobody spoke with an accent.

It was easy for me to see that they were normal, which meant we were not. I knew nothing of the communities of Holocaust survivors around the world; of places where survivors banded together to cope and share stories, their children growing up in a pack, with a wider perspective. Dad had wanted to marry a Canadian girl and start a new life. In her own way, Mom wanted a new life, too. As a result, I grew up feeling there was nobody quite like us—a Holocaust survivor father, a Canadian mother, a family tipping toward newness and pleasure in any way we could.

CATHY AND I TOOK DANCE together and when I think of joy in childhood, I think of Thursday nights, when I was transported into a realm of ease and weightlessness. My leg floated up at the barre; the teacher, Myrna, put "Jamming" on the hi-fi and my rib cage moved left-right, left-right. Myrna wore a bodysuit in a silky fabric, cut high on the hip, with leg warmers and black jazz shoes with heels instead of soft soles. I traded my plain black leotard for a purple Danskin and jazz shoes as soon as I could, and worked up a sweat trying to perfect my double pirouettes. Cathy's split leaps were higher but as soon as the music came on, my body had no bones. I felt like a liquid, moving from shape to shape as the thoughts left my head. I could not believe the pleasure of flying around the stage doing a ring of posé coupé turns; the freedom and thrill of taking up too much space.

I SPENT ENDLESS HOURS AT Cathy's house, exploring the strange contents of the kitchen cupboards: packaged macaroni and cheese, white bread, Hamburger Helper, jars of spaghetti sauce. Nobody ate smoked fish or knishes or cabbage rolls. There was no black bread or sweet homemade mustard or slices of beef tongue. Instead, we got to make Chef Boyardee pizza from a box with Cathy's mom, pressing the dough into a cookie sheet and tearing open the bag of powdered cheese.

Cathy spent plenty of time at our house, too, but even better was when she came with me to the restaurants. At that time, Dad was working on plans to transform Teddy's into a two-story food emporium with a deli, bar, dining room, and discotheque. He walked around with blueprints tucked under his arm and a cigarette in his mouth. There would be a DJ booth! And a disco ball! And a dance floor—our very own stage to dance on!

Meanwhile, the Carousel had moved locations and now catered to a downtown business crowd. It was closed on Sundays, when Dad would go to take care of things and that, I knew, was the best possible time to be there. While Dad opened the safe and looked in the till, Cathy and I slipped behind the swinging door of the kitchen. "Ordering," I yelled, picking up an invisible steak with tongs. "One New York, medium rare!" Cathy stood beside me at the cool flat top, playing with the spatulas.

We yanked open the heavy door of the walk-in cooler, careful not to let it latch behind us. "What if we get locked in here?" Cathy said.

"At least we'll have a lot to eat."

Shivering, we stuck our fingers into plastic buckets, hotel pans, and baking sheets, tasting blue cheese dressing, jellied beef jus, whipped cream. There were piles of raw steaks and buckets of anchovies, but I didn't eat stuff like that in front of my friend.

We came out of the kitchen and wandered into the bar, where the soda gun glowed in the dim light. We shot Coke, Sprite, and tonic into tall glasses. We poured grenadine, thick and syrupy, through the little spout attached to the top of the bottle into a little metal cup on a stick. When I dumped the syrup into our glasses, the mixture that had been dull and brown turned a beautiful pink. I shook in Tabasco and grabbed maraschino cherries from the fridge below the counter.

The first sip was the worst, but I knew I wouldn't throw up. Cathy touched her glass to her lips and put it down.

"You're going to drink it?" she said, her eyes huge.

"Oh yes. It's delicious!"

She stared at me as I finished my own drink and reached for hers. We did not waste food. Ever.

MOM WAS AWAY ON A bridge weekend the night the renovated Teddy's reopened. Dad toured me through the new kitchens—one upstairs and one downstairs—and he showed me the dumbwaiter—an actual elevator!—the cooks would use to move supplies up or down. On the main floor, in addition to the deli, where we would serve our classics, there was a bar with dark wood and Tiffany lamps. Upstairs featured a book-lined dining room and, at the back, the pièce de résistance, a small dance floor with a DJ booth and disco ball, just as Dad had promised.

The reopening party was packed and sweaty. "What should I do?" I yelled, so Dad could hear me over the music.

"Whatever you want," he shouted back, grinning. In black velvet pants and a sparkly top, I roamed from room to room, floor to floor, kitchen to kitchen. Donna Summer crooning from the speakers and waiters pushing through the dance floor with platters of garlic shrimp and filet skewers. At the center of it all, Dad was the happiest I'd ever seen him—dancing, laughing, hugging, shaking hands—and I was there to soak up his glow.

11

The Mini-series

With all the excitement, the sadness within me became wispy and vague. I wasn't always sure it was there and I didn't know what it was called. But the two things that happened next made it sharp and pointy and impossible to ignore.

Toward the end of sixth grade, everyone was talking about an upcoming TV mini-series called *Holocaust*. The teachers at my school told us to watch. Lisa and Suzanne were already away at university, but my parents and Julie, also, planned to watch. Nobody made me—I had already taken up my lifelong role as the sensitive one, and I could have found a way to disappear into my room. On the other hand, nobody stopped me, and I didn't want to be left out. I was on the edge of an abyss: the blackest truth was about to invade my bright fairy tale.

We gathered around the family room TV. I don't remember the mood being tense. Behind the opening credits, a synagogue burned and collapsed, making my pulse quicken. Twenty minutes later, a Jewish boy was tripped, kicked, and beaten by German kids on the soccer field. The hairs on the back of my neck prickled. By the time soldiers were smashing windows, I was sweating and shivering. They ransacked Jewish shops, burned books, threw produce into the street. The grandfather was beaten and forced to march with a drum around his neck. The grandmother sobbed on her knees in the street.

Head swimming and hands over my ears, I ran downstairs and put on a record to drown the sounds coming from the TV. I heaved over the basement toilet, but I couldn't eject the bad feeling from my body. Dad's carefully constructed stories of bravery and heroism evaporated. *He* was the beaten boy on the soccer field. The grandfather I never knew was the humiliated gentleman forced to drum. My dead grandmother was the old woman, kneeling on the road. Looking back, I see how mild *Holocaust* was compared to reality, but that April night, it didn't matter. I suddenly understood that the world could hold pure evil, and that evil had been directed at us.

Flooded with recognition, I felt the magnitude of what I'd been carrying click into place, and I lost the insulation Dad had worked hard to give me.

THE MINI-SERIES MIGHT NOT HAVE had the lifelong impact it did if it hadn't been followed, a few months, later by my first experience of real-life antisemitism. Cathy and I graduated from our little Jewish school and got ready to start different junior high schools. At the same time, Julie was leaving for university, and I would be home alone with my parents, who continued to be preoccupied with our businesses, comfort, and pleasure. They loved me, but their attention was elsewhere.

That September, my cozy little life became dangerous and violent. At my new school, girls fought outside at lunch and you could be shoved into a locker for looking at the wrong person. I felt like I'd fallen through a hole into a different universe, and I scurried down the halls in fear and confusion.

———

THE FIRST TIME I WAS THREATENED, I was in the bathroom before a school dance, dressed in a sweater vest and wool skirt, like a typist on her way to a job interview. I was an easy target.

"See that girl right there?" someone said from behind me. I was washing my hands at the sink, and I looked into the mirror to see two blond girls near the stalls. I didn't know them, and it took me a second to realize they were referring to me.

"That's the girl I'm going to pound into the wall at the dance if she doesn't keep her eyes to herself."

I hurried out of the bathroom and walked straight home. "Oh no, that dance is on a different day," I lied when Mom asked why I was home so early.

The school had a rough atmosphere, so at first I didn't realize I was being targeted because I was Jewish. But soon a girl named Debbie started to call me Jew-this and Jew-that. When I came back from winter vacation with my olive skin darkened with a tan, she came up with N——Jew, a confusing combination of words I couldn't begin to process. My one friend that year, a girl I'd known since we roamed the ravine as six-year-olds, suffered worse than I did. They made fun of her Yiddish name and tossed her books around in the social studies classroom while I sat on my hands, blood whooshing in my ears.

I needed to get out, but I wasn't sure how to describe the situation to my parents. There was no way I was going to tell them about being called Jew-anything. I felt a queasy kind of shame, and I knew not to bring that shame into our house. Dad had worked hard to separate us from everything he'd been through; to make sure we were accepted, comfortable, successful. I wasn't going to ruin everything with my stupid little problem. No, I needed to protect him the way he had protected me. But maybe I could say something to Mom.

ONE COLD DAY, I WALKED home for lunch and found Mom in the kitchen getting ready to host her bridge ladies. "Mom," I said, taking a Stouffer's microwave meal out of the freezer. I opened the box and took out two plastic pouches. One contained a solid off-white mass with orange bits; the other was a block of frozen rice.

"The girls at school are really different." I stabbed the bags with a fork and put them in the microwave.

"Different how?" she said, cutting a cucumber into batons.

"Well, they sort of like to fight," I said with a little laugh. "Like that's what people do for fun." The microwave dinged and I leaned across the counter to rotate my half-thawed lunch and put it back in for another minute.

"Who's doing that?" Ranch dressing oozed into a glass bowl.

"Kids I don't know? Kids who come on the bus? I'm not sure who they are."

She had the cucumbers in one hand and the ranch dip in the other. "Just stick with the good kids," she said. "The kids you know from last year."

I picked up my thawed lobster Newburg and followed her into the family room. She set the cucumbers and dip down on the hearth and went back into the kitchen.

I sat at the TV with my lunch, searching for a way to tell her about the locker room. Any day, I would be tossed into the running shower by four or five girls—they took your arms and legs and swung you right in, letting your head bang on the yellow tile floor. I wanted to explain it all, but I couldn't find the first sentence. Creamy lobster sauce soaked into white rice and I scooped it up with a spoon. Fred and Barney got into their foot-powered car. Mom came back into the family room. I opened my mouth but no words came out.

I sat there, silent and thinking. I thought so hard my brain hurt but, still, I couldn't think of what to say. "Mom?" I began.

"Almost done, Bon Bon? It's twelve thirty. You should head back to school."

I STARTED WEARING MY GYM uniform under my clothes so I could avoid the locker room altogether, and somehow, I got to the end of the year without anyone laying a finger on me. In the summer, my parents finally heard me and arranged for me to move to Cathy's school the following fall. My friend's transition to junior high had been smooth and easy. She met Allison, Beth, Angie, and two different Susans, all of them genuinely welcoming and nice. They included me right away but, for months, I worried that an invisible mark would show up on my face or my clothes, in the sound of my voice or the smell of my hair.

12

Café au Lait

All the teachers at my new school were smart and nice, but Ms. Harasym, the French teacher, was the best one of all. While our mothers were Mrs. and our unmarried teachers were Miss, she was young, possibly divorced, and the only Ms. I knew. She wore crisp white shirts with popped collars and slim pants that zipped up the side. *"En français,"* she said, and we fell over ourselves to comply.

Until then, French had been the most lifeless subject I could imagine, but Ms. Harasym changed everything. Instead of the bushy perm of the day, her hair was cut in a short pixie, with pointed sideburns that accented her high cheekbones. She ran a trip to Paris for the ninth graders, organizing bottle drives to help make it accessible to everyone. But if you wanted to go, you had to speak French the whole time. She had a sharp side—she wouldn't hesitate to call you out for talking in class or arriving late—and we didn't want to disappoint her.

I'd traveled before. In late December, my parents sometimes took us away to escape the cold. At a Maui motel, I put a quarter into a vending machine and a sweating can of pink nectar popped out. We ate papaya with lime, carefully scraping out the seeds. "Did you know seaweed is edible?" Julie said. We picked rubbery green stems off Kāʻanapali Beach and ate them with Wish-Bone dressing.

But Europe was a different type of trip, requiring at least two planes, many hours of travel, and unknowable sums of money. We were originally from Europe, yes, but that was different. In fact, given their firm preference for the New World, Mom and Dad didn't consider such a trip, and most schools didn't offer them.

Except ours. On a cool March morning, we arrived at Charles de Gaulle—Ms. Harasym, maybe twenty teenagers, and a teacher friend she brought to help chaperone. After spending the night on the plane, sound seemed warped and everything I looked at was fuzzy at the edges. There was a marvelous smell, too—a mix of foreign cigarettes and perfume that clung to my hair and clothes after I left the arrivals hall. Settling into a seat on the tour bus, I pressed my face to the glass as we started to move, absorbing more sensations: the slanted sunlight of the Parisian early morning, smudges of green trees and red roofs whizzing by, hunger tinged with nausea and a fluttery feeling in my abdomen.

We arrived at the pension and went straight to breakfast, served in a type of basement, with stones piled up to form walls and a curved ceiling instead of the flat popcorn panels I was used to.

"*Un café, s'il vous plaît?*" I said to the aproned woman who raised her eyebrows at me.

"*Café au lait?*"

"Uh, *oui.*"

I'd just started drinking coffee at home, either black like my parents did or, if we were at the store, whitened with cream from the little triangular cartons that sat on the tables. What the waitress dropped off was entirely different: a smooth broth the color of butterscotch, foaming, warm, and served in a cereal bowl. Alongside the bowl of milky coffee sat a roll on a saucer, crescent shaped, flaky, and toasty brown. When I picked it up, I discovered it weighed almost nothing at all. Was it hollow? I broke the strange pastry apart, showering the tablecloth with crumbs, and dunked it into the bowl. Crisp and spongy, warm and cool, sweet, slightly bitter and even vaguely barnyard, my first café au lait–soaked croissant just about blew my mind.

WE CAME UP FROM BREAKFAST and Ms. Harasym asked us to gather in the lobby so she could hand out our keys. "Cathy, Beth, Allison, and Bonny," she read from her clipboard. I went limp with relief. By that stage, my place in the group was everything, a fact my mother mentioned with pointed regularity. "You're so worried about your friends. It's always about your friends," she said most Friday nights, as I hurried to clear the table after dinner and join everyone in the woods near the school. "Your sisters were much more interested in the family."

There was no use arguing because it was true. My sisters had grown up as a trio. I was on my own and I knew what it was like to be on the outside. I never wanted to be out there again.

IN MS. HARASYM'S PARIS, EVERY shop, bakery, and restaurant was more charming and delicious than the one before. How many times did we walk to that crêpe stand in the eighth arrondissement, watching traffic spin around the Place de la Concorde? They made the crêpes on an oversized griddle with a special wooden tool and handed them to us hot, seasoned with lemon and sugar, or a fiery orange brandy called Grand Marnier. Ms. Harasym planned real French dinners, too. We ate escargot drenched in garlic butter and rich stews with olives, tomatoes, and a meat they said was chicken. "What chicken do you know with bones like this?" Cathy said, holding up an unfamiliar-looking joint. When we found out it was rabbit, she was full of outrage, but I was not as upset as a girl who'd had a pet bunny should've been. I wondered when we would eat it again.

———

ONE NIGHT WE WENT TO Montmartre to see the glowing Sacré-Cœur and the artists with their paints and easels on the cobblestones. We stopped for a snack, and I ordered a café au lait, my new favorite drink.

"*Non*," the waitress said. "It is nighttime now. Café au lait is for breakfast. I'll bring you something else."

It was called espresso and it came in a cute little cup. The liquid was dark and oily, and when I tasted it, thrillingly bitter. Nobody paid any attention when I ordered another, and then two more after that.

Later that night, I lay in bed, heart pumping wildly, eyes pinned open. One by one, my friends fell asleep, leaving me alone with my new disease. Magical Paris turned strange and eerie. The minutes turned into hours. I started to shake, then weep, certain I was dying and would never see my family again.

It was after two when I crept through the silent hotel to my teacher's room. I put my ear to the door. Was that laughing? My knock was as light as a knock could be, but Ms. Harasym opened up right away, wearing a long cotton nightgown and holding a bathroom glass in her hand. The friend she'd brought on the trip was jumping on the bed like a little girl. The two of them were wiping tears from their eyes.

"S-something is wrong with me. I can't sleep," I stuttered. "Should I go to the hospital?"

Ms. Harasym stopped laughing and looked at me. "You drank espresso, yes?" she said.

I nodded miserably.

"How many?"

"Four."

My teacher disappeared for a moment and came back with an empty glass. She walked over to a little table and poured several glugs from an amber bottle. "You're going to be fine. Drink this."

The Grand Marnier smelled like oranges and lighter fluid. I hesitated. Ms. Harasym smiled and lifted her chin. There was nothing else to do. I tipped my head back and poured the fiery potion down my throat.

I wiped my mouth with the back of my hand and gave the glass back to her.

"*Ça va?*" she said.

"*Oui.*" And off to bed I went.

13

Blueberries

Soon we all moved to high school. There was a new energy crackling in the air and suddenly, boys were everywhere. I liked Matt, who came by my locker to chat with me between second and third periods, and Bobby, who electrified my shoulder when he touched me to give the address of the party on Saturday night. It wasn't just me. My whole group of girlfriends, the circle I'd worked hard to situate myself within, began to bend and morph under the stress of a new force. Something was happening to us. We were just trying to keep up.

At the exact time when I wanted to disappear into this compelling new world, my parents started to take too much interest in me. Mom assessed my changing looks and developing body in a way that made me squirm, even when she had nice things to say. "You have a sensational figure," she announced one day, as I was on my way out to meet my friends. I felt embarrassed and exposed, missing the days when I roamed the ravine in my hand-me-down windbreaker, the rest of the family busy with grown-up things that didn't involve me.

Baba, at least, treated me the same way she always had, and her apartment was a safe place, away from the pressures of growing up.

My sleepovers were less frequent than they'd once been, but I still loved that huge old-fashioned furniture and the little kitchen that never cooled off because it was always in use. Standing at her Formica table, we stretched strudel dough so thinly I could see her tablecloth's red-and-yellow pattern through it. After we loaded on the apples and raisins and cinnamon sugar, Baba picked up the tablecloth and jerked it to make the dough roll over on itself in a heavy, bumpy log.

As every fifteen-year-old girl has to learn, change is inevitable, and for me it happened, irrevocably, on the day I came home from school, thinking about a boy named Bruce, and found Mom sitting on the couch, staring into space. "Mama had a stroke," she said robotically.

"A what?"

In a monotone, she explained that Baba couldn't talk or move the right side of her body. "C'mon. We're going to the hospital. She needs some things."

We stopped at Baba's apartment on the way. Just inside the living room, I opened the heavy buffet, looking for the paper bag of candied fruit that had always been there. I loved the glazed pineapple rings Baba bought for her fruitcakes, and the sticky apricots she ordered from California. I stuck my head inside the empty cupboard and inhaled, but all I smelled was wood.

In the kitchen, the glass with the mermaid sat there, overflowing with drips from the tap. When was the last time we made varenikes, windows open to catch an August breeze?

We mix flour and eggs and oil into a smooth dough. "It has to rest now, Bondles. You can't rush it." We watch The Price is Right *while we wait, and when we come back to the kitchen, we roll the dough, not too thin. "See how it doesn't jump back?" Baba says, her rolling pin making that clicking sound as it moves over the smooth surface. We cut circles with the lid of a Mason jar. The windows steam up as she fills each round with a spoonful of flour-*

sugar mixture and an impossible heap of wild blueberries. The dough stretches obligingly as she folds it over and pinches it closed. Then she drops each varenika into a huge pot of boiling water. "Be careful not to tear them," she says. "The blueberries will leak into the water and turn everything gray like nobody's business."

"Okay, Baba."

To go with them, she makes a blueberry sauce that is so dark and rich, sometimes the filled varenikes and the sauce together are too much for me.

"Bondles, I'll make something special for you." She slices up the scraps of dough left over after all the circles have been cut and tosses them into the boiling water. She fishes out my "doughies" with a slotted spoon and hands me a little bowl of them, swimming in melted butter, with just a drop of purple sauce over top.

WHILE MOM RUMMAGED AROUND IN the bathroom, I went into the bedroom and breathed in pikake, Baba's favorite perfume. I opened the closet and found my old housecoat among her voluminous muumuus. In one pocket of the shoe organizer on the back of the closet door, I located my slippers and walked around the apartment with my heels hanging over the backs until Mom said we had to go.

THE HOSPITAL SMELLED LIKE CANNED mushrooms and antiseptic. I stood by the bed looking at Baba's white face and the clear plastic tubes in her nose. One corner of her mouth pointed downward. She couldn't get a sentence out. "I want, I want . . ." she trailed off.

"Baba, what? What can I get you?" I picked up the plastic cup and tried to put the straw in her mouth. She closed her eyes. She was wearing every piece of jewelry she owned—a thin gold rope and a strand of pearls and an amethyst ring on her index finger. Her hands were cold, her gnarled knuckles dry and swollen.

WHEN SHE WAS WELL ENOUGH to leave the hospital, Baba had started to speak again, the words coming slowly. Her face looked almost normal, her cheekbones just a little more prominent, the skin of her neck a little looser. I thought the scare was over and, with relief, turned my attention back to the confusion of high school.

A short time later, Baba was readmitted to the hospital with heart failure. I didn't know enough to worry. Baba had already survived a stroke, hadn't she? But not long after, the phone rang at night. I came into Mom and Dad's room in my nightgown.

"It's Mama," Dad said as he put down the receiver. "She's worse. They want us to go."

I watched Mom put on a gray sweater. She fixed her hair and fussed with a scarf, tying it around her neck.

"Bye," they said, and I went back to bed.

IT WAS LIGHT OUTSIDE WHEN they came back and told me Baba was gone. I stared at Dad, my right eye twitching. "What do you mean?"

There was a strange void as we stood there in the front hall—a sucking vacuum, a pressure drop—but soon it was taken up with Mom's anger. "Can you imagine," she said in that hard way of hers. "I was fussing with my clothes and my hair when my mother was lying dead in the hospital?"

I didn't understand, at first, that Dad had told us Baba was worse when she was actually gone already. I didn't realize that he couldn't bring himself to say the words, that he waited until they arrived at the hospital so someone else would be the one to tell Mom that her mother had died. I absolutely didn't consider how many people Dad had watched die, and the scars that might have left inside him.

MY SISTERS CAME HOME FROM university for Baba's funeral. It was December and the ground was frozen. Clumps of icy dirt hit the top of the plain casket and made the lid jump. I was sure it would pop off. Shiva was at our house. Mom put out a whole smoked turkey and people cut off slices to make open-faced sandwiches on rye bread. Baba wasn't there to bake pecan puffs and brownies, but we still had some of her baking in the freezer.

My only grandparent had disappeared, but my grief was choked and confused. I thought the hurt was everyone else's and I didn't know what I had the right to feel. I was the youngest, after all, still afraid to take up too much space.

IT WAS YEARS LATER WHEN I started to dream about her. She was an earth mother with long silver hair. She was a blaze of white, telling my fortune with her tea leaves. Everything about her had been generous and ample: her body, her food, her love. She had modeled a kind of intuition and wisdom—a female power I was eventually able to name, but only much later.

14

Noodles

My parents hated the winter, especially Dad, who had cruel arthritis in his back, neck, and shoulders, surely caused, Mom said, by the heavy labor he'd been forced to do as a child. They decided to buy a condo in Arizona, where they could go to escape the cold, a week or two at a time. Being able to afford a second home was a big deal to them, a sign they'd arrived, and they excitedly ordered a houseful of nice furniture, but when it came time to set the place up, Baba had just died and Mom couldn't leave. My sisters must have been busy at university and that's how Dad and I ended up going down, just the two of us, one winter break.

As we drove from Sky Harbor airport into Scottsdale, I took in the Seussian cacti and the red mountain in the shape of a camel's back. I had a vague headache from the champagne we'd been served on the plane. "You see," Dad had said, holding up his glass, sunlight streaming in from the airplane window, "why waste time sitting at the airport waiting?" We'd arrived late and the flight had been over-sold. "I told you they'd bump us up to first class," he said. This was signature Dad thinking and although it could have ended in a mess, it had worked exactly as he said it would.

———

INSIDE THE CONDO, EVERYTHING MOM and Dad had ordered—beds, mattresses, lamps, sofas—was in crates and boxes in the center of the carpeted living room. We took for granted that Mom was the arranger: the maker of plans, the payer of bills, and the solver of problems. In normal times, she would've had the place set up in advance, or arrived with a plan to get the job done before bedtime. But these were not normal times and Mom was back home, tying up her mother's estate. If her muted response to her mother's death was not enough to convince me of her pain, this rare lapse should have been.

But I wasn't thinking about Mom. Dad eyed the boxes and said, "Oh! Let's take a look," unfazed by the task before us. We began to work on opening the crates with our bare hands, flinging pieces of cardboard around the room.

A FEW HOURS LATER, WE'D unpacked some pieces, but the work was slow going. There were at least a dozen boxes we hadn't touched when the sun dipped low in the sky. We'd picked up a few basics, but mostly, the cupboards were bare. Other people would've ordered in, but Dad hated takeout. Instead, he put a pot of water on to boil. He mixed eggs and flour and water into a paste, his tongue sticking out a bit in concentration.

"This is how my mother made noodles," he said as I wiped out the inside of the new fridge.

"Your mother made noodles?" I turned to look at him. His memories of Udel, the grandmother I'd never had, were always so vague and amorphous. "You've never said this before."

"I know. It just came to me now. Isn't that funny?"

He turned the water down to a simmer and dropped the batter by the spoonful into the pot. Soon, floppy yellow disks floated to the surface like little jellyfish, and he scooped them into a bowl with a blob of butter. Tender, hot, and almost sweet, they slid down my throat so fast that he smiled and mixed up more.

AFTER DINNER, WE THREW TWO mattresses on the floor of the big-gest room and slept like that, without mattress pads or sheets or blankets. "Let me tell you something," he said in the dark. "Are you listening?"

"Yes, Dad."

"The most important thing is to enjoy life. Just marry a nice boy and be happy. That's all. That's the secret."

"But Dad," I said, "how can I just be happy all the time? What about problems?"

"What problems? You have everything going for you."

"But—" I had the urge to argue. I didn't know why.

"You shouldn't let anything upset you. You are cute and smart and you have a beautiful life. Don't spoil it."

I could feel something stuck in my chest, like I'd swallowed a bal-loon and my throat couldn't close because of it. I opened my mouth, but no sound came out.

"I am your father," he said. "Listen to me."

I rolled onto my side to relieve the pressure in my chest. Soon, Dad started to snore softly while I stared into the unfamiliar garden until finally, I fell asleep.

LATER THAT WINTER, MOM AND Dad wanted to go back to Arizona to finish the place. There was no school holiday in February, but I was a good student. They pulled me out.

My chemistry teacher that year was Mr. Anastakis, a laconic, un-smiling man with a long face like Abraham Lincoln. While Mom and Dad shopped for pillows and rugs and I sat at the pool with a paperback, Mr. Anastakis taught my chemistry class about atomic mass and the method for calculating the protons, neutrons, and elec-trons of every element in the periodic table.

Children of immigrants are sometimes raised with intense pres-sure to achieve, but that wasn't my pressure. My parents wanted my sisters and me to be well-groomed and attractive ladies-in-training.

Achievement wasn't actively discouraged—they were proud of us when we did well—but feminine virtues like beauty and charm were more highly valued. As the youngest of the group, the very least in terms of achievement was expected from me. I liked to do well, and most years I won school awards for a high average, but my academic performance was secondary. My main job was to be lovable, gregarious, and happy all the time.

Back in school the following Monday, Mr. Anastakis held a pile of white pages in his bony hands. He went around the room, impassively distributing the pop quiz, face down. When he came to my desk, I tried to make eye contract. "I wasn't here last week," I reminded him quietly. He shrugged, laid the test in front of me, and kept walking.

When I turned over the page, the questions looked like hieroglyphics. I glanced over at my friend Allison, moving her pencil busily. My palms started to sweat and I heard a strange *wa-wa-wa* sound in my ears. I scribbled down some stuff from earlier lessons and asked to go to the bathroom. When I handed my half-blank test to Mr. Anastakis on the way out, he seemed to smile.

There were three stalls in the pink and black school bathroom—feet at the bottom of two of them. I banged open the third door and stood over the toilet. When I saw black smudges in front of my eyes, I sat with my head down, staring at the ground until my vision cleared. Then I washed my face and went back to class.

THE TEST CAME BACK WITH a score of 43 percent and Mr. Anastakis's angular scrawl indicating it needed to be signed by my parents. Stricken with shame, I brought the test to the table as we finished dinner that night. It was crumpled from the way I'd shoved it into my bag at school, before anyone could see. Mom was in the kitchen when I handed it to Dad. "What's this?" he said, and I held my breath as his eyes flicked over the page.

There was a pause and I stiffened. Dad rarely lost his temper, but when he did, it was scary. It would start with a growl, very quiet but building to an inevitable crescendo. "Awwwwww shit!" he'd yell, and then words would fly out of his mouth—swear words, words he never used—as his anger took hold and intensified like a tornado. I'd witnessed it only a few times when he argued with Mom, and once or twice at my sisters. If he screamed at me like that, I would crumble into a million pieces. I would evaporate. I would die.

Instead, his eyes fell on me softly, and he smiled. "Sweetheart, it's okay," he said.

"What? You're not mad?"

"It's just a test. It doesn't matter."

"But 43 percent! This has never happened before. You must think—"

"Listen to me," he said more forcefully. "It doesn't matter. I do not want you to be upset." His eyes bore into me as he took the pen from my hand and signed the test.

I left the dining room to find my schoolbag, flooded with relief. I was so lucky. People's parents grounded them, screamed and yelled, told them they were a disgrace. All he wanted was for me to be happy. So why was I crying?

15

The Suitcase

Signed up for a school ski trip that early spring, I headed down to the basement to look for my skis and boots. I opened the door to the furnace room and was hit with a blast of hot air. Unlike the rest of our house, it was a mess of stuff: suitcases, boxes of my sisters' old books and binders, storage bags full of clothes hanging on racks. The furnace turned itself on noisily, making me jump. A trickle of water ran into a drain in the concrete floor.

I found my equipment and was about to take it and hurry upstairs when something among my parents' gray and black suitcases caught my eye. It was bone colored, with a little bit of tarnished brass trim visible at the corners. I grabbed the handle and lifted the boxy, old suitcase. It wasn't heavy, but I could hear soft movement inside when I shook it.

I sat on the concrete floor to snap open the clasps. A cascade of black-and-white photos I'd never seen tumbled out. I picked up a small square with rough edges. A thin young man in a white open-collared shirt and a melancholy expression looked right at the camera. In another, the same boy squinted in the sun, his arm around someone I didn't recognize. My mouth went dry as I sat there, looking at a version of my father I wasn't sure I wanted to see. Before I'd even made a decision, I was stuffing the photos back in the suitcase and taking the steps up two at a time, suitcase in hand.

SINCE THE NIGHT OF THE mini-series, I had managed to think about my background less and less. The Holocaust wasn't taught in school, and Dad had been careful with his stories after my mini-series melt-down five years earlier. It had been he who had comforted me that night. "Sweetheart," he'd said, "just put this out of your mind. For-get it even happened." I didn't forget—of course not—but with Dad's help, I was able to tiptoe around the edges of the abyss with-out falling in. He mentioned the war here and there in passing, but he didn't dig into details. The only time I really had to face the Ho-locaust was at Jewish youth group. Most of the evening and week-end programs were fun, but from time to time the beast would rear its head, and I'd find myself frozen in my chair, watching black-and-white images flickering across a screen set up in a gym. I'd start to feel a familiar revulsion and hurry out of the room with one of the group leaders trailing behind me. "You can't just leave the program," they'd call at my back, and I'd turn around and explain, again, that my dad could have been any one of those skeletons in awful stripes. I didn't want to find him.

WHEN I CAME UP FROM the basement, Dad was in the family room in a paisley bathrobe, reading the paper. Mom was in Arizona. "Look what I found," I said, holding up the suitcase.

"Oh!" He put a hand to his forehead. "I forgot about that suitcase! Make some coffee. Let's have a look."

I opened the metal clasps and the pictures spilled out on the car-pet. I glanced at Dad to find him smiling and nodding his head hap-pily.

"Look at this one," I said, picking up a curled rectangle and hand-ing it to him. "What are you wearing?"

"That's the traveling suit I bought before I got on the ship in 1947." It was the belted jacket and pleated trousers, the fedora. I picked up another snap of a handsome young man, wind in his hair, driving a boat.

"Is this you?"

"It sure is," he said, taking the photo from me and inspecting it closely.

"How can you be driving a boat? Didn't you just survive the war?"

"We managed to have a lot of fun in Pegnitz. We had money from smuggling cigarettes. And we were free."

I walked into the kitchen to make the coffee and came back to the family room with two steaming cups. *This is okay,* I thought, putting down the coffee and sitting on the floor. *This is nice.* I'd matured since I'd last spoken to Dad about the war. *I'm almost an adult,* I thought. *I can handle this now. And look at Dad. He wants to talk. He needs to talk.*

"Tell me again about the people who dropped the bread," I said, picking up a photo of young Dad with his arm around a girl with dark hair. "And who's this?"

"That's my friend Guta." He leaned back and crossed his legs. "Now, do you want to know about the bread or not?"

I nodded.

"We were on this long train ride at the end of the war—ten days in the cold open cars. There was no food, no water, no toilets. When people died, they threw them off the train."

I shivered, but I didn't stop him.

"It was the winter of 1945, and the train was taking us through Czechoslovakia, deep into Germany." He took a long sip of coffee. "Wait—do you think maybe you should be writing this down?"

"Like on paper?" I said dumbly.

"Aren't you the writer?"

"Okay, hold on."

I RAN UP TO MY bedroom to look for a notebook, thinking about how my stomach had dropped when my English teacher had called me to her desk a week earlier. I'd started hanging out behind the school with the smokers. Had she seen me?

"Yes, Ms. Norwood?"

She'd sat on the edge of her desk and crossed her legs under her pleated skirt. "What do you want to take in university?" she'd said.

I was so relieved by her question that my mind had gone blank. "Uh, I'm not sure."

"It's not too soon to start thinking about it." Her gaze had fallen on me. "Do you think you might want to be a writer?"

I'd swallowed. "I haven't thought about it."

"Well, let me know if you want to talk further. I have a few ideas for you."

"Okay. Thanks, Ms. Norwood."

"That's all," she'd said, standing abruptly. "You can go."

I'D TOLD DAD WHAT MY teacher had said, and he'd beamed with pride. Now, as I took a pen from the kitchen and sat back down on the carpet with my notebook on the coffee table, Dad said, "If you're such a good writer, maybe we should write a book together."

A book together. Me and him. Pride washed over me. And happiness. But also anxiety. And fear. It was so many feelings all at once that I could only nod in response. The pen shook in my hand as I held it over the page. "So, what were you saying?"

"The train went under a bridge," he said. "Don't forget, the top was open. And people were standing on that bridge. As we went under they started dropping things. We didn't know what it was. And then we saw. We couldn't believe it! These good people were dropping bread from the bridge right into our hands. It saved my life."

"Who else was on the train?"

"I was with Abe. We were packed in like sardines." I wrote furiously, trying to soak up the incredible story, trying to preserve the miracle. "People became corpses before our eyes. We wondered if we would be next," he said.

We sat like that for a couple of hours, Dad becoming more and more animated, something heavy lifting off of him. When at last he was done talking, I took my notebook up to my room and slid it into a drawer in my desk. It was only then that I noticed how sweaty I was. I stripped off my pajamas and took a long shower.

I passed the afternoon listening to music in Cathy's basement, pretending to be fine, but when I came home to have dinner, I could only pick at the roast beef and baked potatoes Dad had brought home from the store. "Why aren't you eating?" he said.

"Late lunch," I lied, forcing a few bites.

By bedtime, my teeth were chattering and my chest and belly felt heavy. I thought maybe I had the flu, but my temperature was normal.

I climbed into bed feeling like I'd swallowed a lead anchor. I couldn't get rid of the sensation that I was sinking into the ground. Dad couldn't have known what his stories were doing to me because I didn't tell him. Just like when I was little, I thought absorbing what he had to say was simply my job. If I'd shown him my distress, he would've changed the subject immediately. But he had protected me. Now I had to protect him.

16

Jujubes

If my happiness was all that mattered, I wasn't going to bother working hard at school anymore. Nor was I interested in sitting at home with Mom and Dad, submitting to their prying eyes and over-bearing urges. Toward the end of high school, the escape I was look-ing for presented itself in the form of a serious boyfriend.

Dark haired and handsome, he taught me how to smoke pot and drive a stick shift in his mom's tiny BMW. We went to a parking lot on the Southside where I rode the clutch: *Go. Stop. Go. Stop!* I was nauseous from my own driving, but we made out after, anyway, to Dire Straits's "Romeo and Juliet." Winter Saturdays, the sun pale yellow and low in the sky.

We were parked at the glittering view near my house one frozen night when he brought the last of my innocence to a halt with one sentence. "You have a beautiful body." He said it so softly, I wasn't sure I'd heard him.

"I what?"

"Your body. It's beautiful," he said more firmly.

It was a shocking, thrilling invasion, the idea that he would have any opinion at all about my body. I went home, closed my door, and took off my clothes. I stared at myself in the mirror over the vanity. What was he talking about? This bump? That bone? It seems quaint now, that anyone could live sixteen years in a female body before realizing that it would be judged and evaluated, deemed good or bad, worthy or not, by some guy with his hand under your sweater in a BMW.

HE WANTED TO GO ALL the way. It wasn't a nasty kind of pressure, but it was steady and persistent. My world shifted and narrowed. I abandoned Cathy and those useless A-pluses, my other girlfriends and their romance novels. My sisters were long out of the house so I confided in my diary, writing angsty passages about how I felt. The confusion. The exhilaration. I liked the effect our back-seat adventures had on my boyfriend, and I wanted to see what would happen if we took it even further. What was this new power I'd discovered? What kind of spell could I cast? On the other hand, I didn't want to be a slut.

Yes, no, maybe. I got up on Saturday mornings, exhausted and hungover, to punch the cash register at Teddy's. No matter how late I'd been out the night before, I didn't miss work. I'd started as soon as I was old enough to carry a coffeepot; now I was on the payroll like the real staff. That paycheck, that bank account! I loved to wake up and know I had to hurry. I loved that I was expected somewhere; needed to do a job. I loved driving to Teddy's with Dad when he was often distracted by his own thoughts, and we could just be together quietly, in the car.

MEANWHILE, ON WEEKDAYS, MOM STARTED showing up in the mornings in her slippers and robe, asking if I'd made coffee. I had been enjoying solitary breakfasts for ten years, and all I wanted was to be left alone, but there she was, commenting on my outfit, my hair, my skin.

Something was going on with Mom at that time. Where she'd always been a little sharp, a little edgy, she seemed more overtly unhappy. Instead of playing bridge, she sat on the couch with a bag of

Jujubes, watching *Jeopardy!* every afternoon. Her misery was like a smell that hit me every time I came back to the house. It hung in the air and wrapped around the furniture.

It was all my fault. Or it had nothing to do with me. Both. Neither. I really had no clue what was wrong with Mom. What kid can ever separate their parents' inner lives from the way they're treated?

ALL I KNEW FOR SURE was that I'd always been slightly off. I was supposed to be simple, but I was complicated. I was supposed to be light, but I was serious and moody. I was supposed to be compliant, but I had a rebellious streak. *Why are you so withdrawn/contrary/quiet/sulky,* Mom said. I didn't know why.

It was different with Dad. Although he was the one with the truly tragic past, he was stronger, somehow—sturdier, more resilient, and freer with his love. When Mom was physically or emotionally absent, he was there: leaving work in the middle of the lunchtime rush to pick me up from school when I had a fever; taking me to the hospital when a classroom science experiment blew up my thumb. During our walks and car rides, we talked about things that made Mom roll her eyes: Was there a God? What was the meaning of life? Why did he survive and what would I do with all the strength and power coursing through my veins?

As I neared graduation, I didn't so much outgrow my closeness with Dad as struggle with where to put it. I was changing and emerging, trying to become my own person without losing a connection so deep and vital, my life seemed to depend on it. I had begun to cleave in two: there was the girl who could charm and delight the most important person in our family with a thoughtful remark and, further inside, the kernel of a different kind of woman—conflicted and private, fiercely independent, overloaded with a sense of emotional responsibility it would take half a lifetime to understand.

DESPITE MY HAPHAZARD ACADEMIC PERFORMANCE, I got into university in Toronto, where my sisters were. I packed a collection of skirt-and-sweater outfits in my suitcase and a raw filet mignon in my carry-on. The meat made my shoulder bag heavy, but I didn't con-sider refusing it. It was like the salami sandwiches Dad insisted I take on planes, or the onion bagels he toasted when I was rushing out the door. What if the meat in residence was tough and awful? What if I was, god forbid, hungry?

On Dad's urging, Mom had taken me to buy the most expensive clothes I'd ever had. Not to the mall of my childhood, where I'd sometimes taken the bus with twenty dollars in my pocket to buy jeans, hoping to have a buck or two left over not for the candy coun-ter at which you would order what you wanted by the price, but for the German deli. As the heavy glass door had closed behind me, I'd inhaled the smoky, meaty air, stepped up to the counter and said, "I'll have eighty cents' worth of Bündnerfleisch, please." I'd walked to the bus terminal with my new jeans tucked under my arm and the little brown paper package in my hands, surreptitiously bringing ribbons of the delicate meat to my mouth, embarrassed by my weirdness but unable to stop.

No. Mom took me to a ladies' shop downtown to buy the kind of dressy clothes she and Dad thought I would need for university. My parents' projection was a powerful force, and they were guided by the life they imagined for me. Dad had a particularly romantic vision of university, fueled by all that he had missed. Arriving from Europe at seventeen, he watched his peers go off to what could only be the best time of their lives while he, orphan and refugee, found a job and learned how to make a life on his own. He knew he was missing out, but he didn't waste time and energy on self-pity. He could do nothing to change his own past, but he could give his children differ-ent lives. We would be happy, educated women in elegant clothing.

The clothes weren't my style, but I'd wear whatever it took to make my escape. My parents and I never got around to talking about a career, and nobody paid attention to my major. I was simply head-ing out to have the best time of my life. Exactly how that best time would happen was not explained.

17

Vichyssoise

The day after Labor Day, I stood outside a great domed building on campus in a drizzle. It didn't look like a classroom. "Con Hall," said my printed timetable. Groups of kids streamed past, not even glancing at me.

"Where is the—?"

"Is this—?" I walked all the way around the building before finally finding the door at the beginning of the second pass. Inside, I climbed the risers of the circular auditorium to an empty seat. The professor was a stick figure on the stage. Seventeen hundred people were in that class and nobody—boy, girl, man, or woman—spoke to me.

The dorms weren't much better. I'd picked English lit as my major but ended up with the pharmacy girls, who all seemed to know each other. Off they went to chase the engineering boys while I sat in the common room with a book and a bowl of popcorn. My sister Lisa's freezer became home to my filet and I never saw it again.

I put on my pleated skirts and haunted the campus. I'd entered a liminal space and I floated, disconnected and untethered, in the antechamber between what had come before and what would come next.

THE FOLLOWING SCHOOL YEAR, I moved into the first home of my own—a tiny eighteenth-floor apartment with a sparkly view of downtown that reminded me of Dad. Best of all—my own kitchen. It was the size of a coat closet, separated from the main room by a pair of swinging half doors that barely cleared the appliances lined up against the back wall: a mini electric range, a stainless-steel sink, and a piece of countertop just large enough to hold a dish rack. In the corner stood a wobbly white refrigerator that teetered whenever I pulled the handle to open it.

I went out to comb the neighborhood for food. Less than a block away, I found two flower shops that doubled as greengrocers. Out front were buckets of yellow sunflowers and pink blooms the size of saucers. Inside, the cement floors were wet and the employees wore green aprons. I went into one shop, then the other, sniffing the fresh herbs and ogling the raspberries. That first night, I took a shiny eggplant back to my kitchen for supper. How many times had I made it with Baba, letting the purple skin turn black and charred under the broiler as the insides became soft and custardy? I pricked the orb with a fork and roasted it in my little oven until the plasticky odor was replaced with the smell of home. I didn't have any peppers or vinegar or Baba's ancient grinder, so I sprinkled my roasted eggplant with salt and ate it with a spoon.

THE NEXT DAY, I NOTICED a French place on the same block as the grocers. It was about four in the afternoon and inside I found two women setting up for dinner service. I stood on the harlequin-patterned floor and gazed into a display case at the front of the restaurant. It was filled with things to take home—poached salmon and delicate French beans with toasted almonds and a ceramic crock brimming with a white liquid.

"May I help you?" called one of the aproned women in an accent that reminded me of Paris. She came up behind the counter and waited.

"What is that?" I said, pointing to the crock.

"Vichyssoise."

Some kind of sauce for the fish, I figured. It looked so cool and silky, but one glance at the price and I walked out, empty-handed.

I WAS LUCKY. MY PARENTS paid my rent and they paid my tuition. I didn't have much cash but I had a credit card I'd overused the year before, prompting an unpleasant phone call from Mom. "Do you know how much you spent last month?" she'd said. I didn't know, because I was unfamiliar with the basic concept of a budget. All I knew was that I was always short of money, and that I didn't like asking for more. It's obvious now that I should have had a job and the responsibility of managing my own spending, but my parents didn't want me to work and go to university at the same time. "You don't need the extra pressure," Dad said. "Just relax."

WHEN CLASSES BEGAN, I WALKED to a small square building dwarfed by the gargantuan library next door. In the lobby, people in black turtlenecks were engaged in passionate conversation. A sign above a staircase read PRODUCTION BOOTH and pointed up.

I'd arrived at the university's fledgling cinema studies department. If I'd learned anything during freshman year, I'd learned that taking five courses of heavy reading at once was stupid and despite my love of books, despite my lack of a social life, despite everything, I'd fallen behind, needing to write papers on books I hadn't finished during a series of all-nighters at the end of the term. I'd passed, but there had been another round of discouraging marks, another don't-worry-about-it talk from Dad.

Fine, I'd said to myself. If Mom and Dad didn't care what I took, if none of it mattered, I'd take cinema, the birdiest of bird courses, where all you do is watch movies and sit around talking about them. And that is how I meandered away from the staid English department, into courses that were surely the most interesting, modern, impractical lessons the entire university had to offer. I didn't dream of being a filmmaker any more than I'd dreamed of being a writer. I was like a duck being kept idle for its liver.

I pushed open the door to Room 112 and found myself in a theater with upholstered seats on a gentle gradient, sloping toward a stage. As I walked down the aisle, my eyes landed on a familiar shape—a boy with a head of curly hair and a large body. Was that Josh from twentieth-century lit last year? He turned his head toward me and smiled and I hurried to where he was sitting and slid gratefully into the seat beside him.

THE FIRST THING JOSH SHOWED me was how to eat lunch for sixty-five cents. I was always leaving my apartment late, always finding myself famished after class. I forgot my wallet or my wallet was empty. Josh took me to College Street, where the loose change at the bottom of my book bag bought a steaming pork bun that I ate standing next to him on the sidewalk.

As the weather turned cooler and we learned about the French New Wave, Josh took me to Chinatown proper, where a bowl of hot and sour soup was just a few coins more than a pork bun. My socks were always soaked on these days, the smell of vinegar and chili mixed with wet wool. My nose ran and my feet steamed.

A DIFFERENT DAY, ANOTHER HANDFUL of coins in the bottom of my bag. Instead of going to Chinatown, Josh drove his little white car to a place called Kensington Market. I didn't know it had once been called the Jewish Market, populated by merchants selling live chickens and ducks, fresh fish and herring, pickles from barrels. Josh and I bought Jamaican beef patties and the streets smelled like pot.

Around the corner, there was a coffee and spice shop, a store with cheeses stacked so high they filled the window, a fishmonger. Walking to the car, we passed a used bookstore. I felt a pull, but Josh wanted to get home. "Can I have five minutes?" I said. "I'll meet you at the car." I hurried into the store and headed straight to the cooking section, grabbed the first two books that caught my eye, paid, and rushed to meet Josh.

Back in my apartment, I opened the beat-up copy of *Mastering the Art of French Cooking* to the index. Venison, vermouth, viande, and there it was—vichyssoise. Not a sauce at all but a cold potato soup.

It was a couple of days before I had time to pick up a bag of potatoes and a bundle of leeks. I simmered the vegetables in stock, puréed tiny batches in my mini chopper, and pushed everything through a strainer. I added cream and salt and pepper, tasting for balance and the perfect velvety consistency. Soon I was eating vichyssoise for breakfast, lunch, and dinner. I just couldn't get over it. I'd been raised on the best meat my parents could afford and lobster whenever possible. How could something as humble as cold potato soup be so delicious?

18

Stew

I saw Josh at school or his house, but I didn't have him over. My apartment was my fortress, and inside its walls, the years of secret slicing and frying in my mother's don't-make-a-mess kitchen melted away. I stopped on my way home from class and picked up whatever I felt like eating: deep green spinach that I sautéed with onions and dressed with a little cream, tomatoes that I peeled, chopped and cooked into a thick sauce I ate with a spoon. If I had too much work, I opened a can of sardines and ate them on hot toast with a squeeze of lemon juice and a sprinkle of watercress.

I dated here and there, carefully hiding it from Josh for reasons I didn't examine. You weren't supposed to sleep with guys after only being out with them once or twice, but sometimes, I did it anyway. It's true that they never called after that, but I didn't really want them to. When I locked the apartment door at night, I felt a surge of joy at being the only one with a key.

ONE SATURDAY, I WOKE UP to snow on the ground and an empty fridge. I was out of everything—coffee, eggs, bread, fruit, vegetables. I decided to head back to Kensington Market. It was a long walk, but I hadn't been able to stop thinking about that wall of cheese, that fragrant spice shop. Trudging south and west, my boots were soaked in no time.

When I got to the corner of Baldwin and Augusta, I saw that the streets were full of people despite the muck. Someone sat on a crate playing the steel drums. At the spice store, the Portuguese shop-keeper was grinding coffee to order and the air smelled pungent and delicious.

After my intensely carnivorous childhood, I hadn't been eating much meat, but it was such a cold day. I was drawn into a butcher shop in search of comfort. The strong funk inside made me think of Baba, boiling lung as I got ready for school.

"Can I have a little of this?" I said to the butcher. It was some kind of pork with a thick layer of fat, and the cheapest thing they had.

The butcher eyed me with naked curiosity. He was wearing only an apron over a T-shirt, and my eyes landed on a familiar blue-green marking inside his arm. An involuntary shudder ran through my body.

"This?" He pointed to the fat-striped hunk of meat. "Leave this for the shegetz." My eyes snapped to his face. Did he just say shegetz? I'd only heard that particular word for non-Jew a couple of times. "How about a nice brisket?" he said, reaching for a flat red slab.

I shook my head. You had to buy a huge piece and besides, I wouldn't know what to do with it. "Or this?" He gestured to a pile of red cubes. "You can make a good stew with this for a few bucks."

"No, thank you," I said politely, ignoring the familiarity that was in the air between us. He was obviously a survivor, but I didn't want to talk to him about his story, and I didn't want to tell him ours. I had wrestled the whole Holocaust into a little box at the back of my mind, and to function like a normal person, I needed it to stay there. Coping was all about containment, I'd learned. I wasn't going to let a stranger mess with my strategy.

———

WE AGREED, FINALLY, ON A thin minute steak that he cut for me with a big knife. As I walked home, I avoided thinking about what country he'd come from and what camp he might have been in by thinking about what he'd wanted to sell me.

Stew. Growing up, it was almost a dirty word. We were not stew people any more than we were brisket people. Cabbage, soup, certain preparations with ground beef—they all fell into the category of poor people food Mom didn't eat, make, or even want in the house. "Revolting," she'd say, and Dad didn't disagree. If we were what we ate, it would be steak and lobster all the way, baby.

I sensed the irony long before I could articulate it. My parents had grown up eating the exact foods they came to reject—potatoes and cabbage rolls and cheap cuts of meat, if there had been money for meat at all. And most of all, stew. Stew was in my blood.

Dad talked about it often when I was little, a dish with a strange name his mother prepared for Shabbat: beans, barley, potatoes, a bit of meat, and a lot of water went into an oven-proof pot. His mother and the other women in the neighborhood walked their pots to the local bakery on Friday afternoon and slid them into the baker's big bread oven. After davening on Saturday, they returned to collect the steaming vessels and walk them home for a midday meal. The bakery oven was neither turned on nor off during Shabbat, and in this way the dish was a miracle meal for those who couldn't "work"—in this case cook—from sundown Friday to sundown Saturday. The name of this dish was cholent, and it occupied such a huge place in Dad's memory and my imagination, it seemed almost mythical. "The cholent was so delicious," he sometimes said with a dreamy look on his face, "I could never eat enough of it." Or: "My mother made the best cholent of anyone. When she brought it home, the whole apartment building could smell it."

My mom could have made cholent for Dad at any point, but she never did. I suppose Dad could have even made it himself, but that never happened, either. It was almost like cholent was too powerful and better left as a dreamy memory. That Dad's favorite childhood dish was a type of stew, which was Mom's most hated dish, was something nobody tried to reconcile. It was one of many contradictions—between Mom and Dad, between past and present, between scarcity and plenty. I didn't dwell on it. I already knew very well that contradictions were simply part of life.

THE NEXT SATURDAY, I CAME home from Kensington Market with a brown paper package of meat.

"I'll have two pounds of shank please, cut across," I'd said to the butcher.

"What do you want with that? It's not like you're Italian."

"I'm trying something new," I'd said, in a way that didn't invite conversation.

The other used book I'd picked up that day with Josh was *The Silver Palate Cookbook* and in it I'd found an intriguing recipe for something called osso buco. It called for a huge amount of meat—sixteen pieces—so I'd cut it back. I didn't have white wine but I had white wine vinegar. I didn't have tinned tomatoes but I had a few fresh ones. I added olives, capers, extra marrow bones. The recipe said to serve it over saffron rice, but wide, flat egg noodles were easier.

My osso buco fed me for three days. I ate everything, every last bit of sauce, every noodle. I saved the bones for the end, sucking out the marrow as I hadn't done since Baba had made them for me when I was little.

THE SNOW WAS STARTING TO melt when Mom called to say Dad needed surgery. "It's the artery in his neck," she said in a weak voice I didn't recognize. "It's clogged." I dragged my suitcase out from under my bed and tossed in sweaters and boots. The birds were coming back to Toronto, but it would still be cold at home. I wrapped *Mastering the Art of French Cooking* in a pair of jeans and zipped up my case.

By the time I got to the house, Dad was home from the hospital, a bandana tied jauntily around his neck. I couldn't see the incision, but electric shocks of empathy shot down my legs all the same.

"Dad, I want to cook for you," I said as he lay on the sofa. I ran upstairs to get my cookbook. "How about something from Julia Child?"

"Tell me what's in there."

"Ratatouille, coq au vin, beef bourguignon . . ."

"Beef bourguignon? What's beef bourguignon?"

"Like a French beef stew."

"It will be like cholent!" he said, a little too excited.

"Dad, take it easy."

"That's what I want."

I looked at Mom. Was she going to let me make a complicated stew in her spotless kitchen? "I'm going to need some special ingredients," I said, testing.

"I'll get my coat," she said.

IT WAS SNOWING WHEN WE drove to a big grocery store across town. Mom was nervous on the slippery roads, jerking the steering wheel tightly back and forth, slowing to a crawl in the gloom. She seemed worn-out all of a sudden, my capable mother, and I wished I were the one driving. Not that she would have let me.

When we got home, I dragged a chair into the kitchen so Dad could supervise the cooking. I cut the large cubes of meat into smaller chunks. I cleaned pearl onions and button mushrooms and sautéed them in butter. Dad was so happy, watching and licking his lips. I uncorked the bottle of Burgundy we'd picked up on the way home and began to pour it over the browned meat, vegetables, and herbs. "A whole bottle?" Mom said doubtfully.

A COUPLE OF HOURS LATER, there were a few inches of snow on the ground and the kitchen windows were steamed. I served the beef bourguignon in deep bowls, with crusty bread on the side. The mushrooms and pearl onions were enrobed in a rich sauce, but when I poked a cube of meat with a fork, I could feel it was still tough. Mom took a couple of polite bites, but Dad dug right in. "Delicious," he said, eating too fast for his semi-reclined position.

"Oh god, Dad, slow down. You're going to choke!"

"What kind of meat did you use?"

"Stewing beef, like the recipe calls for."

"Don't you think it would be better with tenderloin?" he said.

"No. It's tough because I didn't cook it long enough."

"Yes, let's make it again tomorrow with tenderloin," he said, ignoring me. "Toby, don't we have a filet in the freezer?"

19

Creepy Salad

I pinned batik hangings on my walls and laid a row of cloisonné ball candles on the windowsill beside my bed. It was the late '80s and my twenty-one-year-old form teetered on the edge of self-discovery—rifling through racks of vintage clothes in Kensington Market, record bins, stacks of books; dog-earring the pages of the university course calendar, searching for the outfit, the album, the professor, the way of looking at the world that would feel like home. Not Mom and Dad's home; the home I needed to make for myself. I was trying—god I was trying—but it was a random, messy process, riddled with confusion, experiments, and many mistakes.

JUNIOR YEAR ENDED AND I was reluctant to go home for the summer. I knew two boys named Paul and Andrew from Michigan and during the school year, I had taken the train to visit them in Ann Arbor. I'd fallen for that cozy town—its bead shops and tie-dye, foot-long hot dogs and old-fashioned soda shop. Instead of heading back to Edmonton, I came up with the idea of taking a summer course at the University of Michigan. Mom and Dad weren't at all keen—the needless risk of traveling alone, the expense—but somehow I found a way to manage it.

It would have been better if I had talked over a detailed plan with my parents. We could have looked for gaps, assessed risks, come up with contingencies. But that would have meant puncturing the smooth, pleasing world I had worked hard to create for them. Instead, I told them I had everything figured out and that I'd be perfectly safe. Then I got on a train and headed off into that strange summer when I was doubly displaced, first staying in Toronto instead of going home, and then going to Michigan, where I knew exactly two people.

In Ann Arbor, I met Paul's younger brother, Joey. He had floppy dark hair and a loose way about him that was different from anyone I knew. He was a creative soul and he walked around with a notepad and a pencil, writing and reading his poetry. I was drawn to his freedom, his utter lack of self-consciousness. How could I be more like that?

Joey and I soon became a couple and at first, everything was exactly as I wanted it to be. Paul had helped me find a sublet near the university, an empty house shared during the school year by four girls. I went to class and wandered in the shops and shot pool with my friends at the campus bar. I discovered a farmer's market with white cherries the size of plums.

Joey had a red car, and he planned a trip to a place called the Pictured Rocks. It was dusk when we got to the shores of Lake Superior, and I had trouble making out the shape of the rocks we'd driven six hours to see. "Aren't they beautiful?" Joey said. I remember the shock of the lake, icy pins and needles that stung my legs and made it hard to breathe. It was July and we camped on the beach with Joey's friends.

We headed home on Sunday, exhausted from a weekend of partying. Joey was too tired or too stoned to drive, so it was decided that I would take the wheel while he slept in the back. In the dark, the route seemed even longer on roads I didn't know. My eyelids grew heavy, each blink a little longer than the one before, each reopening a little more difficult. My mother had raised me with a mortal fear of falling asleep at the wheel, and as I steered through curve after unfamiliar curve, I saw myself dozing off as the car careened off the road and into the forest. I turned the music up. I rolled down both windows and sucked in the bracing night air.

Joey woke up and started yelling that it was too cold.

"I have to have the windows open or I'm going to fall asleep!"

"So what is it, freeze or crash?"

We both cracked up at that, a good howling laugh that swept away the tension. The windows stayed open, I turned on the heat, and he went back to sleep.

BACK IN THE LITTLE RED car a week later, Joey was about to drive through a crosswalk in town when he realized that people were crossing and slammed on the brakes. The car jerked backward, my body jerked forward, and my head hit the windshield.

I wasn't cut or knocked out. People crossed in front of the car, tsk-tsking, saying something about seat belts. I didn't get it until I noticed the windshield on my side, shattered in a spiderweb pattern. I was amazed by the beautiful design my head had made in the glass. I felt a dull throb inside my skull, but it seemed far away, separate from me somehow, confusing and remote. It took several more beats to notice that Joey was driving again, and he was angry.

"You broke my windshield," he said. "What the fuck. You broke my fucking windshield." He didn't have money for a new one, he said. What was he going to do?

He dropped me off and I sat on the couch in my sublet, wondering how I could pay for Joey's new windshield, and whether I had a concussion. It didn't occur to me to call home and talk everything over with my parents. The less they knew, the better.

AS SUMMER WORE ON, JOEY got on my nerves more and more. He was always around, sitting on my couch, taking up all the air with his poetry. His glass left a white ring on the coffee table, he let the toilet paper unroll all over the bathroom. One day he went back to his place and I finally had a chance to miss him. Feeling badly about our bickering, I decided to surprise him with dinner.

The house had an overbaked backyard, and I found some dill weed growing in a shady area near the fence. *Mom's creepy salad,* I thought. I went to the grocer for onions and Persian cucumbers and ripe tomatoes. Early in the day, I mixed up a dressing of oil, vinegar, salt, sugar, and tons of that dill, chopped fine. Closer to dinnertime, I broiled chicken thighs, added the tomatoes and cucumbers to the onions, fussed with the seasoning.

I can't say what we fought about that night. I can't say for certain that he was drunk. We weren't finished with dinner but we were standing, and I was upset that the sweet surprise I'd planned was turning sour.

"But look," I said. "I made you dinner."

"A little greasy salad," he sneered.

That insult stung more than he could have known. "Don't be an asshole," I probably said. When he lunged at me, it wasn't a punch or a slap but more of a hard shove, a shove in which his hand caught my mouth a moment before I flew into the wall. I was on my feet as my face hit the cool, hard surface.

Click. I heard myself grasp what was happening. A surge of adrenaline sent me up to the bedroom. I slammed the door. There was blood in my mouth. My fingers shook as I pressed numbers on the phone on the nightstand. "Come," I told his brother. I dragged a chair to the door and pushed on it as I listened for Joey's footsteps on the stairs.

Soon I heard low voices. The front door closed and from the bedroom window, I watched the three boys drive away in Paul's pickup. They left Joey's red car in the driveway.

I BOARDED A TRAIN THE next afternoon, and some hours later I unlocked my apartment door and headed into the shower. Wrapped in a towel, I wiped steam from the mirror and stared at my wet face. My top lip was puffy, and there was a cut inside, near my right front tooth. My nose was maybe a little swollen. Really, I was okay. You're lucky, I told my reflection. It could have been so much worse. Yes, you're fine.

Still in my towel, I called home. "Hi, Daddy. I'm back in Toronto now. I just wanted to let you know."

The TV was blaring. "Hold on," he said. When it was quiet, he came back to the phone. "Where did you say you are? Are you okay?"

"I'm good," I said, brushing away hot tears. "I just felt like coming back. Nothing is wrong."

"Mom isn't here but I know she'll want to talk to you. Call back later?"

"I will. Love you."

THERE WERE ONLY A COUPLE of weeks until Labor Day. The city steamed around me, bustling with growth and industry and purpose. The roads were clogged with traffic; the sidewalks full of people. Everyone seemed to have a place to be. When I think about what happened next, I think of the brand of Verdicchio that was all the rage at that time; its curvy bottle and little scroll of story attached. Soon I would encounter that wine in the apartment of the man who would become my first husband.

20

Verdicchio

When Jeff first asked me out, it wasn't for a real date or, at least, I didn't know if it was a date. We were at his parents' house for dinner and he invited me to his place in an offhand way. Because he was someone I already knew, it seemed like he was just being kind. Like maybe he felt sorry for me.

I'd spent a lot of time at his parents' when I'd first come to Toronto—they were something like family friends—and he'd seen me there in my pleated skirts when he came by before or after work. He was friendly, but a teaser.

"Congratulations," he'd said to me a couple of weeks after I'd first arrived. We were standing across from each other at the island in his mother's kitchen as he wolfed down a breakfast of raisin toast with Cheez Whiz. It was maybe the first time he'd spoken directly to me, and a pleasant warmth crept into my arms and legs.

"Thanks," I said slowly. "Uh, why?"

He stuck a piece of toast into his mouth and swallowed. "That zit at the end of your nose is finally gone!" His green eyes flashed at me.

I came to understand that this playful irreverence was part of his charm. Whenever his mom invited me for Friday night dinner, I'd watch the way he strode into the room—adored son, brother, cousin—warm and smiling, tossing out sweet or salty one-liners. His confidence was like a charge in the air. When he got close to me, I felt a current of energy between us, but I couldn't begin to trust that he felt it, too.

THE ROSH HASHANA OF MY last year of university, Jeff's mom asked me to make Baba Sarah's matzoh balls for her chicken soup. "Thanks for inviting me," I said, arriving early and leaning over to kiss her on the cheek. Her blond hair was pulled back, her face pink with the warmth of the kitchen and her efforts.

I tied an apron over my flowered dress and got to work separating eggs. I added matzoh meal to the yolks and beat the whites until they held their peaks. I folded them into the yolk mixture and shaped the balls with wet hands before carefully dropping them into boiling water. Some people like their matzoh balls dense, but Baba's recipe was so fluffy, the balls barely held together. Jeff's mom nodded appreciatively as I fished them out with a slotted spoon. At my elbow, her chicken soup simmered away, replete with herbs and parsnips. She was a gourmet cook, a wonderful cook, and it was the first time I realized that you could put more than chicken, onions, carrots, and celery in chicken soup. In fact, you could put whatever you wanted. She pounded garlic for a veal breast that would become unctuous and sticky and, when I opened the fridge, I saw fennel and orange slices arranged on plates for a composed salad.

A few hours later, the quiet dining room came alive. Voices rose and fell, silverware clattered, glasses clinked. I helped Jeff's mom lay out the desserts on the sideboard against the wall, and it was there that Jeff materialized beside me. When he'd not paid any particular attention to me during dinner, I had been both disappointed and relieved, but as he watched me trying to choose between lemon meringue pie and brownies and chocolate chunk shortbread, he piped up with a running commentary: "Oh, going for the brownies? The brownies are good, really good." I slid the server under a large square.

"But I wouldn't miss this"—he pointed to his mother's apple cake, dusted in icing sugar—"and these cookies are my favorite." He picked one up and took a bite.

"Okay, yes, yum," I said, piling desserts onto my plate.

"So, how's student life?" I looked up to find his eyes on me. A few crumbs clung to his bottom lip.

"Oh, you know. Movie watching is hard work."

He rewarded me with a dazzling smile. "Looks like it agrees with you." I swallowed but I didn't say anything. "Hey, I have an idea," he continued. He was working on extracting a piece of apple cake with long, elegant fingers. "Why don't you come over to my place and have dinner?"

I didn't know if I'd heard him right, and he was looking down at the cake, so I couldn't see what his eyes and mouth were saying. My whole body buzzed with joyful confusion.

IT WAS ANOTHER WARM TORONTO fall. The Blue Jays were on a meteoric rise and everyone was awaiting the completion of the Sky-Dome with its amazing retractable roof. Transformation was in the air.

Half an hour before I was due at Jeff's, my bed was piled with the entire contents of my closet. I didn't know what to wear to this dinner that was maybe a date and maybe not a date. At last, I settled on yet another skirt, this time slim and pink, locked my door and stepped into the elevator. I'd put on makeup and done my hair. I didn't know what I was going to, but I knew that whatever it was, I needed to look my best.

"IT'S OPEN," HE SAID WHEN I knocked on his door. I stepped into an apartment not that different from my own, but bigger and decorated with brown furniture. He seemed like a full-fledged man, an adult, but really, he was just a few steps ahead of me in growing up. His apartment, his suits, his job—he was trying, just as I was trying. But I didn't look at it that way then. He seemed comfortable and secure and nestled within his family and his city, completely in his element. After the mistakes I'd made in Michigan, how could I not be attracted to that certainty?

He was sitting on the couch but got up as I entered, and I was moved to see him, finally, in Levi's, with a nice amount of wear on the back pockets. He seemed almost surprised to see me, and he hurried to do up the two top buttons that had come undone.

We made small talk as we moved into the kitchen and he took a package of pasta from the cupboard and put water on to boil. "Do you like spaghetti?" Out came a jar of Ragú.

I might have been a little meek and I might have been out of my element, but I wasn't stupid. I knew what the son of a gourmet cook was communicating with a box-of-spaghetti-and-sauce-from-a-jar dinner. This was not an important night.

I don't remember if we had a salad, or if there was dessert, but crystal clear is that bottle of wine and the way he pretended he didn't know if he had wine or not. "I'll check," he said, getting up from the little table by the window. When he came back, it was as if the wine had been just kicking around. "Oh, I have a bottle after all," he said, applying a corkscrew. It was much later when he admitted that he had gone out and bought the wine right before I came over, choosing that Verdicchio because he thought the shape of the bottle was sexy. What he'd passed off as insouciance that night was something else—caution, uncertainty, maybe even insecurity. But in the moment, I was paying attention to different details and what caught my eye was a little piece of parchment, rolled up and attached to the bottle as decoration. My life was about to become that story, attached to something larger and unspooling in a way that seemed preordained and mysterious, even to me.

21

Coconut Cream Pie

Soon the awkwardness melted away. Jeff came around in his Jeep to pick me up and we sped away from the sacred arches and stone corbels of the university, into the throbbing center of the city. "Ciao, Roberto!" he said to the salt-and-pepper-haired host at Cibo, an Italian place where I tasted my first gnocchi gorgonzola.

He had a lust for life that felt familiar and right. At the latest hot spot, we walked through a black-and-gold gate and ate baked brie oozing onto a puddle of raspberry coulis. When he went to the washroom, I looked into the eyes of a woman across the bar, accidentally inviting her to come over in her knee-high boots and sweater dress to ask if she could buy me a drink. She was still talking to me when he came back.

"What have we here?" he said, smiling.

Her angular face fell. "I was just leaving." She turned back toward the bar, but her attention added an erotic charge to the evening. I suddenly felt gorgeous and just a little bit wild.

THE GLITTERING CITY CONTINUED TO open up. One night, we zoomed to the best restaurant in town. "You have to try the coconut cream pie," Jeff said, after our server cleared our dinner plates. When the elegant wedge arrived, he drizzled a line of melted chocolate from a tiny vessel over trembling white chocolate curls. The first forkful dissolved in my mouth, ethereal and bitter and sweet. I went in for another, and another, my fork clinking into his, each mouthful melting into the one before. Soon I was dragging the bottom of the plate, trying to scrape up the last of the coconut custard and a few remaining shards of crust. By the time he leaned across the table to kiss me, I was lightheaded. "Told you," he said.

I FINALLY PACKED UP MY silly skirts and put together an outfit befitting a fourth-year film student: black Levi's from Kensington Market, a midriff-baring sweater, little ankle boots. Somewhere along the way, I picked up a red leather blazer.

The world was in some ways very different then and at the same time, not different at all. "Aren't we provocative," said my feminist film professor, the first time I wore my new outfit to her class. I felt my face heat up but I didn't get angry. Neither she nor I realized the irony of a feminist professor calling out a girl for her choice of clothes.

She screened Maya Deren's *Meshes of the Afternoon* that day, and I watched multiple versions of a woman refracted through a dream. The woman chased a hooded figure with a mirror for a face. She entered and reentered a house, climbing and arching over a staircase. Near the end, a man entered the frame and took the woman up to bed, where she lay down beside a flower.

The leaves burned red and time ran backward. Instead of getting cooler that October, the heat intensified. The Jays seemed to be on their way to the World Series and it was impossible not to get caught up in the fever. Had we been to a baseball game or just watched one on TV the night Jeff and I tumbled into bed? He had no air-conditioning in his bedroom, but there was a window unit in the living room. He'd already opened the couch into a bed that night, either in anticipation of getting me into it or simply because he was sleeping there himself, I didn't know. He put those beautiful hands on me and my provocative clothes fell to the floor.

It was a sticky night, a night ripe for a storm. We were tangled in his bedsheets—my knee, his shoulder, my hair. I was drinking in sleep, dreaming of a man with a mirror for a face, a flower, a key— then a thunk and a crack. I sat up. Lightning flashed across the sky. Jeff woke up, too, and together we watched papers fly and swirl in the air around us. Awestruck and paralyzed, we sat there, caught in the whirlwind. The air conditioner had fallen out of the window onto the little balcony and the wind—whether blowing in through the open window or sucking out—had created a mini cyclone. For a few minutes, even he didn't know what to do. Finally, he got out of bed, closed the window, and we went back to sleep.

I MANAGED TO KEEP A foot in each of two worlds for several months. I went to class, wrote papers, met this or that friend at the library or for a slice of pizza. But when Jeff came around, I felt an overwhelming pull. I became the kind of girl who canceled plans if her boyfriend called, the kind of girl who didn't think about whether it was right or wrong or even what she most wanted. This is what I'd been raised to do—give myself over to a man completely, and I simply couldn't stop myself. Bit by bit, I abandoned the friendships I'd worked hard to establish, my purple apartment and my books, the progress I'd made carving out my own path. I fell completely out of my own orbit, into his. It was so much easier, so much more secure. I don't remember feeling lost. What I remember feeling was grateful. I wasn't aware of any power I might have had or power I was giving up.

"LET'S NOT TELL OUR PARENTS," Jeff had said early on, and I'd agreed. Six years was a big age difference and since our families knew each other, going public was bound to be a hassle. The result was that I didn't speak to my parents for days or sometimes even weeks at a time. I didn't want to call from Jeff's place and lie outright; their calls to me rang in my empty apartment.

One cold November Sunday, I stepped into my place and looked around. I'd been stopping by only long enough to change clothes or books and now there were piles of jeans and tops everywhere, and when I opened the fridge, a terrible odor wafted out. I picked up the dirty laundry, got a garbage bag to throw out the rotting vegetables and moldy cheese, scrubbed the refrigerator shelves and bins. Back in the main room, I took a deep breath and pressed playback on my answering machine.

Mom: "Bon Bon, we haven't heard from you for a few days. Give us a ring."

Beep. Dad: "Oh, this is the machine again? I don't like talking to a machine. Call me."

Beep. Mom: "Why are you not picking up? Where are you?"

Beep. Dad: "Bonny, this is your father. Did something happen to you? I want you to return my call."

"I HAVE TO TELL MY parents," I said to Jeff at wing night later that evening. There. I'd said it. Noticing I was holding my breath, I exhaled, long and slow. Jeff took a sip of beer, put his pint down, and smiled. "Yes, you're right."

"Really?" My chest expanded and I started to laugh. "Do you really think so?"

"Yup, it's time. Let's tell everyone."

I STOOD IN THE KITCHEN in Arizona, ready to make my big announcement. After such a long buildup, I'd convinced myself that Mom and Dad would be mad. Well, not mad, exactly, but disapproving or scornful or unhappy in some other way. I didn't realize I was projecting onto them a vague sense of apprehension that was really my own.

"I have a new boyfriend," I said, standing near the fridge as they finished breakfast in the little dinette. My throat felt constricted, but it was too late to stop. They sat there, staring at me with their forks hanging in midair. I told them his name, a name they knew.

Dad cleared his throat. Mom put down her fork. Someone outside started a lawn mower. Finally, Dad's face broke into a smile, then a chuckle. "That's what you call a May-December romance," said Mom, catching Dad's eye and smiling as well. They both became animated, asking me how long we'd been seeing each other and whether they could call him to say hello. Wait, what was happening? I stood rooted to my spot in the kitchen, their voices spiraling around me. Where was their shock, their worry, their pointed questions about whether this was the best thing for me. They were so obviously thrilled. Too thrilled. I wiped inexplicable tears from my cheeks, dialed Jeff's Toronto office number, and handed them the phone.

IT WAS THE FOLLOWING WINTER when he got down on one knee in the shower, with a ring. I'd known it might be coming—I'd let slip that my parents thought we'd dated long enough and an engagement ought to be imminent—but he still managed to surprise me. I looked at the ring, a beautiful anchor. It was heavy and it would hold me in place and tell me who I was. I felt my life lurch forward.

"Will you marry me?"

22

New Year's Eve

Before the Holocaust, before the war, when my father was a little boy in Poland, we were Ger Chasidim. It's a group within a group within a group. Chasidism was born as a spiritual revival movement in eighteenth-century eastern Europe, part of the more general category we would call ultra-Orthodox Judaism. Ger Chasidim speak Yiddish, dress in a particular way, and adhere strictly to a panoply of religious laws. Affiliation is passed down from one generation to the next, not just a religious identity but a sociological one as well.

During my father's short childhood, the head of the Ger dynasty was Avraham Mordechai Alter, and if you plug that name into Google, the photo that comes up shows one of my father's uncles in the rabbi's entourage, two from the right. It's a bit like being photographed with a king.

Even as a young child, my father was aware of this proximity to religious greatness, a type of status he called yichus. He actually had yichus on both sides—the uncle in the entourage was on his father's side, and that was on top of the yichus on the other side, carried by his mother, the daughter of Shlomo Rothblat, whose tomb we would later find in Warsaw.

THE CHILD OF AN IMMIGRANT will accept foreign words without discrimination or judgment, grasping their meaning and nuance while never needing a definition. I didn't hear yichus used out in the world; the people I knew didn't clog their sentences with these ancient, guttural sounds. But on Dad's lips, the word was natural, beautiful even, and he talked about it so often, I knew just what it was: an old type of status more meaningful than looks or education or money.

Dad brought this fragment of life from the old country with him, like a message in a bottle. Although it had no relevance to our situation in Edmonton—we weren't religious, let alone Chasidic—he spoke of this lineage all the time. No matter how much he lost, what he refused to lose was his sense of what it felt like to be on the inside of that special world—it gave him a kind of power, a deep well of strength. The tales of yichus mixed up with the cholent and the little dog to help me understand where I came from and who I was.

IN CHASIDIC SOCIETY IN GENERAL, and Gerer society in particular, the most important thing a woman can do is get married. Everything a young girl is taught leads, ultimately, to the marriage canopy, the chuppah. My grandmother's marriage was likely arranged with great care, and if my father's sisters hadn't been murdered, theirs would have been, too. In fact, if the Holocaust hadn't happened, my father's life would have continued that way, as would his children's and his children's children's, for generations.

Instead of diluting Dad's reverence for the values of his childhood, his experiences during the Holocaust in some ways intensified it. What would keep you safer, after all, than the shelter of the marriage canopy? We all knew the story of *Fiddler on the Roof* and, growing up, there may have been some playful "Matchmaker" talk, but there was never any serious thought given to arranged marriages for me and my sisters. Still, the old attitudes were woven into the fabric

of who we were. Dad wanted his daughters to be safe and married;
we wanted Dad to be happy. He was grasping for something he'd
lost. It was natural to try to give it back to him.

Twenty-two was old by Chasidic standards, not that I knew the
forces that were driving me. What I thought was that I was mature.
That I was ready. My sisters were already married, and I had noted,
as only a youngest child can note, the amount of attention heaped
on them as brides.

Standing in that shower, soaking wet and stripped to my essence,
I didn't think about the weight of history, my dead ancestors,
my father's suffering, or traditional women's roles bearing down
on me.

I just said yes.

ENGAGED, I FLEW BACK TO Arizona to visit my parents among the
red mountains and sharp cacti. Mom met me at the baggage carousel; at the sidewalk, I spotted their old blue Cadillac, which they'd
driven down for the season. Dad got out of the car and we hugged
long and hard.

"Here's the kallah! Hi, kallah," he said, using the Hebrew word
for bride. "Are you hungry? I brought you some things to eat in the
car." Mom looked me over in that way of hers, but she just smiled.
Now that I was engaged, I was in a different category and not subject to being picked apart.

We put my suitcase in the trunk and Dad got behind the wheel.
"Saul, you're going to miss your turn. Saul!"

"I've got it. I've got it!"

As we exited Sky Harbor, I rolled down the window and thought
about the end of my childhood. The sun was high overhead and the
air had that beautiful smell. I didn't have a sense of foreboding. Nobody was going to shave my head or make me wear a wig. I was in
love and I was making the most important transformation of my
life, a wonderful evolution I was eager to undergo.

We walked into the gleaming house and Dad asked me, again,
what I wanted to eat. "A roast chicken sandwich?"

"That walnut bread is out of this world," Mom called from the den, where she was lining up all the TV remotes.

"Salami?" Dad continued. "Lox?"

"Um, I don't know what I feel like."

"We have to take very good care of you now that you're a kallah," he said. I was more than I'd been before.

MOM WANTED ME TO HAVE new clothes for all the "entertainments" there would be—dinners and luncheons and parties—so she took me shopping. I forgot about my bohemian jeans and thrifted suede jackets and bought tailored skirts and matching sleeveless tops. "Try on a few more," Mom said. It was unusual to see her so relaxed, so indulgent, and I happily obliged. Shopping bags in hand, we went to lunch at a fancy department store, the room full of ladies dressed in bright colors. The server brought popovers and strawberry butter to the table. We had chicken salads coming, so I was surprised to see Mom, who was usually on a diet, eat and eat, slathering the hot popovers with pink butter and asking for more.

JEFF HAD STAYED BACK IN Toronto, but he was coming down to celebrate the new year, so Mom, Dad, and I shopped for champagne and shrimp and filet mignon. The afternoon of New Year's Eve, I picked Jeff up at the airport and as soon as we walked into the condo, Dad popped the champagne. "To a wonderful year ahead!" Jeff said.

"To our new son-in-law!" Mom said.

"To my wonderful new parents!" Jeff said.

Around midnight, we finally said good night and walked to the pool for a swim in the moonlight. Someone far away was setting off fireworks and we watched from the hot tub before slipping into the sauna and locking the door.

I STAYED A FEW MORE days after Jeff went back to work. The day before my flight, I drove to the mall to pick up my clothes. With my narrow shoulders and shortness, everything had needed alteration. I brought the old Cadillac to a stop outside Ann Taylor. It wasn't like cars now, smart cars that read your mind, knowing when to lock and unlock as if they're part of your body. This car was dumb and so heavy, it felt like a tank when you drove it.

I must have been distracted when I slammed the car door, throwing all my weight into it. I don't know how my right thumb could have been in the way, but somehow the door closed with my thumb inside, not just the tip but a good chunk, almost to the knuckle. The doors locked automatically and, in my shock, I dropped the keys.

I stood in the bright parking lot, caught. The sun beat down on me and I started to sweat through my shirt. I couldn't wriggle out and I couldn't reach the keys to free myself. I was held there, unable to move, trapped. After an unknowable amount of time, I started to scream, and a stranger finally came along and let me out.

23

Lemons

Mom took me to the Scottsdale hospital for X-rays. Despite the pain being enough to make me vomit, the bones in my thumb weren't broken. The nail turned black and fell off and although I worried it would look horrible at the wedding, by the beginning of summer, a new nail, tender and flexible, began to grow in its place.

The wedding was ten days before my twenty-third birthday. My dress had huge shoulders and the bridesmaids wore purple. What it feels like to look back is not the same as what it felt like to look forward. I was young and desired; giddy with possibility, my life a ribbon of pleasure unrolling in front of me.

The ceremony was in a dark green room lined with books and framed flower prints. When Dad walked me down the aisle, we were both crying. The glass crunched beneath Jeff's foot and we floated back up the aisle as husband and wife. At the reception, we sat side by side at a long head table. Dessert was lemon sorbet in a hollowed-out frozen lemon. Later, much later, I would be at a workstation in the back of a restaurant kitchen, scrubbing sand from the folds of hundreds of wild leeks, thinking about who had worn out their fingers emptying three hundred lemons for my wedding. But not that night. I felt like I was going up—up from where I'd come from, up from my worries about fitting in, from the suffocating weight of the Holocaust and the responsibility of pleasing my parents. The band played Jewish music, they lifted our chairs and Jeff grinned at me. I thought, again, how lucky I was. How chosen.

Jeff and I had an energy between us other people could feel and see. "What chemistry," Mom often said. It's true that a couple of times, that energy sparked and clashed. We'd had a few sensational, dramatic fights in restaurants, where I started to yell and he stormed off, tossing some bills on the table. To me, it was just a measure of our passion and the fieriness of our love.

THE MORNING AFTER WE GOT back from our honeymoon, our suitcases sat at the door and he went to the office. "Bye, wife," he said, giving me a kiss. We'd moved into a cream-colored house with spiral staircases, and I spent the next weeks unpacking and setting it up. I put away wedding presents and fielded calls from the two mothers, who were concerned about the thank-you notes. "Make sure you mention the exact gift," Mom said.

There were a lot of gifts. Gravy boats and silver chafing dishes and candlesticks. Somewhere along the way, Julie had given me a book for entertaining, with different spaces to record whom you invited, what you shopped for, and what you served. I got to work cooking dinners and filling in the book. That and the thank-you notes comprised the only writing I did.

I'D GRADUATED WITH MY AMORPHOUS degree a month before the wedding and I'd let the question of what to do next fall through the cracks. Now I was searching. One of my friends was working on a ship—you can't do that if you're married—but another was going to write the entrance exam for law school. That seemed interesting. Challenging.

"You're going to go to law school?" Mom said a few weeks later. She was visiting from Edmonton, and we were sitting at the little kitchen table of the cream house. "What does your husband think about that?" I had baked lemon bars and I noted, as she spoke, that they were a little too sour.

"Does it matter?" I snapped. "I'm just doing the test for fun."

"My, you're short-tempered," she said. "You're lucky you don't have to work. Why can't you just enjoy it?"

To everyone's shock, I aced the LSAT, scoring in the 92nd percentile. Somehow, my success caused more problems than it solved. "You're not really going to go to law school, are you?" Jeff said sweetly. "We'll never see each other."

Nobody barred me from applying. I could have been determined; I could have persevered. But I was trying to squish my complicated, messy self into the role of pleaser, and the way to please everyone around me was to stay in the place left for me. The call of ambition, the yearning for a purpose, the desire, simply, to find myself, were no match for the values I'd internalized. Smile and laugh. Be a good daughter. Be a good wife. So I shrugged amicably and agreed to forget it, pushing my anger and frustration underground until they bubbled out, eventually, somewhere else.

THE KITCHEN WAS THE ONE place where I still knew who I was, and I began to cook like my life depended on it. I baked different kinds of loaves—Baba's molasses bread and challah and banana bread with chocolate chips. I wrapped pastry around beef or salmon for Wellingtons, taking copious notes in my entertaining book. I threw a Halloween dinner party and spent hours hollowing out a pumpkin for each guest, into which I ladled a spicy pumpkin soup. I asked my mother-in-law to teach me Jeff's favorites—favorite chocolate chunk cookie, favorite apple cake. Most of all, when I think of that time, what I think of is the chocolate mousse cake that was all the rage, and the way I made it over and over again, breaking eggs, melting chocolate, whipping cream, until my brain was as jiggly as the center of the cake when it was baked just enough.

ONE DAY I WANDERED INTO a yoga class taught by a soft-spoken woman with a beautiful, lined face. Yoga was thousands of years old, but it was new in our neighborhood and it was new to me. I was soon hooked and week after week, I lay on a mat in the dim light, listening to the teacher's voice. I visualized my breath as steady and eternal as the ocean. I arched and bent, offering salutations to the sun. "Like this," she said, touching my back or my shoulder. It was the first time I realized I could turn my love inward.

Soon I was pregnant, and it was on my mat that I began to feel the baby move inside me. I knew I was finally doing something, *creating* something. I bought pregnancy books and cooked for myself and my little passenger. We wanted greens. We craved spinach and beet tops that I sautéed in olive oil with a little vinegar. We wanted anchovies—an entire tin that I ate without shame, along with a loaf of bread. After being small my whole life, it felt good to get bigger—to take up more space. My hair got thick and my skin glowed. My breasts were enormous. I was double the person I'd been. "Be careful," Mom said to me on the phone when I told her I was getting heavier. "I gained seventy pounds with you."

I WENT INTO LABOR ON a Monday night, and after a few hours of hard contractions, Jeff took me to the hospital. I'd written a birth plan and I tried to hand it, a few printed pages stapled together, to every person I encountered, but no one would look at it. A nurse put me in a bed and strapped me to a fetal monitor. When she called for the anesthesiologist I shook my head.

"That's what everyone says," she scoffed. "You're going to change your mind."

"No epidural," I panted.

She put her hands on her hips and frowned at me. "In an hour, you're going to be begging for one, and if we haven't prepped you, you won't be able to have it." It might have seemed easy to push around a very young woman, racked by contractions and barely able to speak, and she succeeded in getting an IV into my arm. Still, I did not want a needle in my spine. "Get out!" I yelled, shocking us all when she came in one last time to pressure me.

The contractions poured out of me, one flood on top of the next. When the baby crowned, that ripping sensation had to be a mistake, so I stopped pushing. "No, hon," my doctor said quietly. "What you felt—that's what we're here to do. You have to push right into that." I understood that the only way forward was through, so I gritted my teeth and propelled a new person into the world.

24

Oranges

Becoming a mom was the most grounding experience I could imagine. Instead of looking to my husband or my parents for stability, I had the growing sense that I was the anchor for my baby and myself. It was spring and I put tiny Jamie in the carriage, walking the neighborhood as the sun came up. "Good morning," I said to every jogger and homeless person. I had too much milk. I had boundless energy.

I floated along like that for many months. Jeff was as enchanted by parenthood as I was. What did it matter if he was also busy at work, out some evenings, away on business? It was my job to be the twenty-four-hour parent and I threw myself into the role.

When the weather turned cold, I took Jamie to Arizona. Mom and Dad had two fruit trees in their little garden—a giant orange, its trunk painted white to protect it from sunburn, and a small grapefruit tree. In the early mornings, Dad got up with Jamie and me and the three of us headed into the cool dawn with the orange picker, a metal cage on a long pole. "Which one?" Dad said. Wearing his striped bathrobe and a pair of leather slippers, Dad worked the cage around whatever orange Jamie indicated. The emerald leaves of the tree shook as he brought the fruits to the ground and bent to pick them up. Jamie giggled. My family didn't understand the people around the neighborhood who left oranges and grapefruits on their trees or let them rot on the grass, who showed indifference to this fruit that was theirs for the taking. Dad picked the oranges and grapefruits every year, every single one, and stored them in the extra fridge in the garage. Toward the end of the season, he and Mom boxed up any remainders and sent them to people as gifts, or brought them home in a suitcase. Beautiful fruit was not something to take for granted.

ONE WINTER TURNED INTO THE next. In the kitchen, Dad took out a cutting board and I sat Jamie on the counter beside the little electric juicer. "Okay, press," Dad said. Jamie put both palms on top of an orange half until the juicer began to turn and gold liquid poured into a cup positioned below its spout. If I left them that way—to doze on the couch or take a shower—I would come back to find them still at it, the pitcher full to the top and Dad still saying, "Okay, press."

"Now, how about breakfast?" Dad said when the juicing was finally done. We ate one hundred scrambled eggs over the course of those mornings, Dad melting the butter until it got that toasty, nutty smell and scrambling the eggs one or two at a time. "If you want them to be delicious, don't overcrowd the pan," Dad told his little grandson as I spooned the soft eggies into Jamie's mouth.

EVENTUALLY, WE HAD TO GO back to Toronto, where my life was an unstructured void. Jeff worked, he traveled; at times, I didn't know what he did. A great divide opened between us. He lived out in the world while I felt confined to the house. Jamie was now moving nonstop and I chased after him all day every day, exhausted. When I called Jeff's office to ask him when he'd be home, they said he'd left, but I couldn't find him.

Everyone said I needed to get out more, so I sat on the bottom stair of our house, trying to fit my toddler into his puffy blue snowsuit. My limbs were heavy and I was just so tired. What was wrong with me? "Oh god, you must be sick," Mom said on the phone, giving in to her dramatic side. "Could you have MS? I think you have MS."

I SAW A DOCTOR WITH white hair and a stern manner. "I can't find anything wrong with you," she said.

"Okay." I sat up on the crinkly paper of the examination table, buttoning my shirt. "I'm sure I'm just sleep deprived."

As she wrote in my chart, I slid off the table, put on my boots, and slung my purse over my shoulder. My hand was on the doorknob when she said, without looking up, "Unless you're depressed."

Depressed? I had a beautiful baby and a charmed life. How could I possibly be depressed? Depression was like trauma—something you could choose to have or not have, and in our family, we definitely did not have it.

"No," I said, "I'm sure it's not that."

"Alright, then. Bye."

I closed the door softly behind me.

THE HOUSE WITH THE SPIRAL staircases wasn't safe for Jamie so we moved to a fixer-upper in a neighborhood where I knew no one. The distance between the outside world and my internal reality widened. I wanted my marriage to be thick; I wanted it to insulate me like a puffy coat, but I felt it was barely there. We were both just outlines, sketchy shapes going through the motions. He was busy at work and that was where his passion seemed to lie. "I'm building something, you know that," he said.

I began to have flares of anger. I didn't even know I was mad and then I was yelling. I cried at the strangest times. *Just be happy,* I said to myself. *Why can't you just be happy?* Instead, the feeling of dissonance increased. I felt like a cardboard cutout. I knew the real me was too much—too demanding, needy, hungry, unsatisfied. I tried to stay flat.

When I spoke to Dad, I acted my part. "You have a great life. You're so happy, right?"

I knew what he needed to hear. "Yes, of course."

I made it to the following spring. Just before our third anniversary, I woke up and everything was gray—the sunlight, the bedding, my face in the mirror. "Something is wrong," I told Jeff that night. "I think something has to change."

"I don't want change," he said. "Don't you love me the way I am?"

It didn't take much to unravel it after that. A few fights, one disastrous therapy session. When we decided we were done, there was no prolonged divvying up of stuff like you see in the movies. We agreed to share the child we both loved, then he drove away and left everything, even his suits in the closet.

25

Mexico

There was a foot of snow on the driveway when Mom and Dad said they were going to Mexico. "The Coopers have loaned us their condo," Mom told me on phone. "Why don't you bring Jamie down?" In the weeks since Jeff had left, I'd been struggling to hold it together. Sand, sunshine, two extra pairs of hands—it sounded wonderful. "Thanks, Mom, I'd love to," I told her, and I packed our bags.

My parents were settled in the mirrored apartment when we arrived—Mom in a floral one-piece with a matching cover-up and Dad in a white T-shirt and shorts, his face already suntanned. When we hugged, I collapsed against his broad chest. It was good to see him, and I let my guard down completely.

It was over breakfast the next morning that it began, their campaign to get me to go back. They told me splitting up with Jeff was the biggest mistake I could make, the biggest mistake of my entire life, past, present, and future. I cut up little pieces of mango for Jamie, wondering what they imagined. Did they think it had just been a fight? That I had been difficult, hotheaded, childish, just plain dumb?

"I can't go back," I said, a wave of anxiety spreading from my chest to my limbs.

I soon realized there was no getting Mom on my side. She clung to her romanticized version of what my life had been, the way it had looked to her that day they came over for brunch, early on—sun streaming through the windows, Louis Armstrong singing "What a Wonderful World" as we sat down to baked strata with maple syrup and strong black coffee. She'd dabbed at a happy tear with her white hankie.

"I know what I saw," Mom said, crossing her arms in the mirrored condo.

But Dad. I expected more from him, and he expected more from me. A few days later, I was packing Jamie's sand toys for the beach when he came into our room and sat down on the bed. "Just explain it to me," he said. "What exactly went wrong? Who left who?"

I was accustomed to telling him what he wanted to hear, but this time there was no safe script. Instead, I earnestly described the feeling—the hollow feeling. The feeling of not being seen. The feeling that I couldn't live the rest of my life as an outline. I explained that when I said this to Jeff, the marriage seemed to just evaporate. Poof, it was gone. Dad nodded. "Yes, I think I see. I think I understand."

But the next day, as I started to organize the stroller for the beach, he came and said, again, "I think you should go back." I tried harder, working to pinpoint the feelings, to put them into words. Again, he said, "Yes, I see," and then, a few hours later, "No, you need to go back." Soon I was rushing to pack up before my parents were even out of bed, just to avoid having the same crushing conversation. Jamie and I played in the sand and walked to the little market at the end of the beach for fresh coconuts. There was a man there who hacked them in half with a machete and you could scoop out the soft, gelatinous meat with a plastic spoon.

THERE WAS ONE LAST HEATED discussion before Dad drove Jamie and me to the airport. In the car, neither he nor I spoke, and I mistook his silence for quiet resignation. But as he lifted my suitcase out of the trunk and set it on the curb, I took one look at his face and realized that his temper had begun to boil. Words flew out of his mouth then, words of powerlessness and despair. "Do you think you're easy to get along with?" he growled at me. "Do you think you're so perfect?"

People streamed past us into the terminal. Jamie watched me from his stroller with big eyes. "Dad, I—"

"Do you?" he yelled.

"No," I said softly.

"Does he run around with other women? Does he beat you?"

It was as if Dad himself had taken a swing at me.

No, I must have sputtered.

"Well then—"

Winded, I grabbed my suitcase, turned my back and hurried Jamie into the airport. *Just put one foot after the other,* I told myself as I passed through security, walked to the gate, and finally boarded the plane.

I REPLAYED THE SCENE AT the curb the whole way home. How could my father, my rock, my one true person, refuse to understand me? We'd always been connected, but now he had abandoned me. I knew then that I'd been right to mold myself to his expectations. Dad didn't like the real me at all. In fact, the real me had made him furious. The weight of Jamie's sleeping body sagged against my chest as I stared, unseeing, out the plane window and wondered if I'd done irreparable damage. What kind of daughter carelessly upsets her sixty-two-year-old Holocaust survivor father? After everything he's been through?

A reckless daughter, of course. A selfish daughter. A bad daughter. I could still go back to Jeff, I thought. I could do the right thing and crawl right back. I saw myself inside that marriage, the years flying by in a swirl of calendar pages. I saw my future self, old and hunched and gray. And then, looking at my shadowy reflection in the plane window, I suddenly saw that striving to fit what others expect of you never ends. The more you do to please them, the more they expect, so that you work harder and harder just to keep the seamless illusion that you are what they want you to be, all the time getting smaller and smaller inside, while they have no idea what it has cost you to be that different person who is, in fact, a long way from the person you really are, the person your entire soul tells you to be. As the wheels touched down in Toronto and I wriggled Jamie into his coat, I understood something I'd never understood before: disappointing Dad was terrible. But not being allowed to be myself was a life not worth living.

I dragged our suitcase up the snowy front walk, opened the door, and locked it behind us. I tucked Jamie into bed and stayed up late, safe within the shelter of my own four walls. I was a twenty-six-year-old mother headed for divorce. I'd screwed it all up and I was deeply ashamed, but I wasn't going to change my mind.

PART THREE

Toronto

1990s

26

Waffles

The trip to Mexico set off a period of disconnection and lostness, as everything I had believed to be true was called into question. It was almost as if I were starting life all over again. I had cracked out of the shell that had been built around me—to protect me, to insulate me, to keep me on the right path. Now I was a pile of awkward limbs and raw edges, newborn and barely able to see, and all I could do was feel my way, slowly, toward where I imagined the light might be.

My first act of self-preservation was to stop answering the phone. I couldn't bear to talk to my parents, and since my sisters spoke to my parents, I didn't want to talk to them, either. It took everything I had just to get myself and my child through those first post-Mexico days. I had no extra strength for tricky phone calls.

ONE COLD MORNING I OPENED my eyes to find myself lying diagonally across the bed. 5:43 a.m. Jamie was calling me. "Mama! Eep-eep! Mama!"

I stumbled into his room. "Eep-eep! Hi, Baby Bat," I said. He held the rail of the crib and jumped up and down, grinning from ear to ear. "Juice please, juice please," he chanted. I took him in my arms and carried him down the stairs.

The new house still felt strange and empty. In the tiny kitchen, I set Jamie on the counter and made myself a cup of coffee. I was out of juice so I opened a can of peaches and drained the liquid into Jamie's cup. I added a little water, put on the lid and handed it to him. He put the cup to his lips, tilted his head back and went into a juice trance.

A mixing bowl with yesterday's caked-on batter sat in the sink. I eyed my mother's waffle iron, heavy and solid on the countertop. I considered its square shape, its Sunbeam logo, its frayed cord. Saturday afternoons, Julie had used the smooth side of the plates to make us grilled tuna and cheese sandwiches as the snow sparkled outside.

I glanced out the kitchen window. There had been a thaw and now the whole backyard was frozen mud. "C'mon, Baby Bat," I said, taking Jamie into my arms again. We picked our way past the train set snaking through the dining room and the Legos in the hall. In the living room, I kicked over the fort we'd made, replaced the sofa cushions, and nestled Jamie in the corner with a blanket.

"Wanna watch Winnie?" He nodded, sippy cup still tipped to his mouth. I fiddled with the VCR and soon the Winnie the Pooh theme song filled the room. In the kitchen, I ran hot water into the bowl. My limbs were heavy and my head hurt, but I needed to make the waffles. Pouring batter over those plates was so satisfying. I couldn't change myself or the mess I'd made of my life, but damn it, I could press that batter into submission every single morning.

SOMEWHERE ALONG THE WAY, I gave up on getting dressed. It was okay to be in your pajamas until eleven, I told myself. Then one day I didn't get to showering when Jamie went down for his nap. I was just so tired. In the afternoon, we built a castle out of blocks and made play dough. Then it was time to make dinner and go back to bed. So why bother?

We were sitting on the floor doing a puzzle one afternoon when someone rang the bell. I wasn't dressed and I didn't want to answer, but there was persistent knocking and a familiar voice calling my name.

I opened the door to find my brother-in-law holding out a foil container. Julie had sent him over with a care package for dinner.

"Hey, I haven't seen your new house yet," he said.

"Oh, it's not a good time," I started to say, but it was too late. He had already stepped across the threshold. He took in the living and dining rooms, his mouth hanging open. I watched him crane his neck to peer into the kitchen. "Oh yeah," he said with a laugh. "This is a real showplace."

I closed the door behind him and took a look around. Toys were strewn everywhere and the table was heavy with dirty dishes. In the kitchen, the butter was out and the counter was coated with flour. A whisk caked in waffle batter dripped down the front of the cupboards and a garbage bag overflowed near the back door.

I'd been raised to understand that the state of your space reflected the state of your self-respect, and I could suddenly see I'd let both hit rock bottom.

After I put Jamie to bed, I came downstairs and pushed up my sleeves. I collected the toys, carried the dishes to the kitchen, wiped down the counters, and put away the butter and flour. I ran the dishwasher, took out the garbage, and scoured the waffle iron until it gleamed. I got down on my knees with a sponge and a bucket of soapy water to scrub the floor. I wiped up batter, footprints, dust, and hair, but the tiles—old linoleum that had perhaps been light green once but were now gray and scratched and peeling in some of the corners—still looked dirty.

THE NEXT MORNING AFTER BREAKFAST, I pulled on our coats. "C'mon honey," I said. "We're going to the store."

At The Home Depot, I chose thick peel-and-stick tiles in black and white, and an X-Acto knife the clerk told me I could use to cut them. When Jamie napped that afternoon, I started my project, beginning at one of the baseboards with no plan or forethought. It didn't take long to see I was in trouble. The tiles weren't lining up properly, and even worse, some were higher and some were lower because the old floor was uneven. We went back to the hardware store.

"Oh no," said the clerk when I described what I was doing. "You can't just stick them on top. You have to get the old floor off first. You have to scrape." He pulled a tool off the rack and handed it to me.

I scraped at that floor for days, for weeks. The old tiles came off in fragments and chunks and ribbons. In some places, there were pieces of another floor under that. I worked into the night, scraping back the years, the mistakes, the layers. I wanted to get to the point where there would be nothing left to remove; where the ground would be smooth and solid and true beneath my feet.

27

Strawberry Butter

I couldn't have survived that time without Gloria, a therapist I'd found through one of my university friends. I put my dirty hair in a scrunchie and dragged myself to an address in the northeast part of the city. Despite my complicated childhood, my nightmares and my fears, I'd never been to psychotherapy, and I didn't know what to expect. Navigating the late-winter ice, I made my way to the back door of a house and into a warm basement office, where Gloria appeared with two mugs of peach tea.

"So, tell me about yourself," she said as I sat down on her little couch. I started talking and it all spilled out—about Jeff and my parents and the mess I'd made. For the first time in my life, I didn't enjoy food. Jamie grew and grew, but I could barely eat. "How many pounds have you lost?" she said, looking up from her notepad. Real concern leaked through her neutral question.

"Sixteen." I told her I could take off my jeans without undoing them.

"Please eat," she said as I stood to put my coat on. "Soup, crackers, anything."

THOSE APPOINTMENTS BECAME A REASON to get dressed in the morning, a reason to leave the house. At first, I filled the minutes telling Gloria what everyone expected from me, and the agony I felt about letting them down. I thought I was there to learn how to be less like myself, to understand what I'd done wrong to end up in such a bad position. Gloria took the opposite tack. "Where are you in all of this?" she said one brittle March day. I stared, uncomprehending, into my empty mug. I was used to thinking deeply about other people, trying to adopt their whole way of looking at me and anticipating what they wanted. "I don't understand the question," I said.

"How do *you* feel? What do *you* want?" I didn't need to be less like myself, Gloria said. I needed to be more like myself.

"Love your Bonnyness," she told me, over and over again.

SLOWLY, GINGERLY, I BEGAN TO build myself back up. "I was just so busy," I said to Mom and Dad when I started answering the phone again. They weren't great believers in therapy and I didn't want to get into the details of my sessions with Gloria. Still, I knew they were concerned. As was his habit, Dad tried to just will me toward happiness. "Everything is okay," he said. "You can still be happy."

His words started to sound like white noise—kind but irrelevant. What he'd said outside the terminal in Mexico was seared into my brain and, after turning it around and around for weeks, I'd come to understand something, a little piece of hard-earned knowledge that would serve me for the rest of my life: Someone can love you as much as it's possible to love. He can guide you and shield you and tell you everything he knows. He can share the truths he's learned through one of the most brutal events in human history. Still, they are his truths. No matter how vast his experience, no matter how much he has overcome, someone else's truth cannot be your truth. Nobody knows the path you're supposed to take; the decisions you must make to define your own journey toward independent self-hood. That job is yours and yours alone.

I NEEDED MONEY. I COULDN'T sit around waiting to see what would happen in my settlement with Jeff, and I couldn't take money from Mom and Dad, who would've sent it if I'd asked. Money from parents comes with strings attached, and I knew I needed to be free of strings.

What could I do for work? It was too late to go to law school. Cooking made me happier than anything else and, for a brief moment, I considered becoming a chef. But when I was little and Dad had run to the restaurants morning and night, Sundays and Christmases, he'd said, "You won't go into the restaurant business. Okay? Promise me. No restaurants." Our relationship was hanging by a thread already. This was no time to further defy him.

The only other thing I knew how to do was write. I didn't have childcare during the day, but Jeff took Jamie a few nights a week and every second weekend. I started taking postgrad journalism courses at a university downtown, one at a time.

MY FIRST PUBLISHED ARTICLE WAS a piece in a parenting magazine about temper tantrums. That led to another assignment, and then another. Getting my voice on the page wasn't easy, but it felt good. I got to know the editors at the magazine, and we worked well together. When I opened the email offering me the job of associate editor, I was so excited that I screamed. "Mama?" Jamie said, toddling into the bedroom where I'd set up my computer.

"Mama is very happy."

I FOUND CHILDCARE, SETTLED WITH Jeff, and put a new life together. On Mother's Day, I pulled out the waffle iron from the deepest cupboard in the kitchen. "Remember we used to make these every day?" I said to Jamie, old sadness washing over me.

"Yum, waffles!" He was now in junior kindergarten and a big fan of kitchen projects. I took out the flour and sugar and handed him the whisk. I melted butter and cracked three eggs. By the time I spooned the batter into a measuring cup and poured it over the hot plates, I felt lighter.

"Wait," I said, "let's make them even better." Thinking of that happy day eating popovers and strawberry butter with Mom at the fancy department store, I took berries out of the fridge, mashed them, and creamed them into softened butter. I added a spoonful of icing sugar and mixed until I had a nice paste. I lifted the sheet of crisp waffles off the iron, slathered it in strawberry butter, and watched the pink swirls soak in like a salve.

28

Cinnamon

That summer, Jamie and I flew to Edmonton for a visit. Being around Mom and Dad still made me a little anxious, but I was becoming more confident. I had a good job and I was a good mother. Mom and Dad had also calmed down. It wasn't that they approved of my choices, necessarily, but they were coming to accept them. This time, I found a book titled *When Your Son or Daughter Is Going Through a Divorce* by their bed. "Is this yours?" I said to Mom, surprised. Self-help was not her thing.

"We're learning to understand that we're not in control," she said.

I quickly changed the subject. I didn't want to give any more thought to how my failed marriage had hurt my parents. I'd done that nonstop. And thinking about what my failed marriage had done to me, well, that was a subject I'd be unpacking for many years to come.

The truth was, I hadn't really come home to see Mom and Dad anyway. Not two years earlier, in the depth of my misery, I'd run into Michael, my childhood friend. His hair was shorter than the last

time I'd seen him, but there was the nine-year-old boy with the caterpillars smiling from inside a handsome, bearded man.

"How are you?" I'd said, holding Jamie on my hip. "What are you
up to these days?"

He was finishing a master's in poetry at the University of Alberta.
His thesis was taking him forever. Let's keep in touch, one of us said,
and I wrote his number down on a piece of paper from my diaper
bag.

From that day, we'd gradually started to speak and write letters,
first about books and music and then, when my life blew up, about
ourselves. He was good at making me laugh. "Going crazy would be
a relief right now," I'd told him one afternoon, as I paced the living
room in my pajamas.

"Okay," he'd said. "Give your hair one last wash."

Back and forth the letters flew from Toronto to Edmonton, Edmonton to Toronto, burning a path between us. Soon I was listening
for the mail with sensitive ears and a thumping heart. He wrote to
me about art and music and poetry—awakening a creativity I had
buried inside myself.

New leaves were sprouting on the trees when I'd finally found the
guts to write, "Jamie and I need to come to Edmonton. Something
to do with my parents."

"Great," he'd written back. "I'd love to see you."

THE DAY AFTER WE ARRIVED, Jamie and I met Michael at the museum. I felt a warmth in my chest watching Michael take my son by
the hand to closely examine every reconstructed dinosaur, taxider-
mized wolf and bear. That night, after I tucked Jamie into bed, Michael picked me up in his Honda. His favorite bookstore was hosting
a reading he thought I might like. He stopped at a traffic light and
looked over at me. When the light turned green, he put his foot
down on the gas pedal without moving the car into drive. The en-
gine revved wildly.

"Oops," he said, blushing a bit.

"Race car driver," I said.

"I wasn't doing that to impress you. Although if I thought it would impress you, I'd do it again."

THE AUTHOR READING at the bookstore was Michael Ondaatje. His character, Kip, defused a bomb step by step; carefully, gently. On the way home, my Michael took my hand, making my entire arm tingle.

BACK IN TORONTO, I REPLAYED those too-short hours over and over, pining and fretting. There were so many things I'd wanted to say; things I'd wanted to hear.

But there will be lots of time. There will be walks and drives and late nights, talking and listening. There will be pizza and wine and coffee in bed. The gifts will be honest and simple. A cube of soap that smells like grass. A CD of lush piano music. A stack of poems he's written himself and one, that he's typed out, by Ondaatje.

> You touched
> your belly to my hands
> in the dry air and said
> I am the cinnamon
> peeler's wife. Smell me.

YOU WOULD THINK A PERSON who got married too young wouldn't want to marry again, and I didn't, except to Michael. It was a late morning wedding and I wore a satin dress and flowers in my hair. Jamie walked me down the aisle. We served mushroom agnolotti and cinnamon ice cream in ice bowls with nasturtiums and pansies frozen inside.

My parents were thrilled I was remarrying, even if they didn't completely understand the kind of guy Michael was. A man who wrote poetry and loved art? A man who hadn't quite figured out what he would do for a living? I could imagine what Dad was thinking, but the only thing he criticized was our choice of entrée at the wedding. "You're serving pasta? Pasta isn't nice enough. You have to give the people something good to eat at a wedding. I want to serve steak."

I cleared my throat and took a breath. "I'm sorry, Dad. We can't serve steak at eleven thirty. You're going to have to trust me."

It was a warm day, and the ceremony was outside. Afterward, Jamie and my sisters' kids rolled up their pants and waded into a stream at the back of the property. I had hired a lousy band and when we sent them home, someone grabbed a guitar from the back of his car and played Leonard Cohen's "Dance Me to the End of Love." Michael twirled me on the stone patio. I felt like I'd already lived an entire lifetime, but I was not even thirty years old.

FINALLY, MY LIFE SETTLED INTO blissful domesticity. I kept my job at the parenting magazine and threw myself into cooking on the weekends. In fall, I grilled red peppers and pickled green beans. In December, I shredded potatoes for latkes on a box grater, remembering the feel of Baba Sarah's hand over mine, protecting my knuckles. I roasted chickens and learned how to braise a brisket. After years of effort, it was suddenly easy to be me. I had the exact feeling of being inside myself. I wasn't trying to be what other people saw. I inhabited my body and simply looked out.

I became pregnant and, at home with a midwife, we brought Leo into the world. Four years later, Maya arrived to complete our family. I felt myself grow like I did when Jamie was born, again, and then again.

MEANWHILE, MY PARENTS AND I reached a kind of stasis. They came to love Michael and they were happy to see me settled. Dad and I never spoke about what happened between us in Mexico, and I wondered if he'd forgotten it. I tried to forget, too, but whenever they landed in Toronto, I felt a constriction inside. I was on high alert for anything I could interpret as criticism, and I tried to be beyond reproach. Before they came over, I swept and vacuumed and wiped fingerprints from the walls. I put the kids in fresh clothes. Still, they always seemed to notice something wrong—the grass needed cutting, I looked tired. Were they intensely critical or was I intensely sensitive? I still don't know. Maybe I hadn't gotten over the feeling of abandonment, maybe they hadn't gotten over their disappointment. But we didn't talk about it. My life was about Michael and the kids now. I tried to let the conflict fall away.

ONE WINTER BREAK, WE TOOK the kids to Arizona and I watched them climb all over Dad in the light of the Chanukah candles. They touched his stubble and giggled at his accent. He got down on the floor to play with Maya; he picked up that long pole with the basket on the end and took Jamie and Leo out to pick oranges. His good essence was obvious to the kids—I knew they felt it—and obvious to me.

Near the end of the trip, Maya clutched a bag of stale bread in her little hands as Dad took the three of them out to feed the ducks on the pond behind the condo, just like he'd taken me to the ravine near our house. He wrapped them up in that sense of wonder, just as he'd wrapped me.

DAD WAS JUICING THE LAST of the oranges when Leo, who was sitting on the counter beside the juicer, noticed the green-blue markings inside Dad's arm. "Zaida, what's that?" he asked, and I listened to Dad begin to tell what had to be told, slowly, carefully. He was a little boy in Poland when the bad men came. He had to leave his home. There was nothing to eat. His mother was very brave. It was strange and beautiful to remember the father he'd been to me, the father he still was, as he began to teach my children about themselves.

I ran to grab a pad of paper and a pen off my mother's desk, and I sat down on the kitchen floor, listening and making notes. Dad smiled at me and kept talking. *I'm taking notes for the book,* I almost said as a gesture, an offering. But developing in my throat was a lump that made it hard to talk. The next morning, I tore off the scribbles I'd made and tucked them into my purse. Then I put the pad back on Mom's desk, and flew home with my family.

29

Hard Things

'd left a shaky marriage for a stable one, and I was everything I was supposed to be: a daughter, a wife, a mother. I thought I was done searching, but something nagged at me—an abstract inner conflict that was so old and so familiar, I didn't even know it could be separated from my self.

OUR PARENTS TEACH US ALL kinds of things, sometimes on purpose, more often by accident. Mom was very smart, but she disliked challenge and was not in the habit of encouraging her daughters to do anything at which we could fail. Combine that with Dad's intense protectiveness, his constant insistence that we not work too hard and "just enjoy," and I often found myself afraid to reach for challenges; afraid to try.

On the other hand, a tiny voice inside me persistently whispered the exact opposite: test yourself, look for challenges, seek out hard things. I don't know when I became aware of this other voice, small and insistent, urging me to prove myself. Was it after that chemistry test in high school? Or did it begin much earlier, when I tested the feeling of sharp snow on the sole of my bare foot and ate dog food, staring at myself in the mirror at my aunt's house? Did it begin with the first understanding that my father had survived something so terrible, nothing I did could ever compare?

I was used to living with these dueling impulses in my head, even if I didn't quite understand them. I had not yet discovered Esther Perel, the New York–based psychotherapist, herself the child of Holocaust survivors. "One of the main experiences of children of Holocaust survivors is that you ask yourself . . . 'Would I have been able to do this?'" I heard her say years later to Brené Brown on the podcast *Unlocking Us.* "You think, *my problems aren't real problems.* How can you compare with Auschwitz?"

BEFORE THAT, I INTUITIVELY LOOKED for hard things without understanding why, or even what kinds of hard things were the right ones, sometimes surprising even myself with my random impulses.

ONE SUMMER WHEN I WAS young, for example, I'd insisted on waiting tables at a big fish restaurant Dad had opened with a couple of partners.

"That's not for you," Dad had said. "You can seat people at Teddy's."

"Dad, I really want to learn." I wouldn't give up and he finally turned me over to Mike, the headwaiter at the fish place.

In front of my father, Mike was soft and solicitous, but as soon as Dad walked away, he'd hissed, "It's not going to be the cakewalk you're used to."

"Okay," I'd said quietly.

"I'm going to make this as hard as possible."

"Okay."

Mike seemed to have nothing to do but walk behind me as I delivered plates and drinks and the blackboard with the daily specials. "Don't drop that where are your side towels why didn't you use a tray you're making a mess," he'd chanted softly.

One day, I'd lost a whole tray of wineglasses going up the stairs. I didn't mop it up well enough, slipped, and lost the replacement tray as well. The surrounding tables gasped and laughed. If it was a taste of degradation I was looking for, I'd certainly found it.

After six weeks, I had cuts and burns on my hands. My feet were a mess of blisters. Still, I could juggle a full section, carry five loaded entrée plates in two hands, manage the oversized dessert tray on my shoulder. It had been a terrible summer, but at no point did I consider quitting. All I kept thinking was a variation of what I'd always thought: *If Dad could survive the whole fucking Holocaust, I need to at least be able to do this.*

I WAS BALANCING MY JOBS of editor and mom when a major promotion came along to throw things out of whack. Finally, real traction in my career, but what about everything else? Michael now worked in advertising and his job took him out of town often, plus three kids were a lot of kids. "Why do you have to push yourself?" Dad said when I told him. "Why can't you do something easier?"

The night I signed the contract, Michael and I put the kids to bed early and opened a bottle of red wine. Outside, snowflakes drifted down like confetti. I brought the whiteboard from Leo's room and wiped off his math equations with the dry eraser.

"Groceries, meal prep, driving to school," Michael began as I started a list. "Story time, homework, soccer . . ." The marker squeaked as I wrote furiously.

Covered in my messy scrawl, the board leaned against the family room wall and I flopped down beside Michael on the couch. "I don't see how this'll all get done if I'm working longer hours," I said, sipping my wine.

"We'll work it out, babe," Michael said. "Don't worry." My heart pounded as I contemplated my promotion. I'd be supervising a team of editors and helping to steer the overall direction of the magazine. It was impossible. It was thrilling. It was a challenge I was ready for.

My first day, I hopped out of bed to shower and dress before the kids were up. I put on makeup, organized schoolbags, made breakfast. But it wasn't long before my routine started to crack. I found supervising and supporting other editors gratifying, but there were endless deadlines to meet, performances to appraise, pages to read, emails to return. One night at dinner, Leo spilled the water pitcher, and I surprised everyone by yelling at him. When I ran to get a cloth, Michael followed me into the kitchen. "Just so you know, you're radiating a lot of tension," he said quietly.

"No shit," I hissed.

Michael went out of town for work, and I suddenly felt like I had to do everything everywhere. I couldn't stay at the office late, so I came home to make dinner and get the kids to bed, then worked late into the night. I got up at five to continue working before getting the kids to school in the morning.

I began to make mistakes and I started to have trouble catching my breath. I took money out of the bank machine and walked away with my card and receipt, leaving the cash sticking out of the machine. At a traffic light, I sailed through a red realizing, too late, that everyone was honking and screeching to a halt because of me. *Jesus.* I pulled over and pounded the steering wheel. *Get your shit together,* I told myself. *Other people manage kids and a job. Why can't you?*

MICHAEL CAME BACK AND THE May long weekend rolled around. I felt like I'd barely been home, so I planned to spend the entire time with my family—no office, no emails. On Saturday afternoon, we took out the hose and the kids ran through the sprinkler in the backyard. Jamie's eyes were red, and his nose was running; his usual spring allergies. "You okay?" I said, handing him a Claritin.

"Yeah, Mom. I'm fine," he said, swallowing the pill.

The next morning, his eyes were swollen, and he couldn't stop rubbing them. "What do you feel?" I asked.

"Itchy. It's just my usual," he said. But by afternoon, something seemed different. Something seemed off.

"I'm going to take him down to the hospital," I told Michael, looking for my keys. "I know we'll be wasting our time. I just want to be sure."

IT WAS A QUIET SUNDAY. Flowering crab apples and magnolias lined
the streets with pink and white petals. We parked on University Avenue and wandered into the emergency department. The nurse tri-
aged us and told us to sit down. It was going to be a long, boring
wait. I thought of Michael and the little kids playing in the sunshine.

"Mom? I'm kinda hungry," Jamie said.

I went off in search of food and came back with a sandwich from
the hospital cafeteria. He had one bite before he said he was feeling
funny.

"Funny how?" But I could already see it. His top lip was swelling,
and he was doing something strange with his tongue.

"My mouth is itchy," he slurred. He started to shake then, his
whole body convulsing as I tried to hold him upright. I screamed for
help.

Two people in scrubs came with a gurney and rushed us into a
room. Jamie was white, his lips huge. He couldn't talk.

"He's going into shock," the doctor yelled. "What's he allergic to?"

"Pollen and flowers," I said, wringing my hands. They gave him a
shot of epinephrine. His heart rate didn't come down fast enough.
They gave him another.

"What else?"

"Nothing." I clenched my teeth to stop chattering.

"Are you sure?"

"Yes, nothing!"

All night, I sat in a chair and watched my twelve-year-old's blood
pressure on a little screen. At 4 a.m., his diastolic number went
below 30. An alarm sounded and I ran down the hall calling for help,
but the doctors were already on their way. As three of them worked
to stabilize him, I closed my eyes. All my guilt and inner conflict
crystalized in that moment. *Let him live and I'll leave my job,* I prayed.
Dad had been right all along. I had been too greedy, too ambitious,
and now I was being punished. *I will be a better mother—a better woman,*
I promised. *Just let him live.*

IT TOOK ALMOST TWO WEEKS for Jamie to get better. He was discharged from the hospital with a diagnosis of anaphylaxis. He'd been on one antibiotic to clear up a little patch of impetigo on his cheek and shortly after that, he'd been put on a second antibiotic for a sinus infection. The team concluded that somehow, the two antibiotics mixed with his seasonal allergies to cause an intense allergic reaction. It was a sketchy theory, but it was all we had.

A few days later, I walked to my boss's office straight from the elevator. I felt nauseous but resolved.

She seemed to be expecting me. "I'm so sorry," I began, "I just can't do this anymore." I talked about my kids and my guilt and the terror of the past few weeks.

"I understand," she said simply.

I looked at her calm face and wondered, for a moment, if she was happy that I was leaving. Perhaps I'd done a terrible job. On the way out, I stopped and turned to look at her. She sat behind her desk, the whole city at her back.

"Do you think I'm ruining my career?"

"I really don't know," she said. "The same opportunities don't often come twice. But usually, new ones come along to take their place."

30

Lost

When I got home from the office, the kids were at school and everything around the house felt unnaturally quiet—like when you leave a loud concert and the silence has its own sound. Michael, who'd listened to me worry and rehearse my quitting speech to death, was kind and gentle. My parents were, of course, thrilled. "Oh, thank god," Mom said over the phone.

"Now you will finally relax," said Dad. His love and protection were like a heavy blanket on top of me. It was almost impossible to move under the weight.

In the coming weeks, I took the kids for ice cream after school and volunteered on field trips. I wiped noses and schlepped backpacks. The school year ended, and Michael was able to travel for work without conflict. I felt like a good wife and a good mother. But with no hard thing to push against, I wasn't sure who I was.

IT WAS A COOL FALL night when I dreamed of three figures sitting in chairs with special caps on their heads. I was behind a sheet of glass with a controller in my hand, like a joystick. I pushed a button and nails, which were embedded in the caps, shot into the three people's skulls.

I woke up with tears on my face and shooting pains in my stomach. I hadn't seen a therapist since Gloria, who had long since retired, but I was terrified, and I got the name of someone from a friend.

DR. HAYWARD WALKED INTO HER downtown office in drapey black clothes and chunky silver jewelry. She took a full history in fifty minutes. There was no peach tea. When I asked her if the dream meant I secretly wanted to murder my children, she smiled. "This is just a projection of your ordinary feelings of maternal guilt," she said. "Quite normal." I was so relieved that the rest of what she said caught me by surprise. "But I think you do have deep intergenerational trauma from the Holocaust. It's very clear."

Trauma. That word Dad hated. You don't understand me at all, I wanted to say. You don't understand my family. We are proud and strong. We don't dwell on the past—we look forward. For a moment, I found myself paralyzed, sitting in the therapist's office, torn between what I had been taught to feel and the possibility of what I really felt.

And then I was angry. This woman who'd only just met me was coolly summing up who I was with snap judgments and pathetic Holocaust clichés. She didn't know the kind of father I had, and she didn't know me.

"You need to come three times a week," Dr. Hayward was saying. "And once we start, this is a full commitment. It's like buying season tickets to the opera. You can't cancel and if you miss a session, you still pay."

I hurried out of her office, stifling my desire to slam the door. For the first few days, I continued to be angry. But soon there was something in the background, another feeling that was hard to name. Annoyed as I was, I had to admit that hearing Dr. Hayward talk about my trauma as obvious made me feel a little lighter. The weight I'd been living with was real, and if it had a name, maybe I could start to separate myself from it.

I DON'T KNOW WHAT WOULD have happened if I'd agreed to Dr. Hayward's intense program. We might have dug into Dad's urge to protect and my own resistance to that protection. I might have learned, a little earlier, that trauma doesn't always look the way you expect.

But I didn't agree. That much therapy would cost a fortune and I wanted to fully engage in life, not sit in a therapist's office analyzing it. On another level, maybe I was afraid—afraid of Dr. Hayward's approach, afraid of succumbing to darkness. Or maybe I just wasn't ready.

"I've decided not to continue," I emailed her a few days later.

CONFUSED AND EXHAUSTED, I DRAGGED myself to yoga like a dying horse to a pond. I'd always felt at home on my mat and after I'd left my job, I'd found a studio with a low-key teacher not far from home. It turned out she was away that night, and her husband, a tall yogi with an enigmatic expression, taught the class instead. In the warm semidarkness, he sat in a wood chair and called out the poses. I moved and breathed and moved and breathed, following his commands with my eyes closed. During savasana, instead of my usual urge to fidget, I felt my mind leave my body. I was looking down on myself from space. I was flooded with compassion. *We are all just travelers in time,* a voice said. *You will find your place.* The relief was enormous, and as I rolled up my mat I had the sense that freedom was waiting for me. But where?

31

The March

Dr. Hayward had put the Holocaust back into my head, and I couldn't get it out. My sister Julie was also thinking about the Holocaust, but in a much more concrete way. "I'm going to the March of the Living information night," she called me to say. "Why don't you come?"

Since its inception in 1988, the march had been a duty and a privilege for teens in Jewish communities around the world. Participants traveled to Poland for Yom HaShoah in the spring, to listen and learn and walk on the train tracks at Auschwitz and say, "Never again!" The cornerstone of the program was the group of Holocaust survivors who traveled along with the teens and anchored the trip with first-person testimony. It was an amazing program with which I had a complicated relationship.

I was twenty-one the march's inaugural year, older than the typical participant of sixteen or seventeen, and only a few shaky years into my life in Toronto. As I scrambled to find my footing in the big city, I probably wasn't even aware of the trip. Of course, in those years, I wanted nothing to do with the Holocaust anyway. In addition to fear, I was wrestling with many aspects of my identity, the question of belonging chief among them. Growing up, I thought there was no one like us. A Holocaust survivor father, a Canadian mother, two people bent on reinvention. My parents had style and flair and were motivated by the past to do better. They did not want to dwell on the Holocaust.

Once I finally found my place in Toronto, I began to see that the city was full of survivor families and kids, people who had grown up in a pack, with a broader perspective than mine. I hadn't even known how alone I felt until I saw how together they seemed. Here was a whole community of people like us, yet we weren't part of it. What's more, Dad was ambivalent about whether we *should* be part of it.

When my niece, the oldest grandchild, wanted to go on the march, I remember Dad putting up the familiar roadblocks, no less protective as a grandparent than a parent. Why should his children relive his own suffering? What was the point? We should look forward, not back. We should have joy, not pain.

In the end, my niece went on the march, and Dad came around, perhaps realizing it wasn't really his decision to make anyway. After that, various kids in the family marched when they were in high school, and Dad became used to his grandchildren going on the trip.

IN ADDITION TO THE PARTICIPANTS and the survivors, there is a third group that marches, a contingent of adults who act as chaperones. It's widely known as grunt work with a ton of responsibility—to herd and supervise the kids, to make sure the trip runs smoothly—with no personal time. The chaperones are the last to go to bed and the first to wake up. Nevertheless, it's a coveted role and there are always more would-be chaperones than spots.

Julie knew people who had been chaperones and she was interested in the role. She was ready, she told me. She could handle it. Maybe that meant I could handle it, too? As the youngest and the sensitive one, everything seemed to take a little more out of me, but to follow along seemed like a good idea.

———

AT THE INFORMATION NIGHT, THE organizers screened a montage of past marches. Here was a huge group of kids listening to testimony at the Majdanek camp. Here were kids walking on the tracks at Auschwitz. I started to feel a familiar revulsion, but I was in a crowded room, and I couldn't go running out. Instead, I looked at the survivors sitting in the front row: Bill, handsome and professorial with a halo of silver curls; Nate, wise and serious in his black cap. They were beautiful, these survivors, like Dad was beautiful, but when they were introduced at the beginning of the evening, I realized they had something Dad didn't: a means for transformation. By sharing their stories, over and over again, they'd had the opportunity to turn devastation into catharsis, and I thought I could detect the difference in the way they spoke and held their heads.

AFTER THE MEETING, JULIE DROVE me home and we talked about what we saw. Both of us had been struck by the honor and respect paid to the survivors. People had lined up to hug them; the teenagers fawned over them and hung on their every word. They were almost like rock stars.

Shouldn't Dad get to be a rock star, too? There was no way he'd go on the march on his own, but what if the two of us signed up and took Dad with us?

"I'm going to apply," Julie said as she pulled into my driveway.

"Okay, I will, too." I closed her car door feeling hopeful. If everything went well, we'd both be accepted and the two of us could encourage and support Dad, who could take his rightful place with his counterparts as a cherished member of the community.

THE SCREENING PROCESS FOR CHAPERONES is rigorous. I spent days writing my essay and preparing for the interview. I fantasized about the relief of sharing my burden, letting all those kids take up the mantle and lighten my load. Maybe if I could pass the feeling of responsibility on to the next generation, I would stop putting food in our dog's bowl and thinking, every single time, how good the kibble would've tasted to my dad when he was starving at age twelve.

MY SISTER AND I GOT our phone calls on the same day: we'd both made it. All we had to do was convince Dad and at first, it seemed like it might be easy. We took turns calling him to explain the features of the trip and how much there was to be gained. Despite his natural inclination to avoid all things Holocaust, he seemed to be swaying. "The survivors are treated like royalty," I told him.

"Isn't that something," he said earnestly.

He had problems with arthritis in his legs, back, and neck, but we'd be there to help him. He didn't have much experience speaking to huge groups about what had happened to him, but we could get him ready.

Dad continued to play along until it was time to pay for the airline tickets. "No. I don't want to go," he said suddenly.

"Dad, what do you mean? Why not?"

"Because I don't want to."

"But what about—"

"No. Not going."

Maybe he was nervous about speaking to so many people. Maybe he didn't want to make the emotional journey. Maybe he had simply had enough Holocaust for one lifetime. He couldn't be convinced, and he felt no need to further explain himself. He was a person who knew his own mind, and to pressure him would only make him dig in deeper.

Julie was going to go anyway, so I would, too. My money was due, past due, way past due. Any day I would type in my credit card and start to pack. Except there was Julie, leaving for the airport, while I was on the couch in my slippers at home, going nowhere.

32

Paris

On the eve of my thirty-ninth birthday, Michael handed me a heavy paper bag.

"Happy birthday, love."

He had been trying to cheer me up for weeks. Julie had come back from the march exhausted but satisfied, and I knew I'd missed out. On top of that, I hadn't been able to find another job since leaving the magazine, and I felt like a failure.

We were by then living in a house with ochre walls and a good kitchen. My favorite spot in the entire place was a bookcase we'd built into the back wall, just for my food books. Beside my stacks of *Gourmet* and *Saveur* and *Cooks Illustrated* were my beloved *Silver Palate Cookbook* from university and my Julia Child, now held together with a thick rubber band. I had *The Classic Italian Cook Book* by Marcella Hazan and Craig Claiborne's *New York Times Cook Book* alongside a treasured copy of *Larousse Gastronomique*.

"For your collection," Michael said. I opened the bag and slid out *Barefoot in Paris*.

"You remembered!"

"Of course. Who could forget those stories of you running around as a teenager, drinking too much coffee in the City of Lights?"

"Thank you, honey."

I was about to throw out the bag when he said, "Wait, there's something else."

I plunged my hand into the paper envelope and touched a single sheet of paper. The bill, I figured, but when I pulled it out, I saw that it was printed with dates and times.

"What's this?" I said.

He only grinned.

"Oh my god!" I said. "We're going to Paris?"

"We're going to Paris. It's time I took you back!"

WE BOARDED AN OVERNIGHT FLIGHT, *Barefoot* in my carry-on. At the back of the book, Ina Garten had listed where to go for the best bread, cheese, pastry and chocolate; wine, cookware, and more. We followed it to the letter, visiting Poilâne for tartines, Ladurée for our first macarons, and E. Dehillerin for madeleine pans and an assortment of excellent little knives. It was pure pleasure to be there with Michael and to reconnect with an earlier version of myself, so young but already in love with food and everything it meant to me.

Instead of staying in a hotel, we rented an apartment with a big blue door and a little modern kitchen, so we could shop and cook like locals. We walked to the Boulevard Raspail market for fresh vegetables, a gooey wedge of cheese, and a loaf of warm bread. While Nina Simone played on the stereo, I sliced eggplant and zucchini. We dragged hunks of bread through the cheese and polished off a bottle of rosé as my ratatouille simmered on the stove.

At a restaurant near the Tuileries Garden, we ate smoked potatoes with fava beans and pea shoots, then skate wing fried in butter. We passed the menu back and forth over a candle in the center of the table, trying to choose a dessert. When the paper caught fire, I hurried to blow it out as he sang happy birthday.

EVERYTHING WAS PERFECT AND BEAUTIFUL when we walked back to the market for black cherries to bake into a clafoutis. On the way home, we passed by the Hôtel de Ville, Paris's city hall. Something about the poster for the installation inside caught my eye. "What is that?" I asked Michael.

He jogged over to the sign and came back. "It's about the persecution of French Jews during the war."

We stared at each other for a long moment, holding our bags of delicious food. I watched people pour in and out of the building and a peculiar feeling came over me—a feeling, I only later realized, of being seen. It wasn't the exhibit that drew my attention but the people. The real, live people who wanted to know what had happened to the Jews during the Holocaust. I wanted to watch them read and listen and learn. I wanted to see them take up the mantle, share my burden.

We toured the exhibit, which seemed to barely weigh on me, so charmed was I with the French people who'd come to see it. We walked back to the apartment, parcels still in hand, and I baked the clafoutis for a late dessert before bed.

It was the darkest part of the night when my eyes snapped open. The chains and lions and teeth were back. Spidery symbols in red and black. I was shivering and my face was wet. I didn't want to wake Michael, of course I didn't, but I could only lie there for so long. As soon as the bedroom began to lighten, I shook him gently.

"What's wrong?" His eyes weren't even open.

"I had a nightmare," I said. "Like when I was little."

"Oh, honey, let me get you some water."

He started to get out of bed, but I grabbed his arm. "Stay here."

I lay there for a little while with my head on his chest, feeling it rise and fall. When I could lie still no longer, I got up and wrapped a robe around myself. "I have to call Dad."

Michael glanced at his watch. "It's still the middle of the night there."

"It doesn't matter." I didn't want to upset Dad, but this was an emergency. There was a type of reassurance only he could give.

One ring, two, three. "Hello?" Dad's voice thick with sleep.

"Dad? I'm in Paris. Can I talk to you?"

"What's wrong?"

"I had a bad dream." The rest tumbled out of me—my terror, my heaviness, my feeling that I'd never be free.

"It's okay," he said, even as my talk became incoherent babbling. "Don't let it get to you."

"But—"

"Sweetheart, do you hear me? It's okay. It's over and we survived."

MICHAEL AND I WERE HEADING out for breakfast, facing each other in the tiny apartment elevator, when he took my hand and looked into my eyes. "You know," he said softly, "you have to find a way out of this."

"What way? There is no way."

"There has to be a way. You can't just keep going on and on, letting yourself be defined by your fear."

"I don't know what you expect me to do," I said.

"I don't know, either, but you deserve to be free." The elevator stopped on the ground floor, Michael kissed me on the cheek, and I followed him out the blue door, into the street.

33

Passion

In my mind, there was good Europe and bad Europe. Good Europe meant the beautiful and delicious places I loved: Paris; Barcelona, where Michael and I had eaten grilled octopus and padrón peppers one summer when the kids were at camp; a Tuscan villa with the whole family, where we'd discovered bitter honey gelato and purple figs pulled right from the trees. Bad Europe was Poland and Germany, the terrible places of trauma and hunger and death, the places of my nightmares.

Seeing that exhibit in Paris breached the artificial barrier I'd created for myself. Bad ran into good, tainting so much of what I cherished. When I arrived home, I was determined to restore my internal order and I did this, simply, by cooking. I cooked for pleasure and stability. I cooked to rediscover my joy.

I became so absorbed in the kitchen that I stopped sending myself on every random job interview, and I stopped beating myself up for what I'd come to see as my career suicide. Instead of applying for positions I didn't want and wouldn't get, I just kept cooking. When I got bored of French food, I moved on to Italian. I made gnocchi and gnudi; orecchiette and ravioli. I pounded veal and shelled borlotti beans. I brought back the osso buco from my single days and my kids loved it so much, it became known as "awesome buco."

One night, as I scooped tiny meatballs, acini de pepe, and chicken broth into Leo's bowl, he said, "Your Italian wedding soup is so yummy. You should be a chef!"

"That's funny, Leaps," I said, using one of a half dozen nicknames we had for him. "Me a chef."

Inside, I felt the tingling, impatient feeling I had started to recognize as a sign that something important was happening. Chef school. What if I actually did it? I'd never given myself the chance to dive headfirst into this thing I loved, to take it from a side passion to the main event. I thought of Baba and the way she'd expressed her ample creativity through the things she made. I thought of our family and food—intertwined at every turn.

But Dad's words rang in my ears. "Promise me you'll never go into the restaurant business," he'd said, running to the store in the middle of the night to deal with floods and break-ins. "It's no place for you."

GO. DON'T GO. REACH FOR something hard. Relax and take life easy. My dueling impulses were enough to drive me mad. As I cooked dinner that night, I thought about how often I'd let other people or circumstances decide what was right for me. I was forty and I still hadn't found my purpose. The space for work—not just a job but true, meaningful work—had always been squished into the amount of room left over after all my other roles were fulfilled. More than ever, I craved the satisfaction of a challenge; the opportunity to sink my teeth into something difficult.

"WHY NOT?" MICHAEL SAID IN bed that night, when I told him what Leo had said. "You'll love chef school. And your dad will think it's fantastic."

"My dad . . . might be a problem."

"No, he'll be thrilled," Michael said.

"Oh, will he?" I turned out my light. "You don't know him like I know him."

THE NEXT MORNING, I LOOKED up the address of a large culinary institute on the outskirts of the city, spoke to someone on the phone, and went out for a tour. I had a now-or-never feeling in my bones when I paid my deposit. Then I took a breath and phoned Edmonton. I wasn't trying to please Dad because I knew he would not be pleased. Nor was I trying to piss him off, although I knew he might be pissed off.

"COOKING SCHOOL?" DAD SAID, AFTER picking up on the second ring. "So you can make nice dinners for your husband?"

"Dad, c'mon. Is that all I'm good for? No, this is professional chef school. Like a restaurant chef, you know."

"I already told you. The restaurant business is too hard. I didn't send you to a nice university so you can get up at six to chop onions."

"What now?" I heard Mom say in the background.

I took a deep breath and counted to ten. "You did tell me," I said slowly. "But this seems to be something I have to do. It feels important and the feeling is not going away."

"You really like to make your life hard, don't you," Dad said.

"Yeah, I guess I really do."

I listened to him breathing. "Well," he finally said. "It's never a bad idea to become a better cook."

I sighed. "I'm going to be more than a better cook. I'm going to be a great chef."

I DIDN'T IMAGINE THAT I would work in a restaurant, and I didn't imagine that I wouldn't. I couldn't imagine anything beyond two years of immersion in something I loved. The most difficult part was giving myself permission to do it.

Since I was an eight-year-old making secret potato chips in my mother's kitchen, cooking had been my natural form of expression, an intuitive way of using my voice. Now I wanted to speak in French and Italian and Spanish; I wanted to speak Japanese and Portuguese. If food was our family's love language, I wanted to speak better than anyone would have thought possible. Signing up for chef school was submission wrapped in rebellion. Or rebellion wrapped in submission. In any case, I was on my way.

34

Yes, Chef

A few weeks later, I walked into culinary skills lab with a red toolbox in my hand. The blades of my knives glimmered in the fluorescent light as I unpacked them and laid them on a clean towel. Underneath my stiff uniform, a steady thrum of energy pumped through my body. Students all over the classroom were getting to work on our first assignment: consommé. By the time Chef came over to my workspace, my vegetables were beautifully brunoised. I'd separated the eggs and mixed them with ground turkey and seeded tomatoes for my raft. Chef was a heavyset man, tall and barrel-chested, with thick blond hair, cut short. As he approached, I stood a little straighter in my jacket and neckerchief.

"Hi," he said, towering over me.

"Good morning, Chef." I couldn't believe he'd noticed the quality of my work from across the room. Then again, I'd been handling a knife since before most of my classmates were born.

"Do you want to see my cuts?" I reached for my carrots.

He made a dismissive gesture with his hand. "I have a question for you."

"Yes, Chef?" He was so close, I could smell his last cigarette.

"Are you wearing your steel-toed boots?"

"Yes, of course." They were a required part of the uniform.

"Show me, please." I pulled up my checkered pant leg and stepped forward with my right foot. He nodded, took a look around, stroked his chin. Then, without warning, he picked up his own steel-clad foot and brought it down, hard, on the cap of my boot.

A wave of vibration traveled through my body. I wiggled my toes. No pain. Chef wore an undecipherable expression until, finally, his face split into a wide grin and I saw he was missing a tooth. "Hey, good thing you weren't lying," he said. I focused my eyes on a dull spot on the linoleum floor until Chef walked away, chuckling. Welcome to chef school.

WEEK TWO IN CULINARY SKILLS lab. Chef sat at a small table with a fork in his hand. I lined up behind a guy with broad shoulders and a shaved neck. A blue vein pulsated near his left ear. "Next!" Toe Cruncher called. The Vein stepped forward.

I gripped my plate with my side towel. Before leaving my station, I'd warmed it in the oven as Chef had shown us. I'd carefully placed all my different potatoes—croquettes, gaufrettes, a slice of galette duchesse, and my Savoyards—on the school china. I'd dampened a clean cloth and wiped fingerprints and crumbs from the edge of the plate. After a lifetime of evaluation based on written work, I was excited to be graded on seasoning, knife skills, and composition. "Okay, next!"

The Vein retreated and I stepped up to the table. "Hi, Chef." I was about to put down my plate when he said, "Hey, did you know I'm famous?" His head was cocked to one side.

"Uh—no, Chef. How great." I smiled. Heat radiated through the side towel.

"Yup, I played a chef in a movie." He stared at me. My body felt safe inside my uniform. "You should look it up."

"I will, Chef." I felt the class lining up behind me as Chef held my gaze. Finally, he leaned back in his chair and gestured for me to put my plate down in front of him.

"So, what have we here?" He knew, but I walked him through it anyway.

"Nice, looks very nice," he said, putting down his fork. "Just one thing." Bare-handed, Chef hunched over my plate like a potter at his wheel. Applying pressure from the rim, he squished the four distinct items I'd made into a messy pile at the center of the dish. The little potato pancakes I'd fried in clarified butter broke apart. Several gaufrettes exploded into pieces. He sat up straight and wiped a thread of cheese from the Savoyard on my towel.

"Why the fuck did you have everything separated around the edges of the plate? Put it together. In the center. Get it? C-plus."

I opened my mouth and closed it again, picked up my plate and walked away. "Hey, you forgot your towel," he called, and tossed it at my back. As I slid four hours of work into the compost bin, I thought of the empty Tupperware I'd brought to transport my creations home. Leo would've loved those crispy waffle fries.

DAY BY DAY, WEEK BY week, Toe Cruncher sliced any romantic vision of culinary school I might have had to ribbons. Instead of fussing over sophisticated French food, cooked in soft afternoon light, the culture I'd dipped my steel toe into was like the army. Yes, Chef! No, Chef! Show up five minutes late and you were locked out of class. Have a spot on your jacket and you might be publicly ridiculed; speak to Chef in a way he didn't like and you'd be mopping the floors after everyone else left. My classmates were young—many straight out of high school—and there were three guys for every girl. Rowdy and full of swagger, they seemed to embrace the emphasis on hierarchy and discipline. Meanwhile, I'd just turned forty.

What had I done? I couldn't believe I'd been stupid enough to leave a good job in journalism only to end up in the brutal service industry. So brutal, in fact, that my teacher would have broken the bones of my foot without a second thought. *What are you doing?* Dad said in my head.

But then came the day Chef swept into the lab with an enormous cardboard box. "All of you, grab a tray and come over." I walked toward the crowd that was forming around Chef, expecting more woody carrots and overgrown beets. When I got inside the loose semicircle, I saw Chef slapping whole fishes on people's trays. Glossy and silver skinned, I recognized salmon, but I'd never seen the other fish. It was gray and flat—only a couple of inches thick—with big eyes protruding from its tiny triangular head. "Dover sole," he said, as the creature almost slipped off my tray. Why had I never seen a Dover sole? It was one of Dad's favorite fish, the thing he loved to order in fancy restaurants. I bent over the tray and sniffed deeply. Nothing but briny water.

Back at my station, I worked on the salmon first, scaling it, removing the head and tail, and cutting along the spine, above and below, to create two filets for poaching.

Time disappeared as I got to work on the sole, laying it on a damp paper towel on my cutting board. I made an incision near the tail and flicked upward to loosen the skin and create a flap. I put my knife down, pressed my left palm on the tail to hold the fish in place and gripped a corner of the skin with my kitchen towel. I tugged as we'd been told to, expecting my fish to rip in half like a sheet of paper. Instead, the skin peeled away from the flesh with a soft tearing sound. When I reached the head, I pulled more carefully so the head would separate from the skin and remain attached, as Chef had shown us. I flipped the fish over and pulled the under skin off as I'd done on top. Bending to get into my toolbox, I took out a pair of kitchen scissors and trimmed the feathery bones on both sides.

The next time I looked up, people were already heading to the marking table. I reviewed everything I'd made: a court bouillon of leeks, white wine, celery, and a bouquet garni tied with kitchen string; poached salmon, barely cooked to a delicate coral. The sole was fried meunière style, with clarified butter, lemon, and minced parsley. On the side, I'd made my first beurre blanc, cube after cube of cold butter swirled into a shallot-wine reduction, magically suspended into an elegant, tangy sauce.

"Nice," Chef said, for once short on words. "A."

I drove home with the windows open, laughing out loud in the cool autumn air. Finally, I was in the right place, doing the right thing, *and I was good at it.* After a whole day of work in the lab, I should have been exhausted, but all I could feel was elation.

AT THE BEGINNING OF OCTOBER, I noticed that one of my weekly labs with Toe Cruncher would fall on Halloween. The lab was from one to five p.m.; I wouldn't get home until six. Our Halloween traditions were elaborate and etched in stone. The kids and I carved pumpkins and roasted their seeds to a crispy brown before I painted faces, tied capes, and positioned bunny ears. I'd talk to Toe Cruncher. He was weird but generally affable. For sure he'd understand.

I stuck around after class one day to have a quiet word with him. "So, Chef, our next lab is on Halloween," I began.

"Hmm, thirty-first, so it is." He crossed his arms and smiled.

"It's just such an important holiday to my kids," I said. "They'll be waiting for me."

"Hmm, yeah, Halloween. Kids love it."

"Yeah. So If I work efficiently and get my lab done by four, could you mark it early?"

"Well, you know, if I don't mark it, you'll get zero."

"I know but—"

"For leaving early, you know? But yeah, I could probably mark you early."

"Thank you, Chef. I appreciate it."

THE LAB THAT DAY WAS egg cookery. I plated my Spanish omelette, creamed mushrooms and quiche Lorraine, and caught Chef's eye. "Go," he gestured with a tip of his toque. I smiled gratefully and skipped out the door. 3:45!

It often poured on Halloween, but that evening was mild and dry. Michael came home in time to hand out candy and the kids and I headed into the balmy night.

A FEW DAYS LATER, I went online to check my grade for the egg lab, but the space was blank. "Hey," I whispered to my classmate Chris at an early demo. "Chef's been slow entering the egg marks, huh?"

"Has he?" Chris whispered back. "I got mine."

After class, I went back to the mark site and saw that blank again. I was about to write Chef to say there'd been a technical glitch when it finally dawned on me. The blank was intentional. Chef had given me a zero.

Tears of frustration sprung to my eyes. I must be crazy, I thought, to want to be able to be there for my kids *and* go to school *and* love what I'm doing *and* feel fulfilled . . . it was just too much wanting. As soon as one need was met, another was sacrificed.

In bed that night, I reached for Michael under the covers. "Oh my god, is that your hand? It feels like sandpaper." The weeks of scrubbing and peeling and chopping had left their mark.

I teared up again. "Yeah, I guess my body is getting a little beat up." In addition to my cracked and peeling hands, I had a perpetually sore lower back and mangled feet from my steel-toed boots.

"This is becoming a little extreme," Michael said in the dark. "Are you sure you want to keep going? You can quit, you know."

I sat up, turned on my light, and took a tissue from the night table. "Quit? Are you serious? I've never felt more alive in my life."

CHEF BROUGHT OUT THE PLEASER in me, and I wanted to be liked. That must have been why it took me so long to see what was right in front of me. But I finally got it one afternoon when I came into the lab early, seeking his advice about some pickles I'd made. "They look fine," I said, as I unpacked my knives and set up my station, "but the garlic has turned a greenish blue. Do you know what that would be?"

"Hmm," he said, leaning against my station, stroking his chin in a now familiar gesture.

"Are the pickles safe to eat?" I prodded.

"I don't know. Probably better not."

"You think? Okay, thanks Chef." I tied on my apron and tucked in my side towels.

"Because, you know, one day you're gonna come in here and say, 'Hey, my family ate the pickles and they didn't make it.'"

"Chef?"

"And you're gonna want me to help you make new ones, you know? Like new kids? And I don't know if I'll be able to help you with that." His palms were spread wide on my stainless-steel work-station as he leaned forward.

I looked around, but nobody was close enough to be listening. With a sick feeling in my stomach, I turned my back to him and switched on the gas burner to start roasting peppers.

BY THE TIME THE GROUND froze, I'd finally learned to speak to Toe Cruncher only when necessary. I wanted to report him, but I didn't know what I'd say. I'd already stopped by the school office to report another chef threatening to throw his knife in class, and the ombuds-man had laughed in my face.

35

Burnt Caramel

At last I found my way into a groove. The alarm went off at five thirty and I slid into my hideous checkered pants. I looked away from my blouses and pumps as I pulled on thick socks to protect my heels from my boots. It was now second term and twice a week I had baking, taught by a haughty chef with purple lips. She came into class with her paper toque perched on her loose blond hair. Put out your hands, she said, and we lined up so she could point out nails that were dirty or too long.

There was a no-jewelry rule and I followed it, except for my wedding band, which she noticed in week two. "What do you think no jewelry actually means?" she shouted in front of the whole class.

Feeling wretched in my now-stained uniform, I took the tiniest liberties. She called me out for everything. One particularly cold February morning, I came to class with a curl tucked behind my ear. She sent me out to buy bobby pins, locked the door, and didn't let me back in.

We worked in pairs in baking lab, and Chef's bullying gave Dan, my eighteen-year-old partner, too much leeway. He bossed me around, talked down to me, blamed me for his mistakes. At a loss, I came home and solicited some expert advice from my teenage son. "Swear at him a bit," Jamie said.

It was right before Valentine's Day, and the assignment was layer cakes. We worked independently on the batter, but we were to collaborate on a shared batch of icing. I creamed butter and sugar in the mixer; Dan was going to add the food coloring. With the motor running, he put in not two drops as he was supposed to but a little stream of red. Instead of soft pink, our icing turned a lurid fuchsia.

I puffed up my chest and threw back my shoulders. "You gotta be fucking kidding me," I said.

"It's fine. It's fine!" he snapped, but it wasn't fine. We earned a mortifying grade and derision from the rest of the class.

MAKING DRY CARAMEL FROM white sugar is a finicky, delicate process. You have to heat the sugar to melting and then lightly brown it, but too fast or too slow, too hot or too cool, too much mixing or too much neglect and the sugar will crystallize, or it will burn. I'd made caramel a dozen times at home, but while I mixed batter for yet another shared cake, Dan headed to the burners at the back of the classroom. "I got this," he said.

"Be careful."

He was gone too long; I knew he was. When he came back, the little copper pot was smoking and an acrid smell filled the classroom. The sugar was so burnt, it looked like black sand in the bottom of the pot. There was no time to start again.

I'd finally had enough. "You don't know what you're doing, little boy," I said as we packed up, my blood pulsing in my ears. I'd seen that smug expression on Chef's face during grading for the last time. "From now on, you do what I say."

BAKING GOT A LOT BETTER after that. I put cake after cake on the decorating turntable, learning to crumb coat and thinking of Baba and her effortless creations with walnuts and coffee and whipped cream and chocolate.

When we made bread, I kneaded the dough by hand as Baba had

taught me, while Dan and the others lined up at the machines. *Smooth and elastic,* she said in my ear, and I worked until the dough obliged. "Not bad," said Chef Purple Lips when she cut into one of my steaming loaves. "You've done this before, I see."

SOME DAYS, I ARRIVED HOME so exhausted, I sat in the driveway, mustering the energy to get out of the car with my heavy toolbox. Maya opened the front door and stood inches from the snow in her stocking feet. "What did you bring us?" she shouted. On the day I staggered triumphantly up the walk with a box of profiterole swans glazed in chocolate, she was so happy I thought she would levitate.

When the last day of the school year rolled around, I jumped out of bed and hurried to class. I'd done it. It felt so good to have chosen a hard thing and to have conquered it; to have found an outlet for the energy that had been trapped inside me. After our final demo, I threw my stained apron and steel-toed boots into the trunk of my car and smoked a joint with Chris and some other classmates before meeting Michael for a celebratory dinner.

FOUR MONTHS LATER, I WAS bringing another hot plate of food to a chef to taste, but my advanced culinary skills teacher was nothing like Toe Cruncher. Italian and soft-spoken, he was a great cook and a patient instructor. The word around school was that he'd lost a child, and when I looked at him closely, I thought I could see traces of grief around his eyes and mouth.

"Your cooking water should be as salty as the sea," he said every class, as though he'd never said it before. "Salt your vegetables on both sides and be careful not to overcook them—they should be a little bit crunché." I came home and told the kids about him. "A little bit crunché," they told each other. "Make it crunché."

The things we cooked were delicious. Braised sweetbreads in wild mushroom sauce. Cornish hens, just like Mom's, with pine-nut stuffing. In week eleven we made herb-crusted rack of lamb, ratatouille, and pommes dauphine. When I presented my rack of lamb, Chef smiled pleasantly, but I could see he was a little bored. He'd probably tasted hundreds of racks of lamb! As he cut a bite and put it in his mouth, he raised his head to look me right in the eye. "It's good," he said with surprise and sincerity. "It's really good."

ROUNDING OUT MY TIMETABLE WAS butchery, taught in a classroom chilled to the temperature of a meat locker. Of everything I did at chef school, the labs and the demos, the dishes from different cuisines, the techniques and skills and styles, this frigid classroom turned out to be the warmest, most comfortable place; the place that reminded me of home.

Chef was a British guy with red cheeks and a hearty laugh. The day we broke down half a cow, he demonstrated various knife skills and we imitated, separating the animal along seams and around bones, tracing the shape of its muscles, developing context for the cuts we were used to seeing at the grocery store. Between turns with the carcass, we blew on our hands to warm them.

After the cutting was done, it was one group's job to go around to all the stations and gather up the little bits of meat we'd discarded. Chef had another group set up a grinder. "Come," he said, clapping his hands, "gather 'round. We're going to make sausage." He laughed as hard as the rest of us at the gesture required to get the casing onto the extruder, but he also had the decency to blush.

There was too much ground meat for the amount of casing. He told my group to take the bucket of leftover meat and form it into patties. Some we laid on a baking sheet just like that; some we shaped around boiled eggs he'd produced from I didn't know where. While we started the long, dreary process of scrubbing and sanitizing the cold kitchen, Chef disappeared.

When he returned, Chef was carrying a steaming tray of the patties and Scotch eggs we'd made, along with buns, pickles, and mustard. "Come, my friends. Come and eat," he called, showing his heart with his delicious offering. You have to be standing in a meat

locker with numb hands and tingling toes to know what a hot sausage sandwich with vinegar pickles really tastes like.

ON THE LAST DAY OF butchery, we did the delicate work of cutting
the filet mignon from a chunk of loin. I'd seen Dad butcher dozens
of tenderloins and my knife moved as if on its own, removing silver
skin and separating the meat along its natural seams. After he'd been
around to mark every table, Chef took one of the filets, sliced it
thinly, drizzled it with olive oil and sprinkled it with salt. "Come and
taste. Who knows what this is?"

"Carpaccio," I said.

"You've had it before?" he asked. I nodded. "Where?"

"At home."

"At home? You must've had a pampered upbringing indeed."

"Yes and no," I said with a smile.

36

Smoke Break

Classes ended but I had one more requirement to earn my chef certificate: practical hours in a restaurant. I couldn't work nights because of the kids, so I got a morning job in the central kitchen of a high-end restaurant group. I woke in the dark and took the streetcar to a warehouse space downtown. Inside the warming kitchen, I rotated through the stations, learning charcuterie, mixing up sourdough, scrubbing crates of beets until my fingers were raw. My chefs and co-workers were all men, some of them decent and kind. Anaya taught me how to make massive vats of soup with apples and celery root. We roasted scallions and blended them into champagne vinegar for salad dressing. "What does it need?" I said, passing him a spoonful of my dressing. "Salt. Only salt," he said, nodding encouragingly.

One day, a forager brought a crate of wild leeks to the kitchen door, their little white bulbs encased in sandy soil. It fell to me, the lowest person in the kitchen, to spend the day at the sink, rinsing the grit from thousands of green folds. I stood there for hours, lost in thought. Who had done the painstaking work of hollowing out three hundred lemons for my wedding, almost twenty years before? There had been so much I hadn't known, but there was no point in blaming myself. That young, young person was only at the beginning of understanding who she was.

THE PLACEMENT LASTED THREE MONTHS and I was set up a few times. I burned an expensive tray of hazelnuts because someone screwed with the oven. I ruined a huge batch of tapenade because a mysterious olive pit somehow found its way into the food processor. "Are you an idiot?" said Anthony, one of the senior chefs.

And there was some light hazing. "Are you a married woman, Bonny?" Ryan, another chef, asked when we were all around the big table. We sat on upside-down pails and milk crates, eating chicken adobo for a quick family meal.

"Uh, yeah," I said cautiously.

"Really? You look like you might be single."

"Or the type to do it with animals," said Anthony. There were chuckles all around. "You sure you don't like fucking animals?"

A younger me would have blushed and cowered. A younger me would have wondered what she'd done to invite the harassment. Instead, I stood abruptly and the pail I was sitting on tipped over and hit the floor. Everyone stopped laughing. I drew myself up to my full five feet, two inches, lifted my chin and walked out of the kitchen. "Smoke break," I said over my shoulder, although I didn't smoke.

I FINISHED MY PLACEMENT A couple of weeks later and decided not to look for a job in a restaurant. I'd spent two years bringing my food knowledge and skill to a professional level. I could butcher a Dover sole, break down half a cow, make a perfect hollandaise, bake an airy croissant. I was tougher and more confident than I'd ever been before. I was also prouder of my original connection to food, my background and my heritage. Everything Baba taught me when I was a little girl, everything passed along by Dad or by blood, was far more beautiful and precious than I'd realized. I'd learned to cook twice over: once by intuition, once by profession, and I had finally earned esteem in my own eyes. Dad had been wrong, but also right: chef school was not too hard for me, but as far as working in a restaurant was concerned, I was lucky to have other options. The kitchen was one place where I had nothing further to prove.

37

Writer's Block

"You're done playing around. Let's start the book," Dad said. I was visiting Edmonton for the first time since finishing chef school and we were, once again, drinking cup after cup of black coffee.

It was a beautiful summer morning, but a familiar heaviness settled on my shoulders and darkened the room. I'd worked hard to find my way to where I was and now it was back, this choked, nauseous feeling, as if no time had passed and I was exactly where I'd started, sitting on the carpet, ready to take notes on the horrors of the Holocaust.

Saying no to Dad was hard but changing the subject was easy. "Is that really what you feel like doing right now?" I said, pushing down my revulsion. "I thought we could take a walk." I was hoping to visit the ravine near our old house, I told him. "We can sit on the bench and look at the buildings."

"Oh, good idea. Let's go for a walk. We can work later."

LATER DIDN'T COME, BECAUSE THAT night I got an email offering me the job I'd applied for: food editor at a Toronto magazine. I hurried back from Edmonton to get organized. I was excited to put my food knowledge to work, and happy to finally be getting back to editing, which had always been a pleasure. I loved to listen for writers' voices in the words and help draw out their intentions on the page. I loved to find the rhythm in their sentences. On a different level, a level somewhat removed from my conscious mind, editing also allowed me to hide, a little, from myself and my complex relationship with writing.

Storytelling had come naturally to me when I was little, but the older I got, the harder writing had become. By the time I was a professional journalist, even small pieces—for the parenting magazine where I worked or the occasional freelance article—came out in strangled fits and spurts. Sometimes it took me an hour to write two sentences. Sometimes trying to write gave me such a headache, I had to lie down.

WHAT GIVES A PERSON A forty-year case of writer's block? Mom and I threw out my work when I was nine, planting a seed of self-doubt, but on its own, I don't know if that one act would be powerful enough to plague me into adulthood.

But the Holocaust. And the book. I honestly can't say how many times Dad suggested I might want to write his story. Many times? Once in a while? Only a few? Looking back, the pressure seems to have always been there, but when I try to get specific, my memory goes fuzzy. It's only the day I found the suitcase that stands out in crisp relief, the feeling of its handle in my hand, the feeling of weight, on me but also inside me. Maybe every child takes on some kind of burden from her parents, the burden of truth or experience that comes along with the awesome burden of being loved. But the feeling of this responsibility was so great, it had almost crushed me.

THE NIGHT BEFORE MY FIRST day as a food editor, I had a look through my case of culinary books and magazines. By that time, my collection had grown to include Elizabeth David's *French Country Cooking,* M. F. K. Fisher's *Consider the Oyster,* and a series called Modern Library Food, edited by Ruth Reichl. A pair of books by Laurie Colwin, *Home Cooking* and *More Home Cooking,* rounded out my collection. I ran my fingertip along the spines of my beloved volumes, so excited to join their ranks in my own small way.

I HAD BEEN AT THE food magazine for a couple of months when my library started to whisper to me. Whenever I walked by, I could hear voices, calling me. Sunday afternoons, the sun low in the sky and dinnertime hard on its way, I took my books down and sat on the floor, happily surrounded. What should I make? Coq au vin, suggested Elizabeth David. No, oyster stew, said M. F. K. How about flank steak, Laurie C. said, with homemade biscuits and spicy gingerbread for dessert?

Instructions on the pages were incidental; what I loved most was the conversation. I was amazed by the closeness I felt to these strangers, and the return of a particular feeling, a feeling I'd first known writing at my desk when I was a little girl. A hot flame of recognition. A tingling. A type of excitement so intense, it verged on anxiety.

ONE DAY, I PULLED DOWN Samuel V. Chamberlain's *Clémentine in the Kitchen,* about a plucky French chef and her adventures cooking for an American family, and reread Ruth Reichl's introduction:

> . . . *I came to understand that for people who really love it, food is a lens through which to view the world. For us, the way that people cook and eat, how they set their tables, and the utensils that they use all tell a story. If you choose to pay attention, cooking is an important cultural artifact, an expression of time, place and personality.*

"For us." I knew I was included in "us" by the way those two letters buzzed around in my head.

And yet, I didn't admit, even to myself, that what I wanted more than anything was to join in with my own book about food. Not so much a cookbook as a book about the way food made me feel. A book about Baba Sarah and our restaurants and the layered, textured role food played in my life. A book about the way food made me see the world.

I didn't admit it because I knew I could write no such book. There was something waiting to be written and it wasn't full of joy and pleasure. The book I had to write was about hunger and suffering and death—a journey into the darkest, most miserable corners of my mind. Since I couldn't write that, I didn't think I was entitled to write any book at all.

38

Fear

Being afraid is no way to live. It tightens your body and it dries out your mouth. It takes up too much energy, sapping what you have left for joy and happiness. It can short-circuit your thinking when you need to think clearly and, most of all, it narrows your world as you retreat more and more from whatever has become too scary, and whatever reminds you of what has become too scary, until the space you can operate within becomes as small and cramped as a cave.

By the time my first marriage fell apart, my fears had eaten up a lot of space that should have been free, and I'd become afraid, simply, of being myself. The shock was this: the worst thing that could happen turned out to be the most important thing to happen. I got divorced and my life shattered, but I did not. I had been deprived in the most benign way—deprived of the opportunity to challenge myself and deprived of the self-esteem I would have gained from overcoming challenges. That divorce, that job I took and left, the trial of chef school—step by step, I began to earn my own self-respect. But there were more fears, deeper layers to peel back, and paradoxically, the older I became, the closer I got to confronting my earliest anxieties.

I WAS STILL EDITING THE food magazine when my parents came to Toronto for Passover. The seder had ended, the dishes were loaded into the dishwasher, when I found myself quietly enjoying a cup of tea with Dad, talking about the meaning of freedom. "Does the idea of freedom make you think of what happened to you?" I said.

"Of course," he answered, taking a sip of tea. "But to tell you the truth, I think about it every day."

I played with the matzoh crumbs on the table, piling them into a little pyramid. "Dad, I don't think I can write the book," I heard myself say. I swallowed hard. "I'm so sorry."

The pause was shorter than you might think. "Oh! I never wanted to *make* you. Of course not." I looked up to find not anger or disappointment but concern on Dad's face.

"So it's okay if I don't write it?"

"Yes, forget it. I want you to be happy. Just forget it!"

If we hadn't dropped the rope that day, I might have stayed stuck in the same place forever. Instead, a weight lifted off me and I felt, maybe for the first time, that my life belonged to me.

MY MAGAZINE CONTRACT ENDED AND I started to pitch food articles to *The Globe and Mail* newspaper. Soon I landed a chef column and my voice began to flow more freely. I still wasn't writing into the deep center of what food meant to me until I picked up an assignment on food waste from a women's magazine. It was a practical article, mostly, a basic service piece. But to me, the topic of food waste was anything but basic and, searching for the right way to open, my fingers typed:

> *When you're raised by someone who once survived on potato*
> *peels and coffee grounds, you develop a pretty healthy respect*

for food. My dad was so hungry during the war, he would've happily eaten a dog he caught, but he knew the SS officer whom it belonged to would have shot him for much less.

My heart pounded in my chest as I stared at the words. It was the most honest thing I'd ever written. I finished the article, hit send, and waited.

The draft came back to me with the first third of the article, the story about my dad and the dog, simply not there. The editor didn't explain why she cut it, and I was too overwhelmed to ask. I felt an almost unbearable pressure in my head, and my blood pumped wildly, as if I were in danger.

It was a familiar feeling. Ever since the mini-series all those years ago, whenever I encountered something out in the world that touched on the Holocaust or felt even vaguely antisemitic, I felt that same paralysis, that same blockage.

There was the shock of being called Jew-this and Jew-that the terrible year I was bullied at school, when I'd been unable to tell my parents. Much later, when I was working at the magazine, I was out for wine with a group of colleagues and people were talking about a man at work they didn't like, how mean he was, how selfish and shallow. Jane, a person I worked closely with, a person who was my friend, said, "What do you expect from a Jew?" Her eyes fell on me and she said, "I'm sorry, but it's true."

There seemed to be nods of agreement around the table. My face froze into what might have been a half-smile. I needed to say something. I needed to do something. The conversation meandered but still, I was quiet. The opportunity to speak moved further and further away while I sat there like a statue. This was a feeling I lived with. A feeling of knowing that what I had to say was so enormous, I didn't trust myself to speak at all.

But I was changing. I'd found my voice through cooking. Now I needed to find it through writing. A few days after I sent back the edit, I gathered my courage and asked the editor why she had cut my first-person lead. She never explained herself, but the next time I saw the article, printed in the magazine, a condensed version of what I'd written about my dad and the dog was back. The piece won a National Magazine Award that year, and one more chunk of my soul broke free.

39

Car Wash

My career as a food writer was booming when Maya had a school break and I booked two tickets to Arizona to visit my parents. All through the years, Mom and Dad's pick-up custom hadn't changed. They came together to the airport, snacks ready in the car. It was the delicious walnut bread, or bags of candy, or dried fruit from Trader Joe's. Once or twice, Dad even brought a whole roast chicken in the car. So when we stepped off the plane and, for the first time in my life, Dad was standing there alone, I had a funny feeling.

"Hi," I said as we hugged. "Where's Mom?"

A big, strange smile spread across his face. "Mom wants you to call her. She has a surprise for you."

"Where is she?"

"Would you just call her?"

I put down my carry-on and fished out my cell from my purse. Dad had left his phone with Mom, he said, so I dialed his number.

"Hello?" said a tiny voice.

"Mom? We're here! Where are you?"

A pause. "I'm in the hospital. I've been hit by a car."

IN AN INSTANT, BABA SARAH'S death came back to me; the way Dad
had received the call from the hospital and told Mom that Baba was
sicker when she had died already. My confusion when, later, Mom
had called Dad out on his little deception. "Can you imagine," she'd
said angrily, "I was fussing with my clothes and my hair when my
mother was lying dead in the hospital?" At fifteen, I didn't really understand what any of this meant, but at forty-five, I knew. Dad's be-
havior was likely a trauma response, some kind of inability to deliver
bad news. He had seen dozens, hundreds, maybe thousands of people die. Who can say what that had done to him? Or the ways he'd
found to cope? Trauma, I by then knew, didn't always look the way
you expected it to.

On the way to the hospital, Dad explained that they'd wanted the
car to be clean for our arrival, so they'd taken it to the car wash and,
as an employee pulled it out, Mom was run over. Her tailbone was
broken, as well as her foot and her hip.

MY FEISTY MOTHER WAS ADRIFT and powerless in the mechanical
hospital bed. It was a shock for me and more of a shock for Maya,
who thought of her Baba Toby as able and chic and glamorous. Dad
wanted nothing more than to make it better. "Let's go out for a
beautiful dinner," he said as we left the hospital. "Let's have a good
time." He wasn't just trying to make us feel better. He was trying to
soothe himself. To find the beauty in life. To look for the joy. "Let's
order champagne," he said at the table a few hours later. It might
have seemed strange if I didn't understand exactly where the im-
pulse came from.

AFTER A FEW MONTHS, MOM'S bones healed but something was still
off. Once in a while, she couldn't read her watch. Sometimes she
stood in the hallway in Arizona, not sure how to find her bedroom.
By the time they returned to Edmonton that spring, their gracious
living had fallen apart. My meticulous mother couldn't hang up a

sweater. She couldn't always read. Cruelest of all, she couldn't decipher the cards for her beloved bridge. The doctor diagnosed it as
mild cognitive impairment, brought on by the car accident or an invisible ministroke. Or both. We never did pinpoint exactly how it
began.

It was a blow to all of us, but to Dad especially. My parents had
spent most of their lives functioning beautifully as a unit. Mom was
the head and Dad was the heart, each complementing the other, filling in the other's gaps. For all of Dad's resilience, he needed Mom.
When they got married, he was alone in the world and he bonded to
her completely. Together, from nothing, they created a family and a
new shared reality. Now the structure she'd provided for fifty-six
years was slipping away. He couldn't stand to see her so unlike herself, wandering around the house, looking for things, confused and
for the first time ever, not quite capable.

They struggled valiantly for a little while, reluctant to leave their
home, reluctant to relinquish their autonomy, but finally, my fiercely
independent father had to admit they couldn't manage anymore.
We put their house on the market and my sisters and I traveled
home in shifts to pack up their things. We found them a nice retire-
ment home near my house in Toronto, and when it was my turn, I
flew to Edmonton, zipped up their suitcases, and brought them back
with me. It was a hot August night. On the car ride to the home,
Dad was quiet but Mom chatted happily, clearly relieved. She had
become anxious trying to manage when she knew it was all too
much for her, and she thought life would get easier.

40

The Tomb

Spring came and Dad called me, sounding excited. I was happy to hear the energy in his voice. The adjustment of moving had been hard and he'd had a difficult winter. Plus, Mom wasn't getting any better.

"Come over," he said. "I want to talk to you."

It was a beautiful day, the sunlight thin but warm. Soon the rhubarb would come back, pink and tart. Soon there would be local asparagus and peas and strawberries.

In the dining room of the home, Mom, Dad, and I sat down and ordered—omelettes for me and Dad, waffles with whipped cream for Mom.

"I had a call from one of the relatives yesterday," Dad began.

"Uh-huh." I was looking around at the other residents and only half listening. "One of the Dod's children," he continued.

"That's great." The Dod had been my father's uncle, his mother's brother, and the only one in the family to escape Poland just before the war, becoming the patriarch of his own family in Israel. Keeping in touch with these religious cousins was important to Dad, but they were mostly strangers to me, especially the men—severe, pious, un-knowable.

"They found a family tomb in Warsaw."

"What do you mean, a 'family tomb'?" I said, digging into my omelette. He knew better than I did that our family had been mur-dered during the war, not buried in Warsaw. Whatever they'd found was unlikely to have anything to do with us. "Probably from their other side," I said.

"I want to go and see it," he announced. "And I want you to come."

I put my fork down and looked at him with my full attention. He had been back to Poland only once since the war, a harrowing visit to Birkenau with Suzanne right before Jamie was born, and he'd been left with nightmares and a determination never to go again. Now here he was talking about going to Warsaw because of some hot tip from a distant relative.

The cousins had this effect on him. With so little family, he clung to these relatives who were, in some ways, more like the people he'd known as a child than my three sisters and me. Now they claimed to have found an actual tomb, a physical marker of a lost world. I didn't believe it and I worried Dad's heart would get crushed. But when Dad makes up his mind, there is no changing it.

"We'll stay in the nicest hotel," he continued, looking at Mom. The woman I grew up with would've stopped him here with an em-phatic, "Saul, don't be silly. I'm not going to Poland." But this ver-sion of Mom was too engrossed in her waffles and whipped cream. The doctor was still calling it mild cognitive impairment. As far as I could tell, there was nothing mild about it.

"And we'll eat in good restaurants," Dad said. "We won't do any-thing sad or depressing. It'll be fun."

Fun? I wanted to stay home with my children and watch the gar-den unfurl. I wanted to stew rhubarb and shave asparagus and drive out to the country to pick fiddleheads. I didn't want to go to Poland. Poland was the scariest place on earth.

"Will you come?"

"Dad—" I pushed my half-eaten omelette away and stood up. My stomach hurt and I needed space to think. "You know what? I've got to work. Can I call you later?"

ADRENALINE WAS STILL PUMPING THROUGH my body as I got ready for bed that night. After the March of the Living fiasco, I'd decided, for the last time, that Poland was not for me. That I simply wasn't strong enough. And now this. It was totally impractical. Dad was eighty-four years old, Mom was shaky and confused, and we'd just gotten them settled. And it was illogical. Dad had refused to go on the march just a few years ago.

All night I tossed and turned, playing out different scenarios in my mind. Around lunchtime the next day, I dialed Dad's number.

"Hi, I'm calling to say I can't—"

"Oh, I'm so glad you called. I just got off the phone with a travel agent," he said. "She's going to arrange the trip. Just a visit to the cemetery and home."

"But the kids. And I have to work—"

"Don't answer now," he said. "Just think about it."

IT'S ALWAYS POSSIBLE TO FIND a reason not to do something. Bowing out, staying home, avoiding risk—these are the paths of least resistance that come naturally to an overthinker like me. In the moment, I can't necessarily tell a prudent decision from a missed opportunity. Sometimes a wisp of intuition might push me one way or the other, but more often, the future is still and opaque. It's only looking back that I will recognize, with surety, a pivotal move I've made and wonder how my life would have been different if I hadn't taken that chance.

Over the next two weeks, I changed my mind, back and forth, canceling and rebooking. I desperately wanted to stay home, but this would surely be my last chance to go to Poland with Dad. The ghost of the book I'd decided not to write floated above my head. Certain opportunities come around only once. Was I setting myself up for a future of regret?

A storm rolled in and thunder shook the house. "Are you up?" I whispered to Michael in the night. "I can't do it."

"Hmm. Stay home, baby." He threw a warm arm across my chest. *Yes, I'll stay home,* I thought, staring at the ceiling. Julie had agreed to go on the trip and would take good care of our parents. Dad was a survivor. He would be fine without me.

FINGERS OF SUN WERE REACHING into the wet garden when I called Dad to tell him what I'd decided. "I can't believe you're really going to miss this. Are you telling me you can't spare three days?"

I felt a pull in my gut. There are things I won't do for my father, but I'm not always sure what they are.

"Okay." I hung up and rebooked for the last time.

SOON I DRAGGED MY SUITCASE from the back of the closet and called Julie. She was traveling ahead of me, and she'd been to Poland already. "What are you taking—jeans? Skirts? What does a person wear in Warsaw in June?"

"Don't forget a raincoat," she said. I chose a pair of jeans, a few tops, and my two Laurie Colwin books to reread for comfort. At the last minute I decided to throw in a notebook, just in case.

PART FOUR

Warsaw

2015

41

Sour Cherries

I stumbled into Chopin airport in a daze. I needed to collapse into someone's arms, but the arrivals lounge held only strangers, and a woman in a baby blue pantsuit, holding a card with my name on it. "I'm Ewa," she said without smiling. "Your parents' flight is delayed. Your sister is out touring. I'll drive you."

I'd held Dad to his promise of a three-day trip and routed myself alone, as expediently as possible, through Copenhagen. Mom and Dad were on a different airline; Julie had arrived in Warsaw the day before.

I rested my cheek against the cool window as Ewa drove and droned on about Polish architecture, which had, she said, been all but obliterated by the war and its aftermath. Everything I looked at was gray—the sky, the buildings, the inside of her car. She gestured toward a building called the Palace of Culture and Science, its pointy spire piercing the clouds. "So ugly. Stalinist architecture in Warsaw," she said. "The Russians continued to oppress us long after the war." And, after a pause, "The Jews are not the only ones that suffered."

Later, I'll learn that during the Renaissance, Poland was one of the most powerful states in Europe, a place both pluralistic and cultured. The Jewish community developed and flourished alongside the Protestant and Catholic majority. After the partition of Poland in 1795, the country began a long decline, culminating in Hitler's easy invasion of Poland on September 1, 1939, and Warsaw's surrender on September 28, 1939. Indeed, the Polish losses were enormous and devastating. But in the car, I just wanted her to stop talking.

Ewa dropped me off at the Bristol, a beautiful hotel, just as Dad promised. The lobby was all old-world chandeliers and creamy marble. When I picked up my key, a plaque told me that the hotel was built in 1901, a place where celebrated Polish painter Wojciech Kossak had an atelier and created his finest artworks. I was more interested in taking a shower.

My parents finally arrived a few hours later, Mom alarmingly disheveled. Her once-perfect hair was messy, her clothes askew. Somehow, Dad was unfazed. "Sweetheart, my sweetheart," he boomed. "Do you like the hotel? Nice right?" I hugged him and he was sturdy as ever, smelling of the lime shaving cream he'd used since I was little. I was rebuttoning Mom's sweater when Julie bounded into the lobby, five feet of energy in running shoes. "Let's get going," she said after we hugged hello.

Ewa was right behind her. "I have the cemetery arranged for tomorrow," she said. "Let's have some lunch."

AT A RESTAURANT WITH A pretty courtyard, the server brought herring and bread and some kind of roast chicken, but what caught my attention was a bowl of baby potatoes, sweet and steaming, slick with butter and green with dill.

In my childhood, a potato was not just a potato. As far back as I can remember, whether coarse-skinned and oblong or smooth and round, potatoes were signifiers of something else—the peels my father stole from the garbage bin behind the Lodz Ghetto kitchen to stay alive or, later, the starchy, watery concentration camp rations that tasted like dirt. Once, after Lisa had been peeling potatoes and had thrown out a few green bits along with the skins, Dad came into

the family room, wild in the eyes. He was about to take out the garbage when a flashback stopped him in his tracks. "You're not going
to believe what just happened," he had said. "I looked into the garbage and when I saw all the chunks of real potato mixed in with the
peels, I got so excited. My heart started to race and my mouth watered."

You'd think all of this would make Dad hate potatoes, and it's
true—they were not a particularly exalted food in our house. I don't
know how old I was when I finally grasped the significance of him
never eating a potato with its skin. Mom sometimes threw in a few
spuds with her garlic-studded rib roast on Friday nights, or brought
scalloped potatoes to the table in a white casserole dish, the top bubbling and brown. But in the better life she and Dad were building for
us, the humble potato was not often on the menu. We served potatoes at the store, of course. Mashed and formed with an ice-cream
scoop and smothered in gravy at old Teddy's and then, after Teddy's
was renovated, baked in foil, cut lengthwise and served beside a
steak. The waitress came by with a stainless-steel garnish carousel to
offer you sour cream, butter, green onions, and bacon bits.

Potatoes are the national crop of Poland and there was nothing
extraordinary about them showing up on the table at lunch. What
made my mouth hang open was the way Dad devoured them, peels
and all, and asked for more. It was as if those potatoes spoke right to
him, not as an eighty-four-year-old man but as a child in the country
of his birth. Those potatoes were not about the war or the Holocaust or survival, but something even earlier. Deeper.

"WE'LL GO SEE THE OLD Town now," Ewa announced after lunch.

A short walk from the hotel, Old Town turned out to be a civic
plaza paved with large stones and bordered by charming, colorful
buildings. It was pleasant, for a little while, to be in a European city
like the ones I loved. There was a clock tower and a smattering of
café tables and umbrellas. When I mentioned that it all seemed a
little too perfect, Ewa explained that everything we saw was a recon-

struction. During the war, the Germans brought in engineers who systematically destroyed Warsaw building by building, more than ten thousand in all.

As we walked along the perimeter of the square, a shop window caught my eye. A few steps later, another one. Soon I realized almost every gift store had them: figures carved of wood, with beards, hooked noses, black coats, and hats. As I looked closer, I saw that most of the mournful figures were holding something shiny, a copper coin the size of dime. "Excuse me, Ewa, what's this?"

"Oh, we call that a lucky Jew," she said, walking up beside me. "Something people keep at home to bring them good fortune. It's cute, right?" A shiver went through me and I forced myself to study her face for a sign—of irony or embarrassment or even humor. She looked back at me with her usual expression of pinched seriousness. I was the first to look away.

THE NEXT DAY, WE TOURED the POLIN museum of Jewish history and the fledgling Jewish community center. In the afternoon, Ewa took us to a famous café for tea and cake. It was the kind of place I usually adored, with traditional local music and wood banquettes worn smooth from a century of use. Everyone else seemed happy with their poppy seed layer cake, but for some reason, mine tasted like glue.

By the time we crammed back into Ewa's car, it was almost evening. She took us past the Umschlagplatz Monument on Stawki Street, two parallel stone walls meant to evoke an open train on its way to Treblinka. Dad wouldn't even get out of the car. "We've come to do happy things," he grumbled. "Those monuments are for people who don't know what happened." And then, in a typical pivot, "What's for supper?"

Dinner was booked at a nearby restaurant, but the cake wasn't sitting well in my stomach, and I begged to be released. "I'm just exhausted," I said to Dad, getting into a taxi. "Please? I'll see you in the morning?"

IN MY ROOM, THE ANXIETY that had been building since I'd arrived welled up and I started to shake. I bolted the door and drew the curtain across the big square window. Homesick and frightened, I got into bed with my clothes on and called home.

"How is it?" Michael said.

"Not that bad," I said. And then, "Awful."

"Oh, hon." Kids laughed and shouted on the other end of the phone. In a moment, Maya would come running up to him smelling of pencil shavings, her purple backpack bobbing on her narrow shoulders. I wiped my wet cheeks.

"Hello? Are you there?"

"Sorry, babe, I'm a little distracted. Just picking up at school. Can I call you later?"

My heart sank. "I'll be asleep."

"Okay. Tomorrow, then?"

"I guess."

"Don't worry. You'll be back before you know it."

I swallowed hard. "Yeah, I'll be back before I know it."

I LAID MY HEAD ON the pillow and tumbled into a deep sleep. My childhood nightmares returned as though no time had gone by. Black lions chased me beside a highway. Cars flew by. The lions shouted, they shot at me. Flashes of red. I couldn't run anymore. My eyes popped open. I sat up, my heart pounding and my T-shirt wet. 2:05 a.m. I stepped into the cool bathroom and snapped on the light. I took off my top, my jeans, my socks, and splashed my face with water. In the mirror, a stranger with puffy eyes and matted hair looked back at me. I put on pajamas and got back into bed.

WHEN A THIN GRAY LIGHT finally crept into the room, I dressed, put makeup on my dark circles, and headed downstairs for breakfast. The hotel restaurant was elegant, with high ceilings and French doors opening onto a courtyard. The smell of coffee and the soft clatter of dishes soothed my frayed nerves. I'd heard there was a prince taking up the whole second floor, and I noticed his entourage in a corner of the dining room, dressed in white and talking quietly into cellphones. As I looked for a place to sit, my heart jumped. On the far side of the room, by the window, sat my father, a little rumpled but essentially unperturbed. The international edition of *The New York Times* was folded in front of him.

"Hi, Dad." I slipped into a chair facing him.

"Sweetheart." He peered at me. "You look tired." He motioned to a server. "Bring her a coffee."

"Did you eat already?"

"No, I was waiting for you." I laughed because it wasn't true, he had no way of knowing I was going to come down, but it felt so good to hear him say it. "The buffet looks beautiful," he added. "Let's go see."

The long table was loaded with breads, Danishes, and juices in yellow and pink and green. There was cereal, scrambled eggs, bacon, and sausages. An area in the center of the room was reserved just for fish—herring with onions and herring in oil, trout gravlax, salmon and whitefish, sour cream, capers, onions, bright orange caviar, and caraway crackers. Next to that, there were many types of cheese from France and Greece and Bulgaria. At the end, I counted five cakes and a crystal bowl filled with sour cherries in burgundy syrup. On a different sort of day, I would have eaten everything.

"Oh," Dad said, as he compared his overflowing plate with my little bowl of sour cherries. "You'll help me." It was more a command than a question.

We sat there, nibbling and drinking coffee, as the breakfast room emptied and filled up again. Julie came down with Mom. It was raining and I ran up to the rooms for extra jackets. Soon Ewa picked us up and drove us to the cemetery. The tomb was waiting.

42

Beets

Okopowa Street bustled as Dad pushed open the creaky cemetery gate, but soon we were enveloped in a mossy silence.
There were slabs of weathered granite as far as my eye could see—
some 250,000 graves on eighty-two acres of land. Many of the tombs
were more than two hundred years old.

The cemetery was in the process of being reclaimed by the forest.
The stones were smooth or crumbling with age; tilting, lifting, almost swaying, as if they'd grown, a little wonky, out of the earth itself. Two chirpy birds chased each other around tree trunks wrapped
in vines. Everything was dripping. Breathing.

"We have to find the shomer," Ewa said. "Szpilman. He's the only
one who knows which graves are where." Soon we were standing in
his bare little office, where Szpilman pocketed a roll of zlotys from
Dad and began typing into his old computer. "Sector 47, row 7,
number 36," he announced, and strode out of the room.

THE SCALE AND CONCENTRATION OF the cemetery were difficult to
comprehend. "Imagine fifty city blocks more densely populated
than downtown Manhattan," I later read, "with all of the inhabitants

living underground." What's more, those 250,000 underground inhabitants far outnumbered the live Jews in all of Poland combined,
an estimated 10,000–20,000. Before the Second World War, the
number had been more than 3 million.

If everyone was dead, why did the cemetery feel so alive? I had a
sensation of crowding—it was almost a sound that murmured just
outside the range I could hear. Hurrying to catch up to Szpilman, I
glanced over my shoulder and was surprised to see only Julie, holding Mom's arm, and Dad, walking alone, kicking loose stones out of
the way.

This place was extraordinary, there was no denying it, but I still
couldn't understand what Dad was expecting to find. We were from
Pabianice, not Warsaw, and the tomb we'd come so far to see
couldn't belong to anyone who really mattered.

Just then, Szpilman made a right turn into the brush. The mark-
ers here were not so much arranged as dropped into place at odd
angles, as if cast down from above. "Okay," he said, stopping
abruptly. He gestured to a huge gravestone with a curved top. "Here
it is."

I reached out to touch the rough granite. "We found it," I called
out to Dad. "It's here!"

"Shlomo Rothblat," Dad said once, then again, fingering the letters and sounding out the Hebrew.

The hairs on the back of my neck stood up. "You see?" Dad whispered, turning to me with tears in his eyes. "It's my name carved
into this old piece of stone."

Dad danced around with his arms in the air, crying his tears of
joy. Mom and Julie walked up and we all hugged and joined hands in
a little hora. There was a pounding in my chest as I watched Julie
take photos of Dad, head held high, shoulder against the gravestone.
I knew I was witnessing a full-circle moment.

AND THEN, THANK GOD, IT was over. We'd done what we came to
do, Dad was satisfied, and as we piled back into the car, I couldn't

wait to leave this strange place and get back to my real life in Toronto.

In the restaurant, we took off our damp jackets and threw them on an empty chair. Julie settled at the far end of the table with Mom and Ewa. I sat down beside Dad, who wore an expression of wonder as he stared into space.

We'd finished all the salami and pickled vegetables when the waitress came out of the kitchen carrying that dubious tray, followed by the chef in his dingy whites. I held my breath as he put a bowl in front of me. "*Dziekuje*." With the surprisingly beautiful liquid in front of me, I bent over to breathe in the smell of clean earth.

I loaded my bowl with garnishes and then, all at once, I started to eat hungrily, tasting the delicious borscht that was becoming more and more familiar with every spoonful. Too soon I was tipping my bowl to scoop out the last sweet-sour mouthfuls, wondering whether you could remember a place you've never been, or know a person you've never met. My father's mother, Udel, daughter of Shlomo Rothblat, must've made borscht from beets like these. It must've tasted just like this. What is a beet, after all, but a living root that grows deep in the ground, a footing and an anchor, hidden and waiting to be discovered. In this dreaded place I hadn't wanted to visit and was dying to leave, I momentarily felt completely at home. Another paradox in a life filled with paradoxes.

43

Smoked Fish

Full and sleepy, I rest against Dad's shoulder. As he hums a Yiddish tune and butters another piece of bread, I start to feel it's all been worth it: the sleepless nights before the trip, the difficulty of schlepping two eighty-four-year-olds to Europe, the ghostliness of the cemetery.

We pile into Ewa's little car and head back to the hotel. Julie pulls out her phone to text home. It's her son's birthday. "How do you say happy birthday in Polish?" she asks Ewa.

"We say '*sto lat.*' "

At this, Dad, who's been napping beside me in the back seat, perks up.

"*Sto lat, sto lat,*" he sings. Ewa is stunned, but only for a second. Then together they sing a snippet of the Polish birthday song Dad has, apparently, stored in the recesses of his mind for seventy-five years.

Niech żyje, żyje nam
Sto lat, sto lat,
Niech żyje, żyje nam!

"With a few more days, your dad will be speaking fluent Polish," Ewa says with pride, oblivious to the complexity of a statement that is nevertheless true. Nobody answers.

Back at the hotel, Mom and Dad rest while Julie and I dash out to a grocery store, as is our custom when we travel. In the produce section, we are amazed by the abundance: piles of strawberries; so many wild mushrooms, you scoop them up with a little shovel; flats of sour cherries, pyramids of beets. We buy a few packages of dried mushrooms and kasha to take home, and hurry back to finish our packing.

I hug Mom goodbye, worried about how she'll manage. Their flight isn't for a couple more days. "Tell Dad when you're tired."

"Don't worry about me," she says bravely. "I'm going to be fine."

Dad is sitting at the window, looking down on Warsaw. He stands up and smiles at me when I come over, and I'm struck by those dimples and the bullet crease above his right eye. "Thank you," I say, wrapping my arms around his generous middle. He smells of comfort and stability. "This was really something."

"Yes, it really was," he says, giving me a squeeze. "I just had a feeling." That his feeling was right should not have surprised me at all.

I STEP ONTO MY FLIGHT alone, tired and relieved. As I shoot through the sky, I fall out of time and space, floating between the life I've lived before, and the one waiting for me on the ground. The sunset goes on and on, beaming in through my tiny window and filling the cabin with surreal purple light.

I walk out of the customs lounge and fall into Michael's arms. "Welcome home, Mommy," Maya says as we open the front door of our house. She hugs me and puts a homemade card in my hands.

"Would you like some raspberries?" Leo asks, holding a bowl out to me.

I shower, put on clean pajamas, and pad into the kitchen. I melt butter and take out eggs to scramble. I dig around in the fridge. There's a little smoked fish. I pour a glass of white wine.

"Well, you did it," Michael says, giving my shoulder a squeeze as I reach for a fork.

"Yeah, and I'm never going back to Poland."

"No, you don't have to."

IN BED THAT NIGHT, MICHAEL encircles my wrist with his thumb and forefinger. "Keep me here," I say, turning toward him. "Keep me right here beside you."

"I will," he murmurs in my ear.

I want to believe nothing further can pull me back across the ocean. I want to believe that, at long last, I've conquered my fear, and I am complete. It will be a little while before I notice a feeling still deep in my chest; a subtle tightness, a little bit of strain. One long struggle has finally ended, but as I will soon realize, a new one is about to begin.

44

Camera

It's late fall, the kids settled back into their routines, when I notice the outline of a little door at the back of my psyche. Something big and alive waits on the other side. I can almost feel the doorknob in my hand, cool and round.

I dig out my camera from the back of the closet and head up to the office on the third floor. The room smells like heat and paper. I sit at the desk, surrounded by books, my old magazine articles, the kids' art. The last red leaves drift into the backyard as I wait for the camera chip to download its contents onto my computer. I tap my fingers and jiggle my knees.

I click on the photo of Dad standing beside Shlomo Rothblat's tomb, chin lifted, eyes bright. The trip has validated him in a way he hasn't had to explain: He was an orphan, his family had been murdered and his whole way of life had been erased. Before the tomb, how could he be sure any of it ever really happened?

I zoom in on the gravestone. The epitaph is a long passage of Hebrew, a chunk of missing lineage carved in stone. I stretch my thumb and index finger on the computer trackpad to enlarge the writing, but my Hebrew is spotty and I can only read a couple of words. I need a translator. Do I have my cousin's email?

Jochevet is one of the Dod's many grandchildren, and Shlomo Rothblat was her great-grandfather, too. In fact, it was someone in her vast family who told Dad about the tomb in the first place.

Jochi is older than me and we live completely different lives. I was in my late teens when, on a trip to Israel, she picked me up from a Jerusalem hotel in 100-degree heat wearing a wig and long sleeves. I knew the purpose was modesty but I was amazed to see how beautifully made-up and glamorous she was.

There are warm feelings on both sides but in many ways, we are strangers. Her life as an observant woman seems oppressive—children and grandchildren in the double digits, nonstop housework, endless acts of service to God and her family. Then again, she might look at mine and find it completely lacking in form and meaning.

What's weird is that we look alike. The same olive skin, dark hair, mildly assertive nose. If I curl my hair in the style of her wig and make an effort with eyeliner and eye shadow, I could be her little sister. I have my own sisters, of course, but this is different. Jochevet is my lost grandmother's niece. Since Poland, the resemblance between us pulses with new meaning.

I forward the photo of Dad at the tomb to Jochi, asking her to translate the epitaph. As soon as her reply shows up in my inbox, I tap Dad's number into my cell. Three rings, four, five. "Hello," he says, stress on the first syllable. It's a statement, not a question. He sold the last restaurant twelve years ago, but he still sounds like he's running to greet people at the door.

"Dad, I want to read something to you."

"What?" The TV blares in the background.

"Are you wearing your hearing aids?" I shout. "Can you turn down the TV?"

"Hold on."

The noise disappears. When he's back on the line, I take a breath and read him Jochevet's translation of the words on his grandfather's tomb, slowing down for the most lavish parts.

שלמה יהודה בן רבי יוסף ראטבלאט
הנקרא שלמה חסיד

Shlomo Yehuda Rothblat
Who was known as Shlomo Chusid

שמות וחושך התחוללו במעוננו
Disasters and darkness have occurred at our home
מה רבו דמעותינו באובדן רוענו
How many tears we shed in the loss of our shepherd
הלך לעולמו במיטב שנותיו
He passed away in the prime of his life
ימי חלדו לא הגיע זקנתו
He did not reach his old years
הוי מה גדלה אנחתנו
Oh how our sighs have grown
דורש טוב הוא לעמו ומולדתו
He demands good for his people and his homeland

השאיר אחריו בניו נטעי נעמנים
He left behind his faithful sons and daughters
בני תורה ישרים ותמימים
Honest and innocent Torah follower
נצח יזכרו צדקותיו וחסידותו
His righteousness and piousness will be remembered for
eternity
יגידו מעשיו עדתו קהילתו
His deeds will be said by his community, our congregation
ויספרו שבחיו בני עמנו
And our people will tell his praises
סוף וקץ לחייו בא בשנת רעות האלה
The end of his life came in this evil year
פה מנוחו עד ישני ישראל לתחיה(יקומו)
Here he rests till the dead people of Israel will wake up

The "evil year" is not written, so I can only guess he died in the early 1900s. He's been given the second name "Chusid" or "Hasid" in place of his real last name to show his status in the community.

"Read it again," Dad commands. "Slower!"

I finish the second reading and there's a long pause. "You see?" Dad finally says. "My grandfather was an important man, a loved man. I always knew we came from yichus."

The trip and the tomb have completed something for Dad. Despite his age, he's found a fresh foothold in the world, a renewed sense of his place. For him, it's a type of closing and I know he's absolutely done. I, on the other hand, am not done at all.

MY GREAT-GRANDFATHER SHLOMO MIGHT HAVE been brilliant. He was surely righteous and devout. To think of life before the Holocaust, of all the earlier generations of our family in Poland, thriving and flourishing and finding joy and meaning, fills me with awe. But Shlomo Chusid lived in a world of men. The great rabbis and teachers were men, study of the Torah was reserved for men, lineage was passed down by men. Thinking of prewar Poland, I see a universe of inequality and deep segregation, with men taking the glory, and women doing the work. The most important thing about Shlomo Chusid, as far as I'm concerned, is his daughter Udel, the lost grandmother I'd always wanted and never had.

The little door swings open and a cascade of feeling pours out. It's no longer the dull, formless ache I felt when I was little, playing in the snow and freezing my toes, dreaming up ways to bring back my dead relatives so I could offer them to my father as a gift.

No. It's sharp now, and pointy; a blade in my chest. I stare into the mirror and wonder which features are hers. The dark skin. The long nose. "Your grandmother was murdered," I yell at my reflection. "Wake the fuck up!" I want to slap my own face. I can't make it sink in deep enough. I force myself to think of her on the platform at Birkenau. It's 1944, and she's kept her children alive through five years of beatings, shootings, starvation. Her only son, thirteen years old, is marched away at gunpoint. Is it minutes, hours, or days before she and her daughters are stripped and shoved into the gas chamber? Did the guards bother to shave their heads and tattoo them first? What is her last thought? I lean over the toilet, retching. I teeter on the edge of the abyss. I could be sucked in for another twenty years. *Enough.* By sheer force of will, I change directions.

I slide into my jacket and walk to the stationery store for pens and a new notebook. Dad mentions his mother every once in a while. Why have I not been taking notes? Some kind of blockage has been knocked free and hot lava flows through my body, burning a path forward.

JULIE GRILLS STEAKS AND INVITES everyone for dinner. The first snow brightens the dark trees. Dad loves the Caesar salad. I talk about Udel until I can feel her as a presence in the room. She energizes the air around me. "She's here with us," I say. I watch my dad and sister exchange glances; they think I've lost it, but I don't care. I need this. "Can't you feel her?"

I put my plate aside and pull a notebook from my bag. Dad sits down beside me and we list everything we know: Born? Warsaw. Died? Birkenau, we think. Udel's mother, Shifra Chana, died in childbirth, Dad says. Her father remarried quickly and had more children, but we know of no living descendants. We don't know if they were rich or poor, but they had their yichus.

How did Udel feel the day she had to pack up and leave everything she knew in Warsaw to marry my grandfather, Betzalel, and move to Pabianice? Was she afraid? Did she tremble getting into bed that night, about to have sex for the first time?

Betzalel's first wife had died, leaving him with a little girl named Franya. He and Udel had two more girls, Chana and Nachama, before my father was born in 1930. The next year, Machla was born and the year after that Devorah, giving my dad five sisters in all. Tensions were already rising in Europe and Betzalel's family money was mostly lost in the Depression and yet, for my dad, the 1930s were imbued with warmth and stability. Udel had only nine years to give my father a foundation that has lasted his whole life, to imprint his brain and shore up his soul. I don't know how she did it.

In the winter of 1939, Betzalel, who had a heart condition, died suddenly, leaving Udel alone with her children. Franya, her step-daughter, had just gotten married. Seven months later, on September 8, 1939, German troops thundered into town.

45

Udel

I am in Mom and Dad's suite in the residence, searching. "Where is it?"

"It's here someplace. Look in there." Dad uses the toe of his favorite white shoes to point at a drawer under the TV. Inside, I find a mess of papers, envelopes, odds and ends. When Mom was well, no drawer would be less than immaculate, but that Mom is gone. She can't walk anymore. She barely even speaks.

"The drawers are a mess, Mom," I say to her as she snoozes in her wheelchair. She opens her eyes, looks at me blankly, and closes them again.

We have only one photo with Udel in it, an enlarged print of a print, grainy black and white and beat up around the edges. I'm wondering if it's lost. "Tell me more, Dad. What was she like?" I'm taking everything out of the drawer now, my heart beating a little too fast. "Do I look like her?"

"Yes. No. I don't know. She was good."

At last, I find it, a group photo from Franya's wedding, women and girls only, some twenty faces in all. The bride is in white and it must be summer because the cluster of little girls sitting in the front

are in short-sleeved dresses. One of them is Dad's baby sister, Devorah, smiling with a missing front tooth. In a group of older girls
standing behind them, one face pops out, another one of Dad's sisters, who looked exactly like him.

The adult women are crowded on the other side of the bride in
dark dresses and suits. "Which one?" I say, as I have so many times
before. Dad points to a sliver of a face. Dark hair. A fullness around
the chin. Maybe a familiar nose? It's not enough.

I WANT TO CONJURE HER. What did she smell like? How did she
move? I long to hear her voice. Dad talks about her goodness, but it's
her bravery I need to grasp. *The New York Times* runs an article about
women resistance fighters during the war and I read it hungrily,
imagining my grandmother with a kerchief tied around her braids
and a revolver in a teddy bear.

The truth is even more unfathomable. An ultraorthodox mother
of six, bred for a lifetime of observance and housework, keeping
herself and her children alive despite the darkest evil surrounding
them. Whom did she charm, deceive, bribe, defy? How many times?
Did she lie with a smile on her face, feeling her heart might blow
right out of her chest? Wanting to feel her strength in my body, I
search for points of connection. For all my efforts to be liberated, is
my life really so different from hers? I cook and clean. I've given
birth three times. It's lowly women's work; the work we have labored over since the beginning of time. It's the most important
work in the world.

SOON I BEGIN TO ASK questions, look for records, read up about
Jewish life in Poland before the war. Like some kind of ancient Kab-
balist, I attach significance to numbers and deep meaning to what
others would call coincidence. She's come to me when I'm close to
the age she was when she died—fifty-two. Obviously, that's a sign?
On a genealogy site populated by a distant branch of family, I find a
record of her birthday: May 27, 1892. The hairs on my arm stand up.

My Jamie, her great-grandson, was born on the same day, ninety-nine years later.

ANOTHER DAY AND SEVERAL MORE cups of coffee as we try to shake the memories loose. "What else, Dad? Tell me more."

"Let me see. Have I told you about the cholent?"

I try not to roll my eyes. "Have you told me about the cholent? Of course, that's all I heard growing up. You said that she—" and then it hits me. Why does cholent have to be some historical dish that we talk about in the abstract? I'm a chef—why don't I just make it?

I comb the internet for information and order a stack of cookbooks from the library. It turns out, Jews have been making cholent for ages, perhaps even as far back as the time of the second temple, two thousand years ago. Some say the dish originated in the Iberian Peninsula with the name hamin, similar to the Hebrew word for hot, and included chickpeas and fava beans. For Jews of European descent, the basic ingredients are potatoes, meat, beans, and barley, but different communities have tailored the dish to their own local influences. In France, cholent bears a striking resemblance to cassoulet, the traditional French bean stew, and there is speculation that cholent came first. Other communities add whole eggs to bake with the stew, an ingredient kids either fight over or won't touch. The common thread is time, the slow overnight cooking that both accommodates the commandment not to work on Shabbat and allows the flavors of the ingredients to soften and become greater than the sum of their parts.

A WEEK LATER, I'M ON MY WAY to Mom and Dad's with a steaming foil package on the car seat beside me. Inside the suite, we transfer the contents to a plate and pop it in the microwave. Dad pokes at my first cholent with his fork. "The flavor is good, but it's way too dry."

"Okay, so more water," I say, scribbling notes on a paper napkin.

"Yes, and what kind of meat did you use? It should have more fat."

"I used what you told me. Brisket."

"It's too dry. And where's the kishka?"

"Kishka? You never said anything about kishka."

"Yes, of course kishka. My mother bought the skin and stuffed it herself with flour and chicken fat."

Memories are strange things. Wispy. Amorphous. They don't necessarily come when you call for them. Instead, they have a way of popping up when you're looking in the other direction.

46

Cholent

I return home discouraged and frustrated. How am I supposed to re-create Dad's childhood if he keeps changing the ingredients?

I take the kids to school, write a few articles, throw in one hundred loads of wash. I forget about cholent for a little while, but by early spring, it's back. *Make me,* it whispers. *Make me!* Single socks are missing, the fridge is empty again. The bathroom sinks are full of hair. I file my latest article, collect groceries, and make a solo escape, leaving Michael holding the bag.

At our cabin two and a half hours northwest of the city, I put my key in the lock and walk into the velvety silence. I pace the wood floors barefoot, smelling my books and talking to myself. Did Shlomo Chusid love his books as much as I do? Did he save them for his children, only to have soldiers in armbands throw them in a pile and light them on fire? I pour myself a scotch and get into bed. My grandmothers come to me in my sleep. Udel is heavy across the hips and sweet smelling. Baba Sarah hands me a bowl of boiled chicken necks. The meat is tender and the bones are soft enough to chew. The next night, I dream of pregnancy and a warm wind in January.

Baba Sarah and I are dipping chocolates, we're playing cards. She tells me I'll soon go into labor.

MY MOTHER AND SISTERS HAD their babies in hospitals, but I when I was pregnant with Leo, I found a midwife named Liz who could deliver the baby at home. Michael wasn't thrilled. As my belly grew and my features blurred, we debated home birth back and forth. "It's an unnecessary risk," he said.

"It's my body," I said.

"But what if something goes wrong?"

He had me there. I can always be persuaded to become anxious.

On a stormy night in July, my water broke with a ping and a gush. Michael called Liz and she came right over. I panted through five hours of contractions on my hands and knees, Michael pushing on my tailbone from behind to offset the racking back pain. I'd agreed to transfer to the hospital before delivery but when that moment arrived, when Liz said, "It's time," rain was lashing the windows and I was draped in nothing but a towel.

"Please," I cried as my body squeezed and convulsed and heaved. "I just can't." And that was that. Leo and, four years later, Maya, were born on our own bed.

I nursed each baby for an eternity. I gave my life over to them completely, suffering when I felt they were holding me underwater but knowing there was no other way. The love was that blinding.

I WAKE THE NEXT MORNING at 6:03, my body coursing with energy. I can hear a trickle of snowmelt running toward the lake. Downstairs, I thrust the mop at the grimy corners and attack the mouse droppings around the fireplace. I turn the broom upside down and drag it against the logs overhead as dust and spiderwebs rain down. In the kitchen, I wipe down the countertops and scrub the sink. I wash the fridge shelves and take out the fruit and vegetable bins to soak in warm soapy water. Best of all is the vacuuming, the sucking up of dirt, hair, old pieces of skin, days burned down to the ends. I'm ready to roll up my sleeves and get to work on another cholent when a different urge comes over me. I brew a pot of coffee and sit down at the dining table with a notebook. And that is when I begin to spin.

Udel is in her kitchen in Pabianice, her Shabbos heels tapping the black and white checkered floor. Her eldest, Chana, has already lined the bottom of the old cast-iron pot with sliced onions and quartered potatoes. Udel goes to the pantry and scoops out a big cup of barley, scattering it over the vegetables. Next, the dried white beans. From the icebox, she retrieves a brown package. She unwraps a morsel of fat-marbled meat and carefully places it on top of the barley and beans. She goes back for the coil of kishka she made in the morning. Chana does the seasoning—salt, pepper, paprika, a little sugar. Udel adds plenty of water. The cholent will cook for almost twenty-four hours; she has to make sure it won't dry out.

The bakery is across the courtyard, not two hundred steps from the apartment. As they enter, a cloud of steam wraps around them. It's late afternoon, but the yeasty smell of the morning lingers. Two challahs and a lone rye sit on the rack behind a counter nobody tends. The place is packed with women and girls, pressed and polished for Friday night. They carry heavy pots wrapped in a rainbow of tea towels. Each woman prepares her own Shabbos lunch and the bakery doubles as a community oven. Udel has tied the ends of her yellow towel together over the lid to make a carrying handle—a convenience when the stew is cold and raw, but essential tomorrow when she will bring it home piping hot.

There is a little boy, the only son of six children. "Why can't we cook the cholent at home, Mama?" he asks.

"I told you, Shloimeleh. You can't work on Shabbos."

"But what if it gets mixed up with someone else's?"

"It won't. Everyone knows their own pot. Okay?"

"So if the oven is on, you are working?"

"Sort of, sweetie. You'll understand when you're older."

At the front of the queue, Mendel the baker perspires through the back of his work shirt. He stokes the fire with a long paddle. It's the end of August 1939, and there is already talk of Germans in Poland. Standing beside his mother, Shlomo tries to make sense of what people are saying over his head. Dead horses in the street? Soldiers taking people's silver in Kalisz?

They get to the front of the line. Heat rolls off the oven in waves, making the little boy's eyes water.

Mendel holds the uncooked pot of cholent while Udel unties her towel, folds it, and piles it on top of the others on the shelf beside the oven. He uses the paddle to slide the pot into the fiery depths.

Leaving the bakery with his mother and sister, Shlomo looks back at the baker, still laboring away. The oven door opens and he catches a glimpse of all those cast-iron vessels, lined up in neat rows. Tomorrow, the hard beans will be soft and scented; the meat so tender, it'll fall apart in his mouth.

Soon, Mama won't be allowed to bring her cholent to the bakery, she won't even be allowed in the street. But he doesn't know that yet. He doesn't know there will be a last time.[1]

That evening, I put on my boots and go for a walk as the sun goes down. The cottage road is wet and pitted, with pines and hemlocks on either side. I listen for chickadees and yellow-rumped warblers, northern flickers, red-eyed vireos, goldfinches. Were there birds over Udel's head when she got to Birkenau, or did the sounds and smells drive them away?

Back in the city, I step into the kitchen, my right hand itchy for the feel of my knife, its heel snug in my palm. I've picked up a long coil of kishka from the kosher butcher and swapped short ribs for brisket. I've combed grocery stores for sweet little potatoes like the ones we ate in Warsaw, and I've sloshed beans around in a bowl of water. I slice onions and rinse barley. I cut the meat off the bones and make a pile of cubes. *Okay, Udel, help me here.* I layer the ingredients into my white Dutch oven and fill it halfway with water. I cover it with a lid and slide the cholent into a slow oven before going to bed.

Around three a.m. I wake up with a start, certain it's dried out. I stumble down the stairs and creep into the kitchen. I open the oven door, take the lid off the pot, and squint into the dim light. The beans are still firm, floating in water. I shuffle back to bed and set my alarm for five.

When I come down again, the kitchen smells warm and the pot is almost dry. Thank god I've come down. Thank god! Standing there in the dark, I'm seized by a sudden mania. I open the fridge and root around. A few cloves of garlic, a branch of fresh rosemary, and another of thyme. A bay leaf. I find a package wrapped in butcher paper, duck legs for tomorrow night's dinner, and toss one in. Sausage would make it even better, but I don't have any and besides, there are limits. I almost forget to refill the pot halfway with water.

A FEW DAYS LATER, DAD calls me, too early. "I can't stop thinking about your cholent," he says, a little breathless.

Michael sits up in bed beside me. It isn't even seven. "All fine," I mouth to him, and he flops back into the pillows.

"It was so tender. So delicious!"

"I'm really happy, Dad." I'd set the table and helped him navigate the driveway's March ice. I'd lit candles even though it wasn't Friday night. Mock Shabbos or séance, I wasn't sure.

"Liked it? That gravy! Those potatoes!"

Warmth spreads all the way to my toes. I take a breath and clear my throat. "Would your mother have liked it?"

"My mother would have loved it," he says softly. "She would have loved you."

It's enough, it's more than enough, it's almost too much. I want to hang up the phone and just lie in bed quietly, holding this inside me. But he keeps talking. "I wanted to tell you something else."

"Yes?"

"The cholent made me remember something I haven't thought of in eighty years."

I'm hanging on every word.

"There was a cake."

"A cake?"

"She made a cake on Shabbos. *Piterkuchen*." He almost spits it out, a strange word I've never heard before.

"Say it again?"

LATER THAT MORNING, I SIT down with a cup of coffee at my computer. "Piterkuchen," I enter into the search field. Joan Nathan, the great keeper of Jewish-Polish food secrets, knows. She calls it not piterkuchen but Putterkuchen, Butter Crumble Cake. I make a shopping list.

47

Cake

I bake the putterkuchen two, three times, fiddling with the moisture, the sweetness, the size of the pan. Each time I wrap up a chunk and take it over to Dad, he remembers a little more about his mother, his childhood. "She baked it Friday mornings," he says one day, telling me the cake should be flatter.

I try again, using a sheet pan instead of a Pyrex. He makes us coffees with his little machine, and we sit to taste the next iteration. "I would have one huge slice before cheder and think all day about having another after school," Dad says. "When the rebbe called on me, I didn't know the answer because I was dreaming about cake."

His memories are flowing now. Friday afternoons, Dad hurried into the apartment, the air smelling like floor polish and chicken soup. He dropped his rucksack and headed for the kitchen. Sometimes another golden slice would be waiting for him with a tall glass of milk. But another day, his mama, all pretty and nice smelling for Shabbos, shook her head. "Sorry, Shloimeleh," she said. "Those poor children down the street never get cake. I wrapped it up and took it to them."

"I remember my disappointment like it was yesterday," he says.

THE TRIP TO WARSAW HAS taken up a comfortable place in my memory when my friend Cindy calls. "I have tickets to a photography show at the art gallery," she says. "Want to go with me?"

There's something precious about the girlfriends you make in your forties. It's not about who you lived beside when you were in school. It's not about your partner's friends from work or the other mothers in the carpool. Cindy is a friend I picked all on my own, for her thrilling laugh, her mane of straw-colored hair, her love of adventure. The only problem is that Cindy wants me to go back to Poland.

She's a travel agent of sorts, leading small trips with another friend named Shari. Because of Cindy and Shari, I've trekked alongside the gelada baboons in Ethiopia and swum the brackish waters of Colombia. Cindy also runs a Jewish heritage trip to Berlin and Poland, a trip she's tried to get me to join. "Sorry," I've said countless times. "I just can't."

ON A THURSDAY NIGHT IN June, Cindy's silver car pulls up and we head to the gallery downtown. The exhibit is the work of Henryk Ross, a Jewish photographer born in Poland in 1910. While he was a prisoner in the Lodz Ghetto, Ross was assigned to take photos for the work cards every inmate was required to carry. When no one was looking, he also took unauthorized photos, surreptitiously documenting everyday life in the ghetto—public hangings, starving children digging for scraps, mass deportations. Ross buried his photos and negatives in a box as the ghetto was being liquidated in the fall of 1944. After the Russians liberated Poland, Ross found his way back to Lodz to dig up his film, unearthing one of the most comprehensive physical records of the Lodz Ghetto.

It is the kind of exhibit I've carefully avoided since Paris—avoided, really, my whole life—and as we walk the polished floors of the gallery, I feel a prickle of anxiety. *Here we go*. I'm about to tell Cindy I've

made a mistake and I need to head home when my eyes land on the
first photo.

It's a black-and-white image of a man in a cap, trudging through
deep snow. I want to breeze past but it's too late—I'm already doing
a familiar calculation. My father would have been in the Lodz Ghetto
at exactly the same time as Ross. They probably met. In fact, Ross
probably would have photographed Dad for his identity card. They
were likely deported from the ghetto in 1944 in the same open cattle
cars.

My feet step forward, bringing my nose an inch from the glass.
On either side of the man, massive slabs of broken stone with Jewish
symbols lie in disarray. They look like tombstones but they're many
times bigger than the man, as if they've been hurled, torn and jag-
ged, from the sky. The man is looking down; I can't see all his features. Still, it's clear: he's too old to be my father. I exhale.

"Bon, you've been to Poland now," Cindy is saying. "You've done
it. Maybe it's time to reconsider the trip. I really think you would get
a lot out of it."

"That's the problem," I say. "I would get too much out of it."

We walk up to the next photo, a child with an armband grinning
at the camera and wielding a baton over another child in rags. I stop
breathing and look closely at one boy. Not Dad. Then the other. Not
Dad.

"THAT WASN'T SO BAD," I say, as we get back into the car. My palms
are dry and my heart beats steadily in my chest. I can breathe, I can
hear Cindy's light chatter. Something is shifting; the tiniest little bit
of space is opening up. After half a lifetime of fear, there's a crack in
the darkness.

"Can I tell you more about the trip now?"

"You can tell me, but I'm still not coming."

Her group will be leaving in September, she says. Nine days in
Berlin and Poland, five ghettos and concentration camps, twenty-
five participants.

"I promise this will be different from the march," she says. We are zooming up the empty streets of Toronto, city lights a blur on either side of the car windows. Cindy knows I applied to be a chaperone and was offered a spot, only to back out at the last minute. Her trip is different, she says. "I have a fabulous guide lined up. And you won't believe the survivor." Like the march, Cindy's trip hinges on first-person testimony. She pulls into my driveway and puts the car in park. "Her name is Hedy Bohm and she's just incredible."

"You understand that just being able to look at those photos tonight was a huge step for me." The car is quiet as we watch my neighbor wheel her garbage bin down to the curb.

"I do understand that."

"And that growing up with a survivor has taught me more about what happened than any trip can?"

"Of course. But maybe this can give you something different."

"Thanks, Cind, but I don't think so." I give her a hug and walk into my house.

As I GET INTO BED that night, I think about how the universe sometimes gives you the right person at the right time. When I was too young to want to talk about my background, so were my friends. Then, as my awareness grew, so did my friends', but in a random way. "Children of survivors are bitter," said a classmate at journalism school, her comment based solely on the fact that I wasn't as religious as she was. In her narrow assessment, my father had turned away from religion out of anger at God.

"People like you either can't talk about it at all, or can't talk about anything else," said another friend when we were young mothers and I first began sharing bits of my father's story.

The peculiar bias against Holocaust survivors within Jewish society has a long history. When the war ended and the surviving European Jews found their way from concentration camps to communities around the world, having suffered unimaginable trauma and loss, locals didn't always want to hear about it. Even the Israel of the fifties welcomed survivors, but not their histories. "People would see the tattoo and look at you differently," Avraham Harshalom told *Haaretz* newspaper in an article titled "Nobody Wanted to Hear Our Stories," published in January 2015. The tattoos and the losses stigmatized the survivors and marked them as damaged, perhaps because to truly empathize with what they'd been through would have been too overwhelming.

When my dad arrived in Edmonton, the local Jewish community was similarly indifferent. Brave and handsome as he was, Dad had a strange haircut and a thick accent. More than once while I was growing up, Mom said she'd taken a chance on Dad and his "DP English," even though Dad spent no time at all in a displaced persons camp after the war. The crack was Mom's idea of an ironic joke, acknowledging that many thought they were better than new immigrants like my dad, although at other times, she made it clear she thought it was the other way around: if anything, she wondered if her charismatic survivor husband was too good for her.

As I turn out the light, I realize that Cindy appreciates Holocaust survivors more than any friend I've ever had, an appreciation bordering on obsession. Their courage. Their strength. She collects amazing stories: a survivor couple in their nineties—the girl saw the boy moving in a pile of dead bodies at Dachau and pulled him out; an octogenarian who fought off terminal cancer with his bulletproof insides. When it comes to my family, Cindy is sensitive but honest. Respectful but fascinated. Like everyone else, she was immediately drawn to my father when she met him; his warmth and his good energy. She thought, at first, he'd be a perfect survivor to accompany one of her trips, and Dad humored her in his typical way. "Oh, that sounds lovely," he said. "I'll think about it." His wiggling out was slow and indirect, leaving me to make excuses. "It would be just too much for him," I told her. "He's not in good enough health." Not a lie but not the full truth, either.

MICHAEL IS AWAY AND I lie in the middle of the bed, tossing and turning, thinking about the exhibit, the faces of the people in the ghetto, Dad, and then—no. I take a few deep breaths and imagine myself on my mat. We are all just travelers in time. I pull myself away from the edge and sleep through the night.

48

Crab Apple Jelly

'm making crab apple jelly when Cindy calls again several weeks later. Baba must have dictated the recipe to me; it's on an old envelope, written in my childish scrawl. I've boiled the small, bright fruit in water and strained out the solids with cheesecloth. I've counted the cups of dark red juice and added sugar in a five-to-four ratio. Now the juice and sugar mixture simmers beside a boiling pot of jam jars and sealing lids. It's a warm August afternoon and the kitchen windows are steaming up.

"I've got a meeting for the trip at my house tonight," Cindy says in my ear. "Come and meet Hedy."

I don't say anything.

"She's just incredible, Bon. She meditates like you. She does tai chi."

"How can I come to the meeting if I'm not signed up for the trip?"

"Oh, it's fine. See you at seven?"

I'M STILL WARM FROM MY work in the kitchen when I arrive at Cindy's pink stucco house and let myself in the front door. The thrum of conversation is in my ears as I walk past the colorful art, the giant ferns, a board of cheese and fruit on the dining room table. In the kitchen, I look for a platter. I've made crab apple jelly squares with my fresh jelly and I want to put them out.

There are maybe twenty people milling around the living room, visiting and drinking wine. In the back corner, sitting against a wall of windows to the garden, I see a woman in a blue caftan with short silver hair. She's on a low stool, surrounded by the upturned faces of people sitting on the floor in front of her, like a kindergarten teacher telling a story. The quality of her voice is too soft to hear.

A path seems to open as Cindy brings me to Hedy. Everyone disappears and it's just me and her. I'm kneeling, I think. "I'm the child of a survivor," I say into her blue-green eyes. "I'm too scared to go on this trip."

She takes my hand for the first of many times and intertwines her strong fingers in mine. "You can do it," she says. "I know because I thought I couldn't do it. You're going to come and I'm going to help you."

IT'S A PARTICULARLY STRONG MOMENT for Hedy, who has just returned from testifying at the trial of Reinhold Hanning in Germany. He was the second Nazi she was asked to help prosecute. Oskar Gröning, the "bookkeeper of Auschwitz," was the first.

It began with a German lawyer and former judge named Thomas Walther, who found Hedy in a March of the Living video on the internet. Walther, who is not Jewish, had realized that the few living Nazi criminals could still be tried according to a facet of German law, and decided to devote himself to seeing justice served. He tracked Hedy to her Toronto apartment and, through a series of emails and phone calls, convinced her to testify. Hedy and the other survivors who testified were successful and both Nazis were charged and convicted: Hanning with accessory to 170,000 murders; Gröning with accessory to 300,000 murders.

I don't know any of this at Cindy's that night. A few days later, I visit Hedy at her apartment overlooking a ravine. She serves me tea and Hungarian pastry as she tells me how difficult making that 2015 trip to Germany was. How, prior to the trial, just the sound of the German language sent her spiraling, how Germany was the scariest place she could imagine. She explains that telling her story in a German court was so surprisingly validating, so healing, it transformed her entire worldview at eighty-four years of age.

Amid my awe, I feel a shameful stab of jealousy. Why can't Dad have this healing? He missed the opportunity to become a March of the Living superstar, missed the catharsis of telling his story publicly. "It's too late to go back," he told me when I asked him to go on Cindy's trip. "I'm done with it all." But, sitting beside Hedy in her apartment that afternoon, I think maybe it's not Dad who needs the healing, anyway. I hug Hedy goodbye, ride down in the elevator, and text Cindy from the street in front of Hedy's building. Two words. "I'm in."

49

Berlin

'm alone when I board an overnight flight to Berlin. I'd gone ahead and booked a ticket by myself, realizing, too late, that perhaps Berlin was not a place I want to arrive solo. "Are you really going to just send me?" I said to Michael. He was busy at work, and we had no one to stay with Maya.

"Bon, this is your journey, whether I'm there or not."

We decided that the people in the group, some of whom are friends, will provide enough support. In addition to Cindy and Hedy, there is Lis, a friend I've traveled with before; Erika, one of the moms from Maya's school; and Stacey, an old friend from summer camp.

The day before the trip, my cousin from Edmonton, who was supposed to meet us in Berlin and room with me, breaks a bone and has to cancel. I was spooked for several hours, sure it was a bad omen. Maybe I should stay home.

"Yes, just cancel!" Dad almost yelled when I drove over to tell him I was having doubts. "How many times do I need to say it: You don't have to do this."

I sat there looking at him as my brain ping-ponged back and

forth. Was he right or wrong? Should I stay or go? All he wanted, all he'd ever wanted, was to protect me. But resisting that protection had come to define my adult life. Staring at the bullet crease above his right eye, I saw that darkness isn't something you can run away from but, rather, something you carry with you. It makes you braver and stronger. It makes you complete. I'd faced hard things before; it was time to face the hardest hard thing and finally see if something new was waiting on the other side.

"I love you, Dad," I said, getting up to hug him. "I'll see you in ten days."

THE WHEELS TOUCH DOWN, AND just like that, I'm in Germany, the cradle of my nightmares. In the arrivals area, everyone is tall and fair. I feel like I'm harboring a dirty secret. Are people staring at me? Do they know? I look down at my wrinkled cotton shirt. No gold star. I put on a pair of sunglasses and lift my chin. It's just Europe, I tell myself. I can do this.

It's a warm morning, and the sun has a soft September glow. As I step out to the curb, a wave of nostalgia sweeps over me. I remember that first time in Paris, so long ago—the pleasant sense of disorientation, the waft of European cigarettes and foreign perfume. I slide into a taxi and give the driver the name of the hotel where I'll meet Cindy, Hedy, and the rest of the group.

My composure is fragile. No matter where I go, home or away, I am instinctively circumspect about my identity. I carry a fear of cops and soldiers and customs officers—anyone with a severe haircut and a uniform—in my blood. Never do I walk around telling people I'm Jewish. But in the cab, apropos of nothing, someone says, *"Ich Juden,"* and that someone seems to be me. Is it a challenge? A confession? Blood pulses in my ears and I expect the driver to turn around and tell me to get out, but he just shrugs. *You freak,* I tell myself. *Act normal.*

The next days are surprisingly comfortable and easy. We walk the cobblestones of Berlin, bending to read the names on the scattered brass stolpersteine that mark the places where people were forced from their homes and deported, or murdered on the spot. The "stumbling stones," created by artist Gunter Demnig, are a play on words: an old German antisemitic saying, when accidentally stumbling over a protruding stone, was "A Jew must be buried here." Rob, one of the guys in the group, finds the stolpersteine eerie, but the burnished brass squares, inscribed with names like Goldschmidt and Bernstein, make me feel right at home.

We visit the Memorial to the Murdered Jews of Europe, then head out for lunch. At the Jewish Museum Berlin, we walk on anguished metal faces, then enjoy a nice Riesling at dinner. A waitress brings me a perfect square of sour cherry streusel cake and I devour it slowly, wondering how much butter is in the bottom, and whether the cherries are fresh or preserved.

In my handsome hotel room, I pull the fluffy duvet around my body and count—seven more sleeps until I can go home. I've become good at blocking unwanted thoughts, so I don't think about Poland. Poland is just a black box. And Berlin isn't so bad. Berlin is rather nice.

The next morning, we visit Humboldt University, where Einstein was a professor and some of the world's biggest breakthroughs in science occurred in the nineteenth and twentieth centuries. When the Nazi party came to power in 1933, Humboldt was one of thirty-four German universities where books were burned; not just books by Jews but a wide and stunning variety, from Hemingway to Helen Keller. In the nearby Bebelplatz, we ponder a monument designed by Micha Ullman: empty bookshelves to hold the twenty thousand books burned at Humboldt on May 10, 1933, visible below the pavement through a glass window. A plaque features a prophetic 1821 quote from Heinrich Heine, a German Jewish poet: "Where they burn books, they will ultimately burn people as well."

The good weather holds. The next morning, we take a walking tour of the leafy Schöneberg neighborhood, also known as the Bavarian Quarter. Before the war, this was a center of intellectual life in Berlin, and many prominent people lived here: Albert Einstein, Gisèle Freund, the photographer, Carl Einstein, the art historian, Gertrud Kolmar, the poet, and Hannah Arendt, the political theorist.

Hedy decides to use the wheelchair we've brought in case she gets tired, and a few of us jockey for the honor of pushing it. It feels good to be standing behind her, handles in my grasp, calm envelope of Hedyness drifting over me.

The neighborhood features a scattered memorial that was controversial when it was first installed in 1993: eighty small signs mounted on posts in a seemingly random arrangement. Each sign states one of the hundreds of decrees designed to systematically deprive Jews of pleasures, rights, livelihood, and, eventually, life itself. On the back of each sign, artists Renata Stih and Frieder Schnock have rendered a simple picture to illustrate, eye-catching in its cuteness.

The first sign they installed was a tabby cat on a blue background. The other side of the sign states, in German: "Jews can no longer keep pets."

Another sign showing musical notes says: "Jews are banned from choral societies."

A clock on a cheerful yellow background indicates: "Jews aren't allowed to leave home after 8 p.m."

Beside the U-Bahn subway sign, a white *U* on a blue background, the artists have created a sign with the same symbol. The reverse side indicates that Jews aren't allowed to use the subway.

A rendering of a loaf of bread means: "Jews in Berlin may only buy food between four and five o'clock in the afternoon."

IT'S TIME FOR LUNCH AND a glassy window full of luxurious meats, cheeses, and sweets catches my eye. As I cross the street, I pass by a childlike rendering of dessert. The back side reads: "In bakeries and cafes, signs must be posted stating that Jews and Poles may not purchase cakes."

A little bell rings as I pull open the heavy door. The smell inside prompts a wave of nostalgia. There are great loaves of butter and piles of salamis studded with fat and peppercorns. I choose a Bündnerfleisch more beautiful than the one from the German deli of my childhood, where I bought a couple of slices of cured meat at a time and let them melt in my mouth before taking the bus home with a new pair of jeans.

The city charms me into a stupor. Because Berlin is smart and conceptual and sophisticated, I can eat. I can sleep. I'm even getting used to the sound of the language, at first so alarming. Nothing seems to pierce the pleasant bubble around me. Less than an hour's car ride away, in Oranienburg, my father was an inmate of Sachsenhausen concentration camp near the end of the war. In bare feet, he marched on the snow and dug ditches. They whipped him so badly, he was scarred into his life with my mom. I know and I don't know. I avoid looking at the map. I keep the information quarantined in my brain. My bubble takes care of me.

ON OUR LAST DAY IN Berlin, we board our bus for a day trip to Lake Wannsee. Hedy takes the mic and starts to tell her story. When she was a child in Oradea, Romania, she came to school one day to find the border had moved and she was suddenly in Hungary. "You Jews here at the front?" the new teacher said in Hungarian. "Pick up your books and get to the back of the class." In May 1944, the Hungarian police, in collaboration with the German government, started rounding up the Jews of Hungary and deporting them to Auschwitz-Birkenau; almost half a million people in all. Hedy was one of them.

We visit the House of the Wannsee Conference, set on the picturesque lake. I imagine the top brass of the Nazi Party sitting at the heavy wood table, engineering the Final Solution. Everything is elegant and genteel. I can hear the chamber music. I can smell the tea and cake delivered by butlers in white gloves.

That evening, we head to the airport for our flight to Krakow. Germany is behind me, and the worst is probably over. I use up my euros on a few bags of Haribo candy for the kids. The heat wave continues and we're all in our lightest clothes, chatting and fanning ourselves as we wait for the flight.

There's an announcement over the loudspeaker I can barely make out. "What are they saying?" I ask Erika, who's sitting beside me.

"There's a problem with the plane," she says. "Our flight has been canceled."

50

Vodka

Suddenly, beautiful Cindy, the organizer of our trip, is overwhelmed with logistical problems. Two red circles appear on her cheeks as she scrambles through the hot airport trying to get twenty-five people, plus an eighty-eight-year-old Holocaust survivor, from Berlin to Krakow in time to begin touring concentration camps the next morning.

I want to be a good friend, but when Cindy announces that we'll be busing through the night, something bursts inside me. I know she needs me to act like a supportive participant, an adult, a normal human being, but a toxic sludge is leaking into my limbs. I start to shake. Fear rises in my chest. I cannot go on a bus. A bus is too much like a train and a train is really just a cattle car and since my father made the reverse journey, from Poland to Germany, with no food or water for ten days, ending up in Sachsenhausen with a train full of new corpses, nobody in my family was ever going to travel that way again. The trip was supposed to be plush and comfortable. Cindy promised me and I promised Dad.

"You've been to Poland," he said wearily when I first told him I was going on Cindy's trip. "Why do you have to go again?"

"Don't worry, Dad," I said. "This is going to be a nice trip, a very comfortable trip."

"You're going to the camps, aren't you?"

"Yes, but the travel will be first-rate. The hotels, restaurants, flights. All very high-end."

"Okay," he sighed. "Don't be afraid to order the most expensive thing on the menu. You don't have to suffer. Have some fun."

THERE ARE FAMOUS STORIES OF women going back to the camps in their most expensive designer clothes, in every piece of jewelry they own. Diamond rings, ropes of gold. They're willing to return, maybe they even want to return, but only if they can separate themselves from the pain and degradation they were forced to endure. They wrap themselves in armor of precious metal and silk and dignity to say, *Fuck you. I am beautiful. I survived.*

"You go ahead," I say to Cindy, standing in the hall of the airport. "I'll wait until there's a flight and join you tomorrow. Can I keep Hedy with me?" It makes absolutely no sense and Cindy just stares at me. "Or maybe I'll catch a flight home from here?" She lets out a little laugh and I resist the urge to shake her.

IT'S A LONG TRIP ON the bus through the night. I settle up front with Hedy, whether to watch over her or to have her watch over me, I'm not sure. Someone gives me an Ativan and I sleep fitfully, like a child with a fever. I dream that I'm dreaming I'm on a bus headed straight for hell.

When we get to Krakow, it's pouring rain and the driver lets us off a block from the hotel. I'm confused. I'm crying. Lis takes my hand and leads me to the lobby. It's a modern prison of concrete floors and sharp up-lighting.

LATER THAT EVENING—OR MAYBE IT'S the next night—I feel a little better. The Ativan has worn off and I've had a shower. I've sat in the cinder block stairwell, phone pressed to my ear, listening to Michael's voice. "I can't, I can't," I moaned.

"Yes, you can."

I'm looking for Stacey's room. Inside, she's pouring shots of vodka and playing music. Most of the women are there. At the center of it all is Hedy, lying on the bed like a queen, head and shoulders on a stack of pillows. Her skin is wrapped in a Sephora face mask. Just her vivid eyes show through. "Hi, darling," she says, reaching for my hand. Some of the other girls are in the bathroom, unwrapping their own face masks.

Tomorrow, we go to Auschwitz. We need to look our best.

THERE ARE BEAUTIFUL PLACES TO visit in this world. Places that make you feel free and alive. Places that soften your rough edges. When my parents took us to Hawaii, we watched the pink sun sink into the ocean from the balcony of the hotel. We weren't a family that took many photos. "Don't worry about the camera," Dad would say. "Take a mental picture. Remember this beauty." As the bus careens toward Auschwitz, my mind clicks through a set of slides. My mother's pretty plant garden in the living room. The color of the rhubarb in the backyard. Dad's glittering ravine at night. Those Hawaii sunsets.

IT'S RAINING AGAIN, AND I'M chilled all the way to my bones despite my wool sweater and raincoat. We walk through the gates: ARBEIT MACHT FREI. Barbed wire everywhere. I want to grab the metal and pierce my finger. Train tracks, watchtowers, deep gray mud. A mountain of empty shoes. A pile of dead people's eyeglasses. A pyramid of gas canisters. Zyklon B, the labels say.

In the bathroom, a splotch of blood on my underwear. I'm forty-nine and I haven't had a period for more than a year.

The concrete walls of the gas chamber are covered in gouges from people's bare fingers, where they tried to climb out when the gas came on. Which ones are Udel's? There seems to be a smell although there is no smell.

In one of the barracks, there are books of names, millions of names. The R book opens itself to the right page and my finger is on our name in a matter of seconds. Everyone is there. Udel and my aunties: Chana, Nachama, Machla, and Devorah. Someone in an office somewhere, creating the lists for these books, didn't know that my dad survived. "Szlama Rajchbart, place of death unknown," I read. Rajchbart. This was what we were called in Poland before Dad passed through one of dozens of checkpoints. Before someone, on purpose or by accident, changed our name to a reflection of the Third Reich.

I'M IN BIRKENAU, SUDDENLY, THREE and a half kilometers away. Did we walk? The sterile museum feeling of Auschwitz is gone. The camp doesn't seem empty. In one of the barracks, I sit close to Hedy and eye the rows of bunks like stacked wooden coffins. I want to get up and check them, but I can't move. I catch only fragments of Hedy's testimony. Her mother is taken away. Hedy calls out, but her mother doesn't turn around. She forces herself to eat soup of dirt and rocks. When she's chosen for slave labor at a factory, there is a bit more bread. In the shower, she doesn't know if water or gas will come out.

Under one of these buildings, there's a hole in the ground where my father hid one night, listening to screaming and gunfire as barracks were emptied. I won't look for it. People are chatting, maybe someone coughs. I'm on the other side of a thick glass wall.

As I stand in front of the crematorium, I close my eyes and see a long lineup of naked skeletons. The women shiver in the cold, their breasts sagging and puckered. The men are behind barbed wire.

A gust of Udel—in my hair, on my skin, then she's gone.

BACK AT THE HOTEL, MY limbs are like lead. I feel the grit of ashes everywhere—in my eyes, in the treads of my running shoes. Just inside the door of my room, I strip off my clothes, shoes, and socks, and walk to the bathroom, where I turn on the shower. The room starts to steam up around me, but I'm glued to the tile floor, staring at myself in the mirror. I stand there for I don't know how long, watching my image disappear in the fogging mirror. *No shower,* I think, and walk naked to the front door where I collect my clothes and stuff everything—T-shirt, sweater, jeans, socks, and shoes—into the little garbage by the desk. I turn off the water and put my heavy body to bed.

The next morning, I feel more like myself. I lie in bed, picturing my wooden countertops and green glass mixing bowl at home. I think about plum cakes with icing sugar and sour cherries simmering in syrup. I want to put on a summer dress and listen to music and drink cold white wine. I want to have dinner with Michael by candlelight. Because I'm my father's daughter, I want to fight the shittiest of the shit with what I know to be whole and beautiful and alive.

Instead, we're back on the bus. I've abandoned any effort to be social with the others, who are laughing and chatting around ten rows back. The wheels crunch on gravel as the bus comes to a stop. "Okay, watch your step getting off," our guide says.

We've arrived at a forest near Tykocin, in northeast Poland. On the morning of August 24, 1941, the German army announced that the town's Jewish population, about 1,400 people, were to report to the square the next day. The soldiers told the people they were going to be transferred to the Bialystok Ghetto. Instead, they were marched to enormous pits in this forest. Each man, woman, and child was forced to stand in front of a pit and shot, their bodies piling up in the holes.

IT'S ANOTHER GRAY DAY. OVERCAST but still. Hedy, who has been to the forest with the march half a dozen times, puts her hand over mine and says, "I think you should stay here with me. This place is very bad." Her fingers are cool and strong, dotted with age spots.

I know the facts, but I don't feel them. "Don't worry," I say as I grab my jacket. "I've already been to the worst place. My family didn't die here. This isn't going to bother me."

Alongside Lis and Erika, I walk to a clearing. There isn't much to see. A square iron fence encloses the mass grave site, dotted with half-burned memorial candles left by past visitors. There are a few individual headstones and brass plates with lists of names scattered around.

We are lighting candles for a prayer when I feel it somewhere in my spine: a vibration that travels up and down at the same time. My hands and feet turn cold and heavy, there's a whooshing noise in my head. What is happening? I look from face to face—who else can feel it? Nobody's expression has changed. I can't stand there a moment longer. I'm already moving when I call, "I'm going back to the bus," over my shoulder.

The walk in couldn't have taken more than ten minutes, but now I can't find the path. I take a few steps to the right and peer through the tree trunks—not familiar. I turn and start off in the other direction—that looks wrong, too. A wind has picked up and the birch trees—the tallest, skinniest, saddest birches I've ever seen, naked except for a puff of leaves at their tops—start to shake and sway. My heart pounds and my knees threaten to give way. Where is the path? "Hello?" I yell, but my voice is taken by the wind. The forest swallows me as I run this way and that, searching for a way out.

When, finally, I scramble onto the bus, Hedy is waiting. "Oh god," I tell her. Tears are streaming down my face. "You were right. All the people are still here."

"Come sit beside me," she says, and she covers me in her extra sweater.

THE NEXT DAY, WE ARE headed for Warsaw. Only two more sleeps until I can go home, but first, Cindy has arranged a stop in Lodz. I'm holding a page of Dad's testimony, recorded by the Jewish archives of Edmonton in 1985. I'm going to read three paragraphs about life in the ghetto to the group. My voice shakes and I think I might throw up, but I get through it. After, there are hugs and hand squeezes. Someone gives me a bottle of water.

Cindy has booked lunch at a nearby restaurant. I'm walking between Lis and Stacey, chatting happily, feeling good, when our guide stops. "Hold on," he says. "Let's wait for the rest of the group. I want to tell you something." He's an excellent guide, full of knowledge and trivia, and he often adds bits and pieces as they occur to him.

It's only when the rest of the group catches up that he draws our attention to the right. "Look at this church," he says. "St. Mary's." It's a soaring red-brick building with two slender towers, clocks, and a series of pointed arches. I don't hear much of what he says after that because attached to the building is a laminated page with the following written in Polish, English, Hebrew, and Yiddish:

St. Mary's Parish Church.
BETWEEN 1940 AND 1944, BY ORDER OF THE GERMAN OCCUPYING AUTHORITIES, IT WAS A SORTING STATION AND A DEPOT FOR ROBBED JEWISH PROPERTY.

As I peer through the glass at the dark wood pews, arched ceiling, and ornate geometric floor, my mouth goes dry. I know exactly what I'm looking at. *In the Lodz Ghetto, I had a job, such a good job!* Dad said as I lay in the back seat of the car. *The Germans brought in all these pillows and blankets, and my job was to open them. The feathers were everywhere, all in the air. Sometimes there were jewels in the pillows—big diamonds and gold and money, just waiting for me to find them. We did this sorting in a beautiful church.*

I yank on the handle but the door is locked. "Dad," I whisper, pressing my face to the glass, "I found your church."

THREE DAYS LATER, I WAKE up in my own bed at 4 a.m. Jet lag. I pad down to the kitchen, make a delicious cup of coffee, look at the moon shining into the dark yard. My whole body thrums with relief and gratitude. In a few hours, Dad will be up and I'll go there to have breakfast. I want to show him the photos I took. I want to show him his church.

51

The Tram

Two weeks later, I'm driving up the 400 alone, windows down, Lucinda Williams in my hair. The late September air feels soft and warm. We've sold the old cabin and we're closing on a new one. High above the ribbon of highway, hawks circle and swoop and soar, ready to grab what they need to survive.

I turn from highway to unpaved road, road to shady lane, until I make a right into the driveway and stop the car on a gravel parking pad. The yellow light pours down on everything—the dark log cabin with its sloped tin roof, the shimmering lake, my bare shoulders. The cabin has a wraparound porch and a screened-in room for playing cards at twilight. It's the kind of place people have in their families for generations. Maybe we can become those people.

The car is full of stuff—sheets and new pots and pans, apples and plums and a half bushel of field tomatoes. Later on, movers will come with a truckload of our furniture and books from storage, things I packed and put away before leaving for Berlin. Tomorrow, Michael and the kids will arrive and we'll celebrate our new getaway. I'll celebrate the hole I've punched in the ceiling of my terror. The light pours through.

I drag a towel from my bag and skip down to the lake on the stone path, through bear grass and patches of black-eyed Susans. Leaving my clothes on the dock, I slip into the new lake for the first time.

LIFE EVOLVES, SOMETIMES DRAMATICALLY, SOMETIMES imperceptibly. When I take a notebook and start writing in coffee shops, somehow, it's both. My pen skips across the page as the daily grind fills my nose. It feels strange not to be told what to say. It feels rebellious and free.

By winter, peace gives way to turmoil. I arrive at Mom and Dad's to find Dad gray-faced and shaky. Mom's illness has taken over, and her agitation is out of control. She can't eat or sleep. She thinks Dad, her best friend for sixty years, is plotting against her. There are no options—we have to find long-term care for her.

I'd like to lock myself in a room and just breathe, but more things happen. Julie learns that an archivist from the United States Holocaust Memorial Museum in Washington, D.C., is coming to Toronto, and she arranges an appointment. At a boardroom table in the Jewish community center, my sisters and I tell the archivist everything we do and don't know about Dad's background: only survivor of a family of eight, ghettoed in Pabianice, then Lodz; sent to Auschwitz-Birkenau; selected for slave labor in Gleiwitz, then Sachsenhausen. Liberated in a field the day the war ended. "Anything else?" the archivist says, taking notes. We don't think so. "Well, we'll see," she says. The museum has access to a vast database of records and documents. "We prioritize survivors who are living," she says. "Give me a few weeks."

WE ARE IN THE MIDST of moving Mom when a zip file labeled "Szlama Rajchbart" shows up in my email. The message sits in my inbox like a black hole. My sisters look at the records, chat about them and move on, but I can't even open the file. I'm afraid of being sucked in.

All I want is to get back to a set of short stories I'm working on when the pandemic sweeps in like a tidal wave, turning our house into an island with flood waters on all sides. Jamie lives in his own place in the West End now but Michael, Maya, Leo, and I—plus our dog, Bruno—are in the house twenty-four hours a day. My coffee shop closes. I wander from kitchen table to second-floor nook to living room, but the sound of three other people on Zoom finds me everywhere.

My frustration is cresting when I meet someone with an empty studio. Would I like to rent a desk? The city is locked down and it's probably against the law, but I pack up my books, pens, notebooks, and laptop and drive to the address she's given me. I let myself in with her key and set up at the desk nearest the front. A few people come and go, ignoring me in the best possible way.

I think I'm there to work on my fiction when, not even a week later, I find myself clicking on the email from the Holocaust museum and holding my breath.

The zip file contains over thirty items, most in German, a few in French and English. There are index cards filled out with an old typewriter and many, many lists. A few forms look like the report cards I brought home in elementary school, but instead of checkmarks beside skills like reading and math, Dad has earned a tick for every camp and checkpoint he has passed through. There is a handwritten list of names titled "Inmates of Flossenbürg," a place I've never heard of, and many records from the Lodz Ghetto.

I forget about my short stories and tape together several sheets of paper to create a horizontal timeline that I pin to the wall of the studio. 1939, 1941, 1943 . . . Using the documents, a map, and the stories I know by heart, I scrawl keywords on different pages: "cholent, Udel, church, Mr. Sharp."

A FOUR-HOUR DAY AT THE studio becomes six hours, then eight. The weather is mild but I wrap myself in sweaters and scarves to ward off a chill that seems to rise from the work itself. I begin to do the kind of research I've avoided my whole life. I still can't watch Dad's video testimony, but I've printed the transcript, which I read in little chunks.

I find cousin Abe's testimony on YouTube, and I watch with my heart in my throat. His family was forced from their home in Lodz into a tiny apartment in the ghetto in 1940, two years ahead of Dad's. Food was so scarce, they made soup for the whole family with one piece of bread, and "cakes" out of flour mixed with coffee grounds. One after another, his brother and father and mother got sick from disease and starvation and died in the little apartment. His sister was taken away and he never saw her again. By August 1944, Abe, then alone, had found Dad and his family, and hid with them as the ghetto was being liquidated. Days or weeks later, they were put on a train to Auschwitz-Birkenau.

ABOUT TEN DAYS IN, I start digging around on the Holocaust museum website. There are dozens of articles and documents about the Lodz Ghetto. Instead of the general stuff I'm expecting, the information is specific and detailed. The more I click, the more I recognize—stories, places, dates, names. Everything begins to coalesce. I open a new file on my computer and start to write.

> *A boy of eleven gets on the tram bound for Lodz. It had finally stopped raining but it doesn't make a difference—he's drenched down to his skin, socks squishing in his shoes. He's shivering, but somehow sweating, too. Although it had open sides, the car is packed and airless. He smells wet fabric and fear. The date is May 17, 1942.*
>
> *He doesn't understand why the Germans made them stand all night in the sports field. Is that what a war is? Standing closer and closer together in a clump as old people and little kids are taken away? Baba looked so small next to the soldiers as they march her off with the other old people. Nothing like the boss she usually is at dinner on Friday nights. Where were they*

taking her? Mama made him crouch down so he wouldn't be taken away, too. He got stepped on and muddy but it worked. He is still here.

This all started two years ago, when the soldiers made them leave their big apartment and fit into two little rooms in the dirty part of Pabianice. That was when he found out what the word "ghetto" meant. They moved in such a rush, he forgot his Shabbos shoes. Now they're moving again. He doesn't know where.

His eyes dart around the car full of people. In the time since all the Jews packed into those few old apartment buildings, he's gotten to know the faces better. Neighbors, shopkeepers, friends. But now the familiar faces look strange, wet with tears and staring at nothing in the gray light.

Mama faces him, but there are so many people in between, he can't see her. He shifts, he stands on his tiptoes. As soon as he finds her dark eyes, her face changes and she smiles a tiny smile. It's like she was waiting for him to look. Chana is beside Mama, holding Devorah under a shawl. Beside her, Nachama carries a soggy paper bag in her arms. One bag of belongings for the whole family. He took Daddy's tallis and left the rest.

His stomach grumbles. When did he eat last? It was before they were marched to the stadium yesterday afternoon. "Shlo-imeleh," Mama said as they hurried to put on their coats, "have this." With his sisters watching, he unwrapped bread and schmaltz she'd saved from lunch, tore a piece and put it in his mouth. "Anyone?" All the sisters shook their heads and looked at their shoes. In the street below, the soldiers screamed in their terrible language. He hated their red-and-black arm-bands and snarling dogs. Every morning since moving into the ghetto, they'd had to line up while the soldiers pointed their guns. The first time he saw them shoot someone, he thought it was pretend. A popping sound, then a man just collapsing in a pile. It was only when they dragged him away, leaving a long smear of blood on the dusty road, that he understood it was real.

As the tram shifts, he feels Machla leaning against his shoulder. He can hold her up—they call him "The Bull" at cheder. Is she sleeping standing up? He pokes her in the ribs and she opens one eye, pokes him back and closes it again.

They were lucky to have Polish friends, Mama said. Every time there was going to be an aktion to round up boys, she sent him to the hiding spot. He didn't want to go with the little white-haired man, but she said to be brave. How often did he hide in the man's shed, beside the moldy potatoes and dusty suitcases? Twice? Three times? In the morning, when the barking and screaming finally stopped, Chana came and walked him home. It didn't take long to figure out which kids had been taken away.

He thinks about the big apartment on Kosciuszki Street, where Baba owned the whole building, and cousin Mickey lived a floor below. Baba and Zaida Mendel had been rich once, but when the Depression came they lost almost everything. At least they still had the store.

A lot of people in the Pabianice ghetto didn't have enough to eat, but Mama had a lot of friends. The Czech lady snuck in to trade loaves of bread for their old fur coats. Customers from the store passed them packages of food when the guards weren't looking, or came in late at night to exchange potatoes for rings and bracelets. Their store had even more stuff they could trade or sell—paints and tools and hardware—but the Germans took the most valuable things and wouldn't let them go there, anyway.

Will there be lunch where they're going? His legs are weak and his mouth watering as he stands on the packed tram, wondering when Mama will make piterkuchen again.

Over someone's shoulder, he can see a patch of sky. Trees whizz by, their leaves small and a bright shade of green. It reminds him of the time he went to the woods with his father. In his head, he keeps a list of what he can remember: A red beard, long, but not as long as the rebbe's. Daddy always busy, either working at the store, studying with the other men, or resting because of his weak heart.

It was like magic, that one time Daddy let him come to the pension in the woods. Daddy sang as he packed his clothes in a burlap sack. "V'taher libenu . . ." In the daytime, they picked cherries and blueberries. At night, they walked in the forest with a candle to keep away the bad spirits. They slept in a little cabin, just the two of them.

He tries not to think of the deep hole in the ground and the banging sound as the clumps of dirt hit the top of Daddy's coffin. "I'm sorry," he wanted to say as they covered Daddy with soil. "Come back and I'll be good." It wasn't his fault; Daddy just had a weak heart, Mama said. Still, he wondered if his father died because of something bad he did.

The car slows and he shifts again to see where they are. Choppy as the movie he went to once, images drift by. People moving, dragging carts. Are they behind a screen? They seem fuzzy and far away. The tram stops and soldiers stride up to the car. They start pulling people off, yelling in German. He loses sight of Mama, Chana, and Nachama. Machla takes his hand and they jump off before anyone can shove or pull them.

"Here!" Mama calls. In a confusing mess of parents searching for children and husbands looking for wives, she's standing with Chana and Nachama. Their skirts almost hide Devorah, sitting on the ground.

Someone is shouting at them in Polish to get in line. As they wait and wait, he looks around. What is this place? The sign says Lodz, but it's a different Lodz from where he once visited Abe's family. He studies the metallic screen he noticed from the train. He realizes it's a fence, stretching as far as his eye can see, and very high. All along it are little red-and-white houses with black stripes. At the front of the line, there's a woman with a yellow armband. She sits at a table, a big book open in front of her.

"Name?"

"Rajchbart," Mama says.

"I need each person separately. You are?"

"Udel."[2]

52

Coffee Grounds

When I come home from the studio in the evenings, I feel like I've been mining in a cave. I don't talk about what I'm doing and I wash my hands compulsively, lest I smudge filth over the people I love. "Just tired," I tell my sweet children when they look at me with concern. Making dinner becomes the best part of the day, even when I can't eat it. I watch my family devour osso buco with lemon zest, beef bourguignon with a crisp endive salad. I bake crumbles and fruit galettes for dessert. I lie in bed, praying for a dreamless sleep before I haul myself back to my desk the next morning, pick-axe in hand.

> One by one, they step up to the lady and tell their names and when they were born. She writes it all in the book. He remembers to give the birthday Mama told him to use, January 5, 1925, instead of his real one, December 17, 1930, because older is better. He takes a deep breath and throws back his shoulders as he says it. Beside each of their names, she writes "Cranach 30, apartment 15."
>
> Another person with a yellow armband and a stick leads

them across the road toward the fence and one of the little houses with black stripes. He can see now the fence is very sharp, with spikes sticking out. A soldier in a long coat with a lot of buttons and a big gun comes out and opens the gate. The man with the stick holds it up over Mama's head and she hurries them in. The metal gate clangs shut behind them. The soldier locks it with a key that hangs from his belt on a chain.

"What is this place?" Shlomo asks softly.

"Ghetto," Mama whispers.

Ghetto? In Pabianice, the ghetto had no guards. Of course, they were told if they tried to leave they would get shot, but the Germans were always saying that. Sometimes they shot and sometimes they didn't.

This is different. He feels like an animal in a cage. When will they be able to leave? He starts to shiver again. Devorah is crying softly but Mama tells Chana to put her down. "They're watching," Mama whispers. "She should look like a big girl." As they walk down the rutted path, weak sunlight leaks from behind a cloud. They pass people carrying things, hurrying, looking down. Not one street is familiar. Not one face. They walk in silence. In the distance he sees a bench on a patch of brown grass. Maybe it's a park. He squints but he can't make out what's on the bench. Is that fabric? Old clothes? As he gets closer, he sees the clothes are sitting upright. A zap of electricity shoots through his body. The clothes have feet and sunken faces. One skeleton brings a shaking hand to its face.

Their new apartment is a single room with a kitchen. If you pull the little beds down from the wall, you can't walk anywhere. There is no water and a bucket for a toilet. Mama goes into the hallway and comes back to say there is one water tap out there for the whole building to share.

That evening, they take the ration cards they were given when they arrived and line up for food. Nobody speaks to them. When they get to the front of the line, an old woman gives Mama one tin bowl of soup. "But we are six," Mama says. The woman just shakes her head. They pass the bowl around in the apartment, each person taking a few spoonfuls of soup and a little bite of potato. "We are all together," Mama says. "That's the important thing. Tomorrow, we'll find more food." They squish into two hard beds. Shlomo closes his eyes, but the moving skeleton comes back over and over again. Someone is crying softly. He doesn't know who.

The studio is closed on Saturdays—I have no choice but to take a break. I drive out to the McMichael Canadian Art Collection, in a different jurisdiction that is not locked down. It's autumn and I follow the leaf-covered path to the sculpture garden, trying to soak up the good after a week immersed in bad.

It's no use. My shoulders are up around my ears, and I'm racked with anxiety. I've been asking Dad questions over the phone, tentatively at first but with growing intensity. He tells me whatever he remembers like it's no big deal, but he's already had at least one nightmare because of my digging. It suddenly feels tenuous, this stability of his. Maybe I should leave everything alone. My old writer's block rears its head and I begin to wonder if I'm up to the task I've begun. If I'm good enough.

Inside the gallery, I stand in front of a painting called Mt. Lefroy by Lawren Harris. "By confounding scale, amplifying depth, and limiting colours, Harris created idealized mountains that are as bold, big and abstract as anything painted in Canada at the time," reads the description. It's a strange place to find inspiration, this Group of Seven painting from 1930, but something clicks. I see that Harris didn't try to create a photographic replica of what was in front of him. He leaned into his subjectivity to turn reality into something new. That's what makes the work his own creation. I take Sunday to rest and when Monday comes, I get back to work.

Shlomo wakes up in the dark and hurries into his threadbare clothes. It's almost winter now, and he puts on two pairs of socks to help with the holes in his shoes. He ignores the hollow feeling in his stomach. It's part of him now. In his old life, children didn't work but he now understands something he didn't know before. If you don't work, you don't eat.

Everyone except Mama is asleep. He finds her in the cold kitchen making a cake with pulverized potato peels, coffee grounds, and a tiny sprinkle of flour. "Wait and I'll give you a piece to take with you."

"No thanks, Mama. I have to go." When he hugs her good-bye, he can feel the shape of the bones in her shoulders.

The huge red church on Zgierska Street is over a kilometer away, at the edge of the ghetto. The air is cool but not as cold as it will become. People are saying there's no wood or coal in the ghetto. How will they keep warm?

As he picks his way through the slushy path, he thinks about all that's happened since they came here last spring. He'd never been as hungry or afraid as he was in those first months. They lined up for food every day. About half the time, they got bread and soup. Other times, nothing. You never knew when you would be the ones to come home with empty bowls. The Pabianice ghetto seems like paradise compared to this. There are no neighbors, good Poles or Czechs. They aren't allowed to have school, so there are no friends.

He's not sure when he started to swell up. One night he was taking off his socks and shoes and Chana saw his ankles, fat as an old lady's.

"Mama!" her voice was loud and high.

When Mama came over, she pressed a finger into his stretched, shiny skin. The mark stayed there for a while before slowly disappearing. He was confused to see tears in her eyes.

"What's wrong, Mama?"

But she was already in the kitchen, slamming the empty cupboard doors.

Only later did he realize being swollen meant you're on your way to dying from hunger. Sometime after that he started spitting out blood. Chana took him to the ghetto hospital, but the doctor said it was a nosebleed, not TB. She was so happy, she kissed him over and over. He didn't know what "TB" meant.

He sloshes past the ghosts sitting on the cold bench. Now he knows they're not dead yet, because every night, the bodies are collected and wheeled to the cemetery. Unless they just died this morning? He looks away.

At last, he walks over the Juden bridge and arrives at the church. The sun is just coming up and he can see his breath. After a guard checks his work card, he opens the huge door and steps inside. The church is warm and quiet, with tall curved ceilings and fancy lights hanging down. Sunlight comes through a colored window, turning tiles on the floor green and blue. All of the seats have been ripped out. The day's work is already piled in the center of the floor. A few of his co-workers have begun to arrive, rubbing their hands together.

They don't talk much as they get to work. Pillows, comforters, quilts, and feather beds—they cut them all open with big knives and try to sort the feathers—chicken in one place, higher quality down somewhere else. Where this bedding has come from he doesn't know, but he heard the Germans send the feathers back to Germany to make new pillows, quilts, and comforters.

By midday, feathers are in the air and on everyone's clothes. Someone comes with a pail of soup for lunch. It's much thicker than the rations, with not just peels but real potatoes. He slips his ration of bread into his pocket.

———

"Hi, Dad, I'm downstairs."

"Come up," his voice booms from my cellphone.

"I'm not allowed into your place. Remember? The pandemic."

"Oh right, I'm coming down."

He walks out of his seniors' residence in a black down-filled coat and soft leather shoes. I jump out of the car and open the passenger door. He slides onto the seat and I put his cane between his knees before closing the door.

"Where should we go?"

"I don't know. Maybe we'll just sit here for a moment." He wants action. I want to live in the spaces between action.

"Can we go out for a nice lunch?"

"Everything is closed. The pandemic, remember?" I leave the car in park and dig out my pen and notebook. "Maybe we can just talk for a little while."

"What are you writing?" he says, watching me take the cap off the pen and fumble around for a hard surface.

"I'm not sure."

"Is it a book?"

"It might be a book." The car is quiet. I hear the low thrum of traffic from Eglinton.

"Is the book going to tell my story?"

"Maybe? Sort of? Yours and mine; our stories."

"Okay, what do you want to know?"

THE WORK IS FLOWING NOW, unspooling like a film I watch in my mind. I sit down at my desk in the studio and sift through printouts of documents, testimony, articles. I don't make decisions about what to write, or what is good enough. My fingers just type.

> As they get back to work, a stranger comes into the church. He wears a brown coat, almost new, and shiny boots up to his knees. Except for the yellow star, he doesn't look like a Jew.

"I need a helper," announces the handsome man.

Volunteering can be dangerous. You might get a reward; you might get shot. The other workers, adults mostly, look down, suddenly busy. Before he has even decided what to do, his arm goes up and he hears himself say, "Me."

The man steps closer and studies him for a moment. "Okay, you. My name is Mr. Sharp. Come with me."

The man strides to the front of the church and steps up on the altar. Shlomo follows, his soup suddenly feeling heavy in his stomach. What if he's made a terrible mistake? "You see this Madonna," Mr. Sharp says, pointing to a red-and-gold-painted lady made of wood, "and these big crosses? We're going to move them." Shlomo runs out of the church to find a cart. When he returns, he and Mr. Sharp pile up the heavy crosses and the statue. "Now follow me."

Shlomo stumbles along behind Mr. Sharp as he pulls the cart on the bumpy road, struggling to keep everything from tumbling out. They're walking through a part of the ghetto he's never seen. The apartment buildings are not so dirty and the people aren't on top of each other. There are no skeletons in the street. At Mr. Sharp's house, they carry the things from the church inside. "Put it all beside the fireplace," he says. As he brings in the last cross, a lady comes out of the bedroom, dressed in a skirt and a clean blouse.

"This is Shlomo," says Mr. Sharp. "He brought our firewood for the winter."

"Hi, Shlomo." She smiles. "Are you hungry?"

As he leaves Mr. Sharp's house, Shlomo carries a whole loaf of bread inside his coat. "Come back after work at the church tomorrow," Mr. Sharp says as he closes the door.

Three, four, five more times, Shlomo works for Mr. Sharp. One night he comes to Mr. Sharp's place and Mr. Rumkowski is there, the boss of the whole ghetto! There seems to be a party going on. There are a lot of people, plates of food, and music.

"This is my friend Shlomo," Mr. Sharp says, introducing him to the adults. "He's an amazing kid. Brave. Strong." Shlomo can't believe what he's seeing. These are the powerful Jews who help Mr. Rumkowski run the ghetto. The Jewish police, the factory bosses, the town council.

Much later, he'll learn that it was Rumkowski who worked them so hard, in a plan to make the Lodz Ghetto too essential to the German war effort to liquidate. He'll find out that when Rumkowski was finally deported to Auschwitz, the Jews there killed him before the Germans could, for his role in sending thousands of Jews from the ghetto to their deaths to satisfy Nazi quotas. He'll decide not to judge whether Rumkowski was a corrupt monster or another person who saved his life.

At the party, Mr. Rumkowski's friends are well-dressed and relaxed. You can only tell they're Jews by their yellow stars. Mr. Sharp lets him stay as late as he wants. Someone gives him a fat, juicy sausage, the best traif he's ever had.

53

Butter

Dad and I work together all winter. Sometimes I interview him on FaceTime, sometimes in the car, sometimes the lockdown lets up and we sit at his little table with steaming cups in front of us. He likes something sweet with his coffee so I bake—brownies or cookies or buttery biscuits. I'm worried about the day he'll ask me to read him everything I've written. I don't want to keep it from him, but it's not ready. *I'm* not ready. That day doesn't come. He gives and gives—stories, dates, memories—not once demanding to see what I'm doing with them. Finally, I have to ask: "Aren't you anxious to see what I'm writing?"

"When you're ready," he says.

"But what if I write something you don't like?"

Like some kind of Talmudic scholar, he answers my question with a question. "Do you know what unconditional love is?"

And because he trusts me, I trust myself, putting more and more words on the page, fulfilling the role that has been mine since the very beginning. Nothing short of a full reckoning with the past could have conquered my fear, but real growth calls for one more step. Leaving the world of the frightened child, leaving confusion and powerlessness, I'm finally able to own the role of storyteller. I scour my soul for pain—not out of guilt or duty or responsibility—but as a means to my own transformation. There is empowerment in this role. And freedom. Sometimes even joy. The joy of finding your purpose and knowing, absolutely, that you are doing what you are meant to do.

One day, Mr. Sharp says, "Shlomo, do you have a family?"

Within a week, everyone has a job. Chana goes to a factory to make corsets. Nachama becomes a hatmaker. For Machla, Mr. Sharp finds wonderful work in a kitchen full of food, peeling potatoes and cooking soup for rations. Best of all, Mama gets a job in the big yard that distributes food.

The lineup for daily soup rations is less terrible. They take their little metal containers and when they get to the front of the line, there's Mama, giving them a ladle full of potatoes instead of watery soup. She has to be careful because there is always a policeman standing over her, but Mama is smart.

Devorah is only ten but even she has a job now, as a pupil with older children in the huge tailoring workshop. They are learning to sew underwear and dresses, for whom he doesn't know. Nobody in the ghetto is getting new clothes. The man in charge lets her in even though she's below the required age. Now, when Mr. Rumkowski announces that children who aren't working have to leave the ghetto, Mama can say, "All my children are working."

Things in the ghetto aren't better for everyone. Sometimes he sees ten, twelve, fifteen starved bodies on the cart in the morning. It takes three or four people to push it to the cemetery. At work one day, a man says he saw the Germans empty the hospital. A soldier drove up with a big truck and two more threw children from windows on the second and third floors into the back of the truck. Live children.

One winter morning, he arrives at the church completely numb. The apartment is so cold, the water in the hallway tap is frozen, and his layers of clothes are falling apart. As his fingers and toes defrost in the warm church, he gets to work. As usual, he takes a knife, cuts open a pillow and throws the feathers on the table. But today, something makes a muted clunk against the wood. What was that? Sifting through the pile of down, his fingers touch something hard.

He looks up, but nobody is watching. He closes his hand around the small round shape, drags his fist across the table, and drops the object into his pants. For the rest of the day, he imagines his right side heavier, dragging toward the ground. Finally, he hurries home in the dark, slipping his fingers into his pocket and touching the now-icy metal again and again. He doesn't dare pull it out in the filthy street.

He bursts into the apartment, calling for Mama, but she's already at the door. She's just gotten home herself. "What, Shlomo? What is it?"

Fingers trembling, he digs into his pocket and pulls out the object: a gold ring.

"Oh god! Where did you get that?"

"I found it at work."

As he describes the feathers, the pocket, the walk home, Mama slips the ring onto her index finger. It doesn't sit flat. It's too big and the stone in the center makes it turn on her bony finger.

"It's a diamond," she says in a whisper. "Shloimeleh, you found a diamond ring."

Mama knows of a man, a Jewish policeman, who buys the things people find. It's forbidden, of course. Everything is supposed to be surrendered. Every day, people are shot for much less.

The next night, as everyone gets ready for bed, Mama puts on her coat.

"I want to go," Shlomo says.

"It's too dangerous for you." Mama pulls Chana's knit cap low over her forehead.

"It's too dangerous for you," he says, but she has already slipped out of the apartment.

He doesn't know how long she's gone. Devorah falls asleep, then Machla. Finally, the apartment door creaks open and Mama comes in, eyes shining, cheeks red. From under her coat, she pulls three enormous loaves of bread.

A few times a week now, he finds paper money sewn into pillowcase seams, jewels hidden among feathers. He doesn't know why he never found them before, or if anyone else is finding things. On the day that he brings home a 100-mark note,* Mama lets him go to the black market policeman himself. He hurries home with a half-pound of butter in his coat, thinking of piterkuchen, delirious with joy.

Soon after, Shlomo arrives at work to find the church locked up. Go to the market, a guard orders. His mind races as he walks. Was he spotted with the policeman? Or maybe the policeman told Rumkowski about him? Every day, more and more people disappear. Now he'll be one of them. He's angry at himself for being careless. Mr. Sharp won't be able to help him now.

The ghetto is huge—four square kilometers—and this is a place he's never been, a bustling marketplace. There is a ring of shops with iron gates open to a huge central area, at least a block long. Instead of being sent away, he's put to work im-

---

* The ghetto had its own currency.

mediately, sorting piles and piles of clothes. He doesn't know whose clothes they are and, at first, he's so relieved to have another job, he doesn't care.

After a while, he starts to notice some strange things. He finds a pair of socks, but it isn't one pair, it's three, one inside the other. There isn't one pair of pants, but four, all together. The clothes are bloody. And they are ripped. "What is this clothing all about?" he asks the people who've been there longer. Nobody knows, exactly, but there are stories. Maybe the clothes belonged to people who were sent away, they say, people not allowed to take anything except what they were wearing. One day, he finds a little piece of paper in a pocket. "We are here and they're killing everybody." Where is here? Killed how? Nobody knows.

*The new sorting job doesn't last very long. After a few months, he is transferred to a factory. His job is to carry parcels back and forth. He thinks there are uniforms inside. That lasts a very short time. For a little while after that, he works sorting potatoes in the yard where they give out rations. After that, he doesn't remember working at all, until Gleiwitz.*³

In August 1944, the liquidation of the Lodz Ghetto begins, with all surviving inhabitants sent to Auschwitz. Historians say less than 5 percent of the Jews who lived in the ghetto survived to the end of the war. My father, his mother, his sisters, and cousin Abe spend twelve hours crammed in an open train. As they get off, women and girls are sent to one side, men and boys to the other. My dad and Abe are marched in front of Dr. Mengele, then taken to Birkenau, stripped and shaved. Dad is tattooed with the number B10602. He spends five weeks in the barracks in Birkenau with his cousin, except for the night he hides in the hole. Yom Kippur falls on September 27. Somehow, they have a shofar.

The next day, the Germans round up about two hundred people, including Dad and Abe, and take them by open truck to Gleiwitz. They are forced to dig deep ditches and lay pipes. They fall under the weight. They are beaten.

On January 18, 1945, they are woken up early to march. They march a whole day without stopping. People who can't march are shot. They are not given any food or water, but Dad and Abe find a sack of animal feed—dried corn and wheat—in a barn.

The next day they march again. The road is littered with bodies. They are forced onto a train. People are collapsing; they're only upright because of how tightly they're packed. Dad and Abe bribe their way into a corner so they can lean against the sides of the car. For ten days, there is no food or water or toilets. The train winds through Czechoslovakia, where people stand on a bridge and drop bread into the open cars.

When Dad and Abe arrive in Oranienburg, a subcamp of Sachsenhausen, the train is 90 percent corpses. They can't even walk off—they roll down the ramp. They are so hungry but even more, they are thirsty. They are taken to barracks and given some coffee and food. They are sent to the showers. It could be gas that comes out of the showerheads but they get lukewarm water. They stay for a long time, drinking. Dad's stomach is as big as a balloon. For about a week, they sleep on a concrete floor, dead and sick people together with the living.

In April, they are moved to Ganacker, part of Flossenbürg concentration camp, in open trucks. There is a stone quarry there. They are digging ditches and building an airfield for the Luftwaffe. When they look up, they see planes. One day, they go out to work and the planes come swooping down. Dad thinks they're going to land but, instead, the planes shoot every German plane on the ground. Ammunition stores blow up as local Germans run and hide. Dad and Abe find some potatoes in an abandoned farm and bake them in the fire of a burning plane.

The German soldiers tell Dad and the others that the Russians and Americans are coming, and they all have to run. Again, anyone who can't march is shot. One night, Dad and his cousin find a place to sleep in a big barn with lots of hay. They hide in the loft and pull the ladder up after themselves. On the morning of May 8, they hear voices telling them the Americans have arrived. They don't believe it. When they finally come out, the big jeep with the white star is there, and the jar of green relish Dad eats until he can't eat anymore.[4]

54

Steak Sandwiches

There is a thaw and the air is soft and warm. I put my car in park and dial.

"I'm here," I say into my phone.

"Come up."

"Dad, the pandemic!"

"Oh yeah. Coming."

Today he's wearing a blue paisley shirt, tan trousers, and those old white shoes. His silver hair catches the sun. I open the passenger door and he climbs in. As I walk around to my side, I take a deep breath. The air smells like cut grass.

"Where can we go?" Dad says.

"Hold on." I dig out my pen and notebook. "I've been going over your testimony. Can we talk about Mr. Sharp? He's such a mysterious figure."

"Yes, Mr. Sharp. I think he was a relative of Rumkowski. I wish I could find him."

"What do you remember about him?"

"He had fancy boots."

"Right, I've got that."

"He had a beautiful girlfriend." Dad smiles.

"What was his first name?"

"I don't know. He really took a shine to me."

"Of course he did," I say, gazing at him, waiting for the right moment. Silently, I count to three before my fingers reach into the pocket of my dress and wrap around my phone. I look out my window. I clear my throat. "Dad," I say, finally. "You know I've been doing research with the Holocaust museum in Washington, right?"

"So?" he says, a little absent-mindedly.

"So. I found something." I pull out my phone and tap open an email. I press on the attachment. I stretch the photo to fill the screen before handing it to him.

"What's this?"

"This is your baby sister, Devorah. This is her work card from the ghetto."

His mouth moves, but no sound comes out. He peers at the phone, pulling the image so big that pretty, dark-haired Devorah becomes a set of sepia dots.

"My god," he says. "I have almost no pictures of her."

"I know."

"She was just a baby."

"Yes, she's ten years old."

He wipes a single tear and for a moment, I'm sure I've gone too far. He shakes his head and swears under his breath. "You see how beautiful she is?" His thick index finger jabs at the screen. "Clean and not too thin? We did so well in the ghetto. My mother took such good care of us."

"When was the last time you saw your mother and sisters?"

"On the platform at Birkenau. We made it right to the end in Lodz. We were on one of the last transports."

The car is quiet for a moment. I think about the hardworking ghetto being liquidated despite Rumkowski—or because of him. I think about our family, almost making it, except not. I picture the cattle car they rode in, surrounded by starvation and disease and death. I try to stop thinking before I imagine my grandmother and my aunties in the gas chamber.

Dad rolls down his window and a cloud of relentless chirping drifts in. "Let's go someplace nice to eat," he says, handing me my phone. "Can we go to the Four Seasons?"

"Dad, the pandemic!"

"Well then, where?"

"I think I know a patio that's open. Do you want to do that?"

"What will they have there?"

"Burgers. Steak sandwiches, maybe."

"Yes, let's go," he says. "Let's go have some fun."

PART FIVE

Home Again

55

Walnuts

Mom's home has been locked down and I haven't seen her for weeks. When they finally let me in to help her eat lunch, it isn't really Mom anymore, and it isn't really lunch anymore. She's a stiff shape in a wheelchair. I can coax her to open her mouth by touching a spoon to her lips, like I would a baby. The home purées whatever they've made for the more able residents into mush, and I put it in her mouth. Chicken and carrots and potatoes or, on Friday nights, something that might have been brisket. The food smells good, Dad says, after he's been there. Like Jewish cooking. Sometimes they give him a plate of food, too, not mushed up. He says it's delicious.

But Mom doesn't like brisket and she doesn't like mush. She enjoys tuna tataki and crisp salads. The real Mom likes crunch. She taught me that walnuts were the most important part of a chocolate chip cookie. She gave me the big knife with the triangular blade, handle first, and pulled out the cutting board. Can you chop them, Bon Bon? Not too small. I was using that knife before I could read.

—————

AFTER LUNCH, I TURN MOM'S wheelchair to face the window. I've brought a black-and-gold silk scarf to tie over her drab gray sweat suit. Everything goes in the wash here and stuff gets wrecked. Wool sweaters shrink to a doll's size. Her glamorous nails have been filed down to stumps. There is no system for valuables. "Please take them away," said the manager of the home. We pried her rings off her long fingers and put the jewelry in the safe at Dad's. Sometimes when I visit him, he's sorting it into piles like a kid with Halloween candy. He wants to look at it, play with it, discuss it. I wonder if he's thinking about the jewelry he found in the pillows in the Lodz Ghetto.

TRAFFIC THUNDERS PAST ON SHEPPARD Avenue. I scour my brain to come up with things to engage Mom. How did you sleep? My house needs cleaning. I read her the newspaper, lingering on politics, trying to coax out her strong opinions. Once in a while, she'll moan or shake her head.

I've taken to wearing loose dresses. My favorite is crossed over at the chest, deep blue, with an Indian print. "Why are you wearing that shapeless thing?" I expect her to say. "You should show off your figure." I've stopped coloring my hair. A white streak reveals itself near the front.

"Do you hate it, Mom?" I ask, trying to lure her into an argument. Her eyes brighten for a moment, then glaze over again and she stares into space. I'm ready to stop editing who I am. But it's too late. Can you see what I'm becoming, Mom? She closes her eyes.

The next time, I bring my new guitar. "I'm learning to play. Can you believe it, Mom?" I pick out the chorus of "Sweet Caroline" and sing out loud, bringing curious looks from the staff and some of the residents. "Remember my dance classes, Mom?" I lower my voice. "Mom," I say, "you should not have made me quit." I want to tell her how abandoned I felt when I got divorced, but even with her in this compromised state, I don't dare.

JUST WHEN THE DISEASE HAS taken everything, it takes more. Mom stops opening for the spoon. He mouth is a tight slash across her face, pinned shut. The staff at the home say they have tricks to make her open. They can work with reflexes. Or a feeding tube?

How revolting, I hear Mom say in my head. Her thin body is bloated and overfed already. Her thighs have ballooned to three times their normal size. When we meet with a palliative care doctor to discuss the options, the ethics, I say, "Please. She wouldn't want this."

Refusing food is something Dad can't understand. He's so disoriented that he steps away from decision-making. My sisters and I talk with the doctor, reach a consensus, and run it by Dad. Mom is telling us it's time. She is exercising her final act of free will. Okay, he says.

We tuck her into bed and her brow unfurrows. We play her favorite show tunes and hold her hand. The doctor says most people go in less than a week. A rabbi comes and Dad says goodbye. She hangs on for another twelve days, then slips away.

WHEN WE GET UP FROM shiva, the rabbi comes to walk us around the block. It's cold and clear and icy. "Watch your father carefully," he says quietly as he knots his scarf. "It's a vulnerable time for him." I feel a buzz around me—electricity in my body, in my brain. My mouth is dry. The buzz is fear.

GRIEF IS NOT WHAT I thought it would be. It comes over me at random moments—a pressure behind the eyes. A crawling under the skin. My insides feel disorganized and chaotic. I get up on a Sunday morning, two weeks after Mom is gone. A light has been left on in the closet. In the kitchen, a few dishes sit on the counter. Each tiny bit of disorder adds to a hot ball of anger growing inside me. I find myself yelling about nothing.

I want to check on Dad six times a day. You only have so much chi, my yoga teacher said, and then it's gone. I want to guard him

like a king. Nobody should upset him, tax him, drain his life force.
How much longer could it possibly last? He is patched together. He
has heart and kidney and lung disease. His glaucoma is so advanced,
he can barely see. Still, he gets out of bed every morning and shaves
and looks for something nice to put on. I need better clothes, he
says. These sweaters are schmattas.

At home, I carry the vacuum from room to room. I scrub the
counters compulsively. I call Dad again and again, bracing against
calamity. After a few months, my body aches from tension and I'm
bumping up against the walls of the tiny box I've put myself in. Michael is going to Barcelona for work, and I decide to go along.

I DRAG MYSELF DOWN THE Catalan sidewalks made of octagonal
tiles. At dinner with Michael's colleagues, I try to arrange my face in
a normal configuration. My stomach roils and gurgles. One heel is
cracked.

I sit alone at an outdoor café, watching the people. A woman
struts by in black boots and a fuchsia mask. A man in a red down
jacket sits on a stool and smokes. The waiter hoists a tray loaded
with cups and saucers and delicate pastries onto his shoulder. He
disappears around the corner.

Through the café window, I see a familiar man reading the paper.
He has silver hair and he's wearing a blue sweater. It's soft, almost
milky. I can't pull my eyes from him. The cashier ambles over. Their
lips move.

I'm ready to go inside and sit down with him. I love your sweater.
Can I see your hands? He pays his bill, leaves the restaurant, and
walks past me. Tears drip down the bridge of my nose onto my
notebook. One day soon, my father will leave me and strangers like
this will be all I have left.

WHEN I GET BACK TO Toronto, thick ice has built up on the driveway. I grab a shovel and lift from underneath, breaking the sheet
into huge satisfying slabs. I pick them up in my mittens and throw

them into the snowy garden. I take myself by the hand and lead myself back from the edge.

At the residence, Dad is doing better than I am. "What do you need?" I say. "What can I do?"

"I'd like to have some cake in the house." He's diabetic and it would be better for him not to eat pastry, but I'm not willing to say no.

It's no time to mess around with new recipes. I pull out Baba Sarah's sour cream coffee cake, written in Mom's smooth, capable hand. I heft my mixer onto the counter and sit down to make a shopping list.

WE WERE NEWLY MARRIED WHEN I sent Michael to the store for groceries. He came home with a bag of factory walnuts, the package an opaque blue except for a little greasy window. "What did you buy?" I said, exasperated. "Don't you know about nuts?"

He started to laugh. "What about them?"

"Stale nuts are terrible. You can't just get them anywhere!" He laughed harder but I didn't see what the joke was. In the house of my childhood, nuts were serious business.

To be honest, even the freshest walnuts are a little bitter. You have to understand their charm. If you aren't careful, that pleasing bitterness can become overpowering. When I was little, Mom opened the package right there in the grocery store aisle and tasted them. If she didn't like them, she put the open package back on the shelf and bought her nuts somewhere else.

IT'S COLD OUTSIDE BUT I walk slowly to the bulk food store near Kensington Market, letting my fingers and toes go numb. Inside, I stand over the walnut bin until no one is looking and sneak a nut into my mouth, like Mom would've. It's sweet and rich with a subtle edge. I take eggs and sour cream into my cart. A fragrant dust rises as I scoop into the ground cinnamon.

Home alone—*Blue* on the Sonos, Joni's unmistakable voice. The sun has set early and moonlight streams into the kitchen. My guitar teacher has been showing me how to drop the E string to get Joni's ringing sound. The warmth of open tuning is one of her signatures. That and her evocative lyrics.

> I wish I had a river
> I could skate away on

I cream the butter, sugar, vanilla, and salt. I watch the paddle go round and round, sifting through my thoughts. I add the eggs, one by one, then the sour cream in alternation with the flour. In the green glass bowl, I toss cinnamon, brown sugar, and a heaping cupful of walnuts. I know the oven is ready by the smell. Batter spreads itself into the springform pan.

I'm about to slide the cake into the oven when something feels off. I squint in the dim light. The surface of the cake is all bumps and clumps, too big and too many of them. Mom handed me that big knife when I was little and asked me to chop the walnuts. But mom is gone and I've added the walnuts whole. I put the cake back on the countertop, push up the sleeves of my sweater, and reach into the batter to break them up with my bare hands.

56

Scrambled Eggs

Back at Dad's, we keep working. I'm still not ready to read my pages to him, but I'm closer. One evening, the talk turns away from the Holocaust. "Do you remember when I got divorced?"

"Of course," he says. "You really took a chance."

"Dad," I say, and swallow hard. "I didn't." The firmness in my tone startles both of us. "I need you to understand this. It was the wrong marriage and I had no choice. Do you understand?"

It's windy outside and he's in his usual chair, back to the window. Behind him, the bare trees are bending sideways. "Yes," he says finally, "I understand. You were very brave. I have so much respect for what you did."

That's it. The last piece. Like one of the old brown leaves skittering down the sidewalk, the last of my burden lifts into the air and blows away.

SPRING COMES AGAIN AND NEWNESS bubbles up. It's tender, of course. Ephemeral and sweet. Stores and restaurants reopen. Something inside me begins to refill.

Four doors down, rhubarb grows in the boulevard between the

sidewalk and the road. Walking home one night, a little drunk from dinner, I yank three long stalks out of the ground. "Bon, stop," Michael whispers as I giddily shove muddy stems into my purse. The green leaves swirl out the top like the ruffles of a blouse.

We had snapper tartare with roasted tomatoes. A wedge of cabbage, charred and covered in fried capers and parsley. A lamb neck, cooked slow, like the chicken necks Baba saved, just for me. A bottle of rustic rosé. A little of life's luster is back. You can't control its comings and goings. You can only hop on when that mysterious machine starts to move.

DAD AND I TALK EVERY day now. I go over to his place and run the tape recorder as we nibble cake off Mom's pretty china. I am driven to work harder than he wants. And I'm in a hurry.

"Slow down," he says. "Enjoy life. Take it easy."

"But Dad, I have to finish this before—"

"I'm going to live to a hundred," he promises. "Now, can you relax?"

I have the same old urge to argue but, instead, I just laugh.

ARBEIT MACHT FREI—WORK MAKES YOU free. My dad and millions like him labored under that lie, getting weaker and hungrier and sicker. Nobody was set free. When I stood under the gates of Auschwitz in a driving rain, I understood Dad's need to protect me in a way I never had before. But sometimes we do as our parents do, not as they say. My whole life, my father has modeled resilience and courage and strength. It's impossible not to try to do the same.

Survival is not one thing—one piece of luck or smarts or intuition—but a million small ones. This choice not that one. This brave move, that good stranger. Careful here. Reckless there.

From my father, I've learned that survival is also a state of mind. "Between stimulus and response there is a space," writes Austrian psychiatrist and Holocaust survivor Viktor E. Frankl in *Man's Search for Meaning*. "In that space is our power to choose our response. In our response lies our growth and our freedom." The need for Dad's physical survival might have ended on May 8, 1945; the need for spiritual survival has been with him every day since. Intuitively, he's always known he has the power to choose his response. Dad has chosen beauty and wonder and joy. Dad has chosen freedom.

I DRIVE OUT TO THE cabin to write—windows open, fresh air blowing through the car. I've packed firewood. Smoked fish. Binoculars. My guitar. Sun lights the trees like gold thread. By the side of the road, I see a white owl as big as a three-year-old child. Impossible. I check the rearview mirror to catch a glimpse of it spreading its enormous wings and floating aloft.

ON MY WAY BACK TO the city in the early morning, I spot a barn in the hazy distance, a farmhouse, and a field. What would it feel like to live there? For a moment, I feel a great lifting of weight and I see everything just as it is, not loaded up with meaning but empty and free. A glimpse of transcendence, and then it's gone.

A few days later, Dad is on his way over. Morning sun shines through the dirty windows. I fluff cushions and toss shoes into the closet. He can barely see but somehow, he notices everything. Is that a hole in your shirt? Can I give you money to get the windows washed?

At the mirror, my skin is wrinkled, but it fits better than ever before. I try to make some order out of my hair. When I was young, I wore it big and loose. I'd be on my way out—to school, to a high school party—and Dad would say, "Your hairs are too wild." And they were. It was a lot of hair for my little face, but wild is what I longed to be.

I dot concealer under my eyes and swipe on some lipstick. It's a little obsessive, this perfectionism of his. Still, there's a certain calculus that just makes sense. Why distract him with ripped jeans and messy hair? There are other ways to be seen and heard. To truly become yourself.

IN THE KITCHEN, I LOOK over my collection of ingredients: Beans and barley? Check. Short ribs, cut flanken-style from the kosher butcher? Check. I even picked up a few marrow bones for good luck. We're going to take another crack at cholent. I want it to taste like his mother's. I want it to taste like magic.

My phone rings and I go out to the driveway to bring Dad and his walker up my two front steps.

"Do you have everything?" he asks, rolling into the kitchen.

"Yes, it's all ready."

"What about breakfast first? Do you have eggs?"

I take out a small frying pan, salt and pepper. Soon the smell of browning butter fills the house.

"One egg or two?" I ask.

He smiles then, those dimples huge across his lined face. "What is this, the war? We don't have to share one egg. Let's have two."

AUTHOR'S NOTE

This book is a work of nonfiction. However, I'd like to note the following:

The names and identifying characteristics of certain people have been changed to protect their privacy, but my parents, husband, children, and several others in the book have retained their real names.

"Julie" is a composite character; an amalgam of my amazing real-life sisters Rochelle, Jerell, and Adell.

[1]This passage has been pulled from my imagination, informed by the stories my father told me about cholent, his mother, and the bakery where she took her cholent to cook on Fridays before Shabbat. Dead horses in the street and stolen silver are details my father remembers being discussed over his head when he was a child, just as the war began.

[2]Notes, testimony, and photography of the liquidation of the Pabianice ghetto can be found in several places, including the United States Holocaust Memorial Museum (USHMM), POLIN Museum's Virtual Shtetl (online), and yadvashem.org. I was able to pinpoint

the date of this event with these helpful sources. My father remembers many aspects of his experience, including the rain, the stadium, and hiding among people's feet in the mud. He also has some sketchy memories of the tram ride to the Lodz Ghetto; my imagination has supplied the rest of the details.

Some sources say the Pabianice Jews spent two nights standing in the stadium but Dad remembers one, so I kept it at that. Sources say the people were sorted into two groups; my father and his family must have been in group A because group B was taken to Chelmno. Dad has the sense that his grandmother was not deported but taken away and shot at some point during this chaotic period of waiting and sorting.

I was able to paint a picture of life in Pabianice and the Pabianice ghetto before this sorting by dramatizing my father's memories of his parents, their store, and his own father's sudden, natural death in the winter of 1939.

[3]I created this lightly fictionalized version of my father's experience in the Lodz Ghetto with the following resources: The trove of lists, forms, index cards, and other records sent by the archivist from the USHMM; my father's testimony, recorded by the Jewish Archives & Historical Society of Edmonton in November 1985, and transcribed into written text in 2009, thanks to the tenacity of my sister Rochelle; Lucjan Dobroszycki's *The Chronicle of the Lodz Ghetto 1941–1944* with its granular detail about life in the ghetto, including several passages about the sorting church which, according to Dobroszycki, was nicknamed the White Factory due to the airborne feathers. I based physical descriptions of the ghetto on photographs, and I invented dialogue based on many interviews and conversations with my father.

Mr. Sharp was a real person and my father remembers gathering the Madonnas from the church, going to his house, meeting the woman there, going to the party and, of course, Mr. Sharp's help in finding work for all his sisters, which made life in the ghetto survivable for his family. My father says people were talking about the hospital being emptied, including the detail of live children being thrown out the hospital windows. It is also mentioned in various accounts, including the Lodz Ghetto entry on Wikipedia.

Yadvashem.org offered additional details about the social and political workings of the ghetto, including the heavy use of child labor. Dialogue and other fine details have been invented to round out the story. Mr. Sharp's relationship with Rumkowski comes from Dad's memory; I have not found any additional information on that in the records.

Many times, my father told me about the money and jewelry he found inside the pillows and duvets he opened in the church. With that background, I invented a specific incident with a diamond ring, Mama, and three loaves of bread. The passage about the butter is imagined as well.

The account of my father sorting clothes in the marketplace for the brief period after the church is locked up comes from his own testimony.

⁴The paragraphs in this section, beginning with "In August 1944," come directly from my father's testimony, edited only for clarity and for the purpose of moving the perspective from first to third person.

Finally, because of the pandemic, I couldn't travel to the USHMM during the writing of this book, but their online archive is exceptionally rich and it was there, many layers deep, that I found my aunt Devorah's identity card from the ghetto.

ACKNOWLEDGMENTS

Huge thanks to my editor, Sara Weiss, who drew the best out of me with skill and patience, and my agent, Michelle Tessler, who believed in this book from the start. Thanks to Kara Welsh, Jennifer Hershey, Kim Hovey, Sydney Collins, Rachel Ake, Susan Turner, Cassie Gitkin, Jesse Shuman, Karen Fink, Emma Thomasch, and the rest of the team at Ballantine and Penguin Random House, who worked so hard to make the book real and get it into the world.

Thanks also to the home team at Appetite: Katherine Stopa, Zoe Maslow, Robert McCullough, as well as Adria Iwasutiak and Kelly Albert, for caring so much about the book and putting it into readers' hands in Canada.

There has been a lot of learning over the past several years, all of it reflected, one way or another, in these pages, so thank you to my former teachers and mentors, many of whom have become friends: Alissa York and David Bezmozgis at Humber; Kim Pittaway, Gillian Turnbull, Harry Thurston, Ayelet Tsabari, Cooper Lee Bombardier, Dean Jobb, and Stephen Kimber at King's. Thanks, also, to Felicia and Ante at Yoga Therapy Toronto. And to Nikku, guitar teacher extraordinaire.

Thanks to my King's community and early readers: AnnMarie, Jess, Seema and the entire Saturday morning writers' group. A lot of this material began there.

I wrote several of these chapters from a hilltop village in Italy— thanks to the La Baldi Residency, especially Valentina. Also, thank you to the Banff Centre for Arts and Creativity, and the Dave Greber Awards for the early support and recognition.

Thank you to my fantastic friends, who cheered me on and sustained me for the years that it took to write this, and to Laurie, Susie, Elliot, and Dena for their love and support. And, of course, to my family of origin: my amazing sisters, Rochelle, Jerell, and Adell, who share and understand the particularities of this heritage, and were much more a part of things than I was able to depict; my unique and complex mom, who left us halfway through my writing; and my rock of a father, who is still fascinating and a little mysterious to me, even after everything.

Finally, thank you to my beautiful kids: Jamie, Leo, and Maya; Samantha, Emma-Kate, Hart, and Robin. I love you all so much.

And to Michael: You are my everything.

ABOUT THE AUTHOR

BONNY REICHERT is a National Magazine Award–winning journalist. When she turned forty, she enrolled in culinary school, and she's been exploring her relationship with food on the page ever since. Bonny was born in Edmonton, Alberta, and lives in Toronto with her husband Michael and little dog, Bruno. *How to Share an Egg* won the 2022 Dave Greber Award for social justice writing.

ABOUT THE TYPE

This book was set in Dante, a typeface designed by Giovanni Mardersteig (1892–1977). Conceived as a private type for the Officina Bodoni in Verona, Italy, Dante was originally cut only for hand composition by Charles Malin, the famous Parisian punch cutter, between 1946 and 1952. Its first use was in an edition of Boccaccio's *Trattatello in laude di Dante* that appeared in 1954. The Monotype Corporation's version of Dante followed in 1957. Though modeled on the Aldine type used for Pietro Bembo's treatise *De Aetna* in 1495, Dante is a thoroughly modern interpretation of that venerable face.